The Meaning of

SHAKESPEARE

RICHARD A. FEIST

RICHARD A. FEIST

The Meaning of

SHAKESPEARE

Volume II

By

HAROLD C. GODDARD

Phoenix Books

THE UNIVERSITY OF CHICAGO PRESS

CHICAGO & LONDON

THE UNIVERSITY OF CHICAGO PRESS, CHICAGO 60637
The University of Chicago Press, Ltd., London

© 1951 by the University of Chicago. All rights reserved
Published 1951.
Printed in the United States of America

82   12 11 10 9

International Standard Book Number: 0-226-30042-0
Library of Congress Catalog Card Number: 51-2288

Table of Contents

Chapter XXIV

Troilus and Cressida

I

How could Shakespeare produce one of the most unblushing glorifications of war ever written and then face right about and utter an equally extreme denunciation of it? How could he write *Henry V*, in other words, and then, within a year or two, *Troilus and Cressida?* There is a "poser" for those who adopt the conventional view of *Henry V* and assume that it *is* a glorification of Henry and his imperialistic conquests. If it isn't, no such problem exists, for in that case Shakespeare is simply saying right out in *Troilus and Cressida* the same thing he said under cover in *Henry V*.

It is not Shakespeare's habit to speak right out. Usually he follows precisely Emily Dickinson's injunction:

Tell all the truth but tell it slant.

Was there any reason why in this particular case he should have abandoned his general practice? There was, and a very plausible one. *Henry V* was written for popular consumption in a popular theater. *Troilus and Cressida* bears all the marks of having been written for a very different type of audience. The author of the preface to the Second Quarto indeed says that the play was "never staled with the stage, never clapper-clawed with the palms of the vulgar . . . [nor] sullied with the smoky breath of the multitude," which at the very least implies that the play was not produced on the popular stage, as indeed it seldom has been down even to our day. It is too weighted with long speeches and philosophical thought to make any general appeal. For whom then was it written? Mr. Peter Alexander has ventured the suggestion that it may have been designed for an audience of barristers at one of the Inns of Court. This assumption, in addition to resolving the paradox mentioned, would go far toward explaining a number of the play's peculiar features.

To begin with what is least important: if the country boy from Stratford, who according to one tradition began his dramatic career by holding horses outside a London theater and whom a university playwright had attacked as an "upstart crow," had an opportunity to present one of his plays before a select group of university men, could he have failed, for all his modesty, to feel the irony of the occasion and would he not have been more than human if he had not indulged in a bit of innocent revenge? Twitted perhaps with having "small Latin and less Greek," how could he resist the chance to reveal to these learned clerks and wits an acquaintance with Latin quite as thorough as their own? The extraordinary Latinisms with which the style of *Troilus and Cressida* is freighted are unique among his plays and in some instances approach pedantry or burlesque according as they are taken seriously or not, though they never perhaps quite cross the line. The long formal debates which the play contains, and its extended aphoristic and philosophical disquisitions, would also be exactly the thing to please a group of lawyers or legal students.

So likewise would be the irreverent handling of Homer and Chaucer, which, as Mr. Alexander says, "is not to be explained away as merely the medieval attitude to the classical story." "That the creator of a Prince Henry and a Hotspur," says Boas, "should bring on the stage in travestied form the glorious paragons of antiquity, an Achilles and an Ajax, is at first sight one of the most startling phenomena in all literature." Yet not quite so startling if Shakespeare had already had his tongue partly in his cheek when he created Hotspur and Henry. When, in the play, Ulysses tells how Patroclus—with Achilles for audience on the bed holding his sides for laughter—mimics the Greek chiefs, Agamemnon, Nestor, and the rest, and when Ulysses complains that all their mighty exploits serve only

> As stuff for these two to make paradoxes,

he echoes exactly the complaint of those who object to Shakespeare's desecration of Homer and Chaucer. But such "debunking," as we say today, of the heroic and romantic is just what would have flattered a group of young wits and worldlings. For them, the more cynicism the better. Bernard Shaw once declared that his *Man and Superman* was written for a pit of intellectual kings. Whether kings or knaves, Shakespeare apparently wrote his *Troilus and Cressida* for a pit of intellectuals. If, then, the superficial taste of his audience happened to coincide with a deep and serious disillusionment on his own part with popular ideas of the heroic and romantic (as plays like *Henry V** and *All's Well That Ends Well* go far to show that it did), the occasion must have offered an irresistible temptation to unburden himself of his innermost convictions, to let himself go, so to speak. If so, the result might well have been what we find in *Troilus and Cressida*. "Would you see Shakespeare's mind unfettered," said Goethe, "read *Troilus and Cressida*, where he treats the materials of the *Iliad* after his own fashion." Unfettered: it is precisely the right word.

It is a mark of an artist that he enjoys conforming to the fetters of his art. Shakespeare seems to have recognized instinctively that it was his function as dramatist to represent, not to recommend or condemn, his characters, and not to be concerned with how the crowd might take them, except to the extent of interesting it. Such comments on his plays as he allowed himself he kept subtle or indirect, burying them often in other plays. Yet occasionally even Shakespeare may have been tempted to speak more openly. He obviously did so in *Troilus and Cressida* and *Timon of Athens*, and to a lesser degree in *Measure for Measure*. They are his only plays that by any stretch of the adjective might be called didactic.

Paradoxically, it is the most scurrilous figure in the play, the most nearly sewer-mouthed character he ever created, Thersites, who seems at times to be the author's mouthpiece, acting as a sort of chorus and commentator on the action and the other dramatic persons. In spite of his evil disposition, vile language, and general nastiness, he utters no small amount of truth—negative truth. A man lost to all decency has no motive for concealment. Thersites delights in dragging everything, himself included, in the mud. A few rare men are above disguise. He is below it. "Lechery, lechery," he cries, "still wars and lechery; nothing else holds fashion. A burning devil take them! . . . war and lechery confound all!" Here the statement of the fact must be sharply distinguished from the attitude toward the fact. Shakespeare's special audience, if he had one, probably on the whole accepted Thersites' summary of the sins of the world and shared his attitude toward them (as they did in another vein the attitude of Pandarus). But Shakespeare, unless he had ceased to be himself, must have discriminated. He obviously recognized the facts, but there is nothing to indicate that he took any satisfaction in them as Thersites so plainly does. No one with justice ever accused Shakespeare of being a cynic. He understood sneering, but where does he himself sneer? Those who hold that he does here must certainly bear the burden of proof. His sweetness of temper in the Comedies is proverbial. Hence in part perhaps the annihilating power

* For a defense of this view of *Henry V* see the chapter on that play in Volume I.

of this play. A man who habitually refrains from profanity can get a tremendous effect from a single stroke of it. But that does not make him a profane man. Neither does the scoffing in *Troilus and Cressida* make Shakespeare a scoffer. It is, in any strict sense of the term, the most intellectual play he ever wrote. But he is a poet, and even in this play his critical powers cannot suppress his imagination. Thersites often expresses the author's thought, but never his spirit. Other characters come far closer to doing that. One in particular, a seemingly very minor one, is enough to save the play, for all the cynical things there are in it, from the charge of cynicism.

"Shakespeare's state of mind when he wrote *Troilus and Cressida*," said a young woman who had just put the play down after her first reading of it, "must have been something like Cassandra's." That strikes me as the best brief comment I have ever heard or read about this play. It could not be better said. The work sounds like the utterance of a man who envisages the end of the world, or, at any rate, the end of humanity. Mankind on the verge of racial suicide because of its sins of violence and lust: that is the picture it paints. Some have even conjectured that Shakespeare himself at this time came close to the precipice. It is an unnecessary assumption. But at least it shows a perception of the abyss that separates those who sneer at the sins of the world from those who fall sick because of them.

As this concern over the sickness of the world suggests, *Troilus and Cressida* was evidently a part of the same creative wave that produced *Hamlet*. It would be illuminating to know the exact chronological relationship of the two plays. *Troilus* is generally held to be the earlier, but we do not know just when the poet may have begun work on *Hamlet*. Whatever their order, the plays are in a sense intellectual twins, or, better, the lesser a sort of intellectual satellite of the greater. The leading characters of *Troilus* can be conceived of with equal ease as the elements or the fragments of the Prince of Denmark. (Even an element or a fragment of Hamlet surpasses an ordinary man.) Hector, for instance, is Hamlet's modesty and nobility combined with his inability to live up to his convictions; Troilus is his alternating feminine fineness and savage masculine fury; Achilles his brooding and inaction transformed in the end to their opposite; Ulysses is his intellect and craft; Thersites his contempt and incredible coarseness; Pandarus his wit and scorn of innocence. All this cannot be coincidence. But whether what we have here is some of the stuff out of which Hamlet was made, or a part of what was left over in the process of his creation, is not certain.

II

To anyone who has not followed the development of Shakespeare's mind, *Troilus and Cressida* is two plays in one. There is the love story of Troilus and Cressida, with Pandarus as go-between; and there is the story of the siege of Troy, with Achilles and Hector and Agamemnon and the rest the center of interest. And the two stories are only loosely interwoven. To take the play so is to miss its main point. As Thersites' words on war and lechery suggest, so close to each other are the two themes that they are really one. What the author is saying is that the problem of lust and the problem of violence, and so of war, are the same problem seen from different angles.

Shakespeare had grasped this fact from the beginning, but his interest in it was increasing. In *Hamlet* (to trace a few of the footsteps of that interest backward), the sensuality of the court at Elsinore is the indispensable soil for the germination of violence. In *Romeo and Juliet*, those two sensualists, Mercutio and the Nurse, are the positive and negative instigators of the blood that stains the love and brings the tragedy of that play. But, still earlier, Shakespeare had written two poems the theme of each of which is precisely the relation of violence and lust: *Venus and Adonis* and *The Rape of Lucrece*. Thirty stanzas of the latter are given to a passage wherein the heroine, seeking to assuage her grief and sense of outrage by the sight of others' woe, stands in front of a canvas depicting the Greeks before Troy. In the story of their siege, and of the City's fall, she beholds the image of her own desecration by Tarquin's lust. Indeed she traces the Trojan war itself back to the same passion:

> Thy heat of lust, fond Paris, did incur
> This load of wrath that burning Troy doth bear.

For aught we know, this may have been the seed from which germinated Shakespeare's profound insight into the connection between lust and war. At any rate those thirty stanzas are plainly the embryo of *Troilus and Cressida*.

The *Iliad* itself is an epic whose central, and whose initial, situation stresses the affinity or identity of lust and war, giving the impression at times of being little more than the record of the plundering expeditions and exploits of early tribes. But then again—as when the Trojan elders, beholding Helen, exclaim, "Little blame that, for such a woman, Greeks and Trojans should long undergo hard things; for to look on her is like looking on a goddess"—it rises into a sublime myth of the relation of valor to beauty, a myth that, long after literal warfare is wiped out, will remain an undimmed metaphor of life. It suited Shakespeare's purpose in *Troilus and Cressida* to stress the earthy aspects of his Greek-Trojan material, perhaps because they fitted so perfectly his growing perception that commotion in the outer world is frequently a projection of commotion within, and war, civil war especially, the best of all possible metaphors for the divided, or, as we say, the neurotic man:

> Kingdom'd Achilles in commotion rages
> And batters down himself.

Lust is the most fiery, the most devastating, the most deadly of the passions. War is the most fiery, the most devastating, the most deadly of worldly phenomena. What if the two engender each other in endless succession? Homer was interested in this question but formulated it in theological rather than psychological terms. Shakespeare explores the idea in this play.

The appalling power with which metaphors of sexual lust illuminate the nature of war, and vice versa, proves that they are based on millennia of human experience. The poets of all time have used these figures. To conquer and loot a country is to rape it: to violate a woman is to conquer her by force and plunder her of her treasure. The violence that attends sex when it is unmitigated by love, and the sexual excesses that have attended war and been its aftermath, are the psychological and historical demonstrations of the consanguinity of the two.* (On an attenuated and "respectable" scale, the same thing can be seen in what happens after a big football victory—or defeat.) The end of both military and sexual fury, this play says over and over, is self-annihilation. Ulysses expresses this idea, as it touches war, in his unforgettable picture of a world ruled by brute force impelled by primitive instinct:

> Strength should be lord of imbecility,
> And the rude son should strike his father dead.
> Force should be right; or rather, right and wrong,
> Between whose endless jar justice resides,
> Should lose their names, and so should justice too.
> Then every thing includes itself in power,
> Power into will, will into appetite;
> And appetite, an universal wolf,
> So doubly seconded with will and power,
> Must make perforce an universal prey,
> And last eat up himself.

A universal wolf that finally eats up itself! such is the nature of force; and the nemesis of strength, to put it more abstractly, is a kind of self-

---

* See *The Rape of Lucrece*, 411–69, and the stanzas following, through 728. And, again, Sonnet 129.

cannibalism. Except for its final figure, Ulysses' speech, as befits him, is grave, almost ponderous. Thersites, in a very different mood, says exactly the same thing of lust that Ulysses says of force. "What's become of the wenching rogues?" he asks, referring of course to Troilus and Cressida. "I think they have swallowed one another. I would laugh at that miracle; yet, in a sort, lechery eats itself." "Two curs shall tame each other," says Nestor of Ajax and Achilles (which will remind readers of *The Brothers Karamazov* of Ivan's terrible "Let the two reptiles devour each other"). "He that is proud eats up himself." "Whatever praises itself but in the deed, devours the deed in the praise." The play abounds in these variations on the metaphor, and in it conspicuously begin those multitudinous references to the lower animals that crowd Shakespeare's Tragedies from now on, culminating in *King Lear* and *Timon of Athens*. Human passions are like wild animals that tear and eat each other, Shakespeare declares, with the added characteristic that they finally devour themselves. Because in later plays, notably *King Lear*, he studies this cannibalistic aspect of *all* passion, we need not here collect the passages in them of which those of Ulysses on force and Thersites on lust are the prototypes.

III

Does some problem of the passions in his own life account for the terrible sincerity and intensity with which Shakespeare stresses and reiterates this theme? The *Sonnets*, especially those to the Dark Lady, have been held to point in that direction, as has the character of Cressida, and, in calmer retrospect, that of Cleopatra.

> For I.have sworn thee fair, and thought thee bright,
> Who art as black as hell, as dark as night.

The accent of such lines, and others like them, has been thought hard to account for in terms of purely vicarious experience.

A deluge of ink has descended over the *Sonnets*, until they are hardly visible. Here is not the place to ask who Mr. W. H. was, or who the Dark Lady. Identifications of them are of only archeological or at best biographical interest. That there was a "real" Mr. W. H. and a "real" Dark Lady I am as little inclined to doubt as that there was a "real" Beatrice in Dante's life. But these persons may have resembled what they gave birth to about as much as an acorn resembles an oak. Of how little account they are to us! "The soul knows no persons." So, while their originals remain unknown, Shakespeare, though few seem to notice, tells us precisely who they were—poetically. Which is all that matters.

Two loves I have of comfort and despair,
Which like two spirits do suggest me still:
The better angel is a man right fair,
The worser spirit a woman colour'd ill.

An angel and an evil spirit, Shakespeare says. Why not accept the statement literally? "Thou art the better part of me." Why not take him at his word? Certainly the plays have afforded ground enough for Shakespeare's belief that man is two men in one, or, better, a man and a woman. Surely the Young Man is Shakespeare's spirituality, the Dark Woman his sensuality. The woman attempts to seduce the man—his earthy to betray his heavenly nature. All other interpretations—however true—are incidental and insignificant compared with these.

To win me soon to hell, my female evil
Tempteth my better angel from my side,
And would corrupt my saint to be a devil,
Wooing his purity with her foul pride.
And whether that my angel be turn'd fiend
Suspect I may, yet not directly tell;
But being both from me, both to each friend,
I guess one angel in another's hell.
    Yet this shall I ne'er know, but live in doubt,
    Till my bad angel fire my good one out.

We read this, and think Shakespeare meant it "in a certain sense"—that it is all just a manner of speaking. Whereas he meant exactly what he said. Poets always do. If only we can find out what it is they have said!

Now *Troilus and Cressida*—the love story especially, but the war story too—is this sonnet writ large. It need not trouble us that the plot does not exactly parallel that of the *Sonnets*, nor that all the women in the play are not sensual, nor all the men spiritual. Symbolically, as in the *Sonnets* with the Platonic tradition behind them, it is proper that a man should represent the celestial, a woman the earthy or sensual principle. But actually both principles are present in both sexes, in the hermaphroditic man. Troilus recognizes this intuitively and, when the full truth dawns over him near the end, calls the two natures of the woman he loves his own Cressid and Diomedes' Cressid. Cressida recognizes it too, also by intuition, and at the close of the scene in the orchard (III, ii), where for a moment she is covered with confusion by a sense of her unworthiness of Troilus' love, she gives us a glimpse of the ingenuous girl, Troilus' Cressid, who is being buried alive under the worldly witty woman, Pandarus' Cressid. (Here perhaps lies Shakespeare's deepest indebtedness to Chaucer.) It is one of those momentary contradictions of themselves in which so many of Shakespeare's characters indulge and which make them complex living beings—a flash of pure sunlight emerging from dark clouds, only to be swallowed up greedily the next instant by still darker and more ominous ones:

> CRES.: I am asham'd. O heavens! what have I done?
> For this time will I take my leave, my lord.
> TRO.: Your leave, sweet Cressid!
> PAN.: Leave! an you take leave till to-morrow morning,—
> CRES.: Pray you, content you.
> TRO.: What offends you, lady?
> CRES.: Sir, mine own company.
> TRO.: You cannot shun yourself.
> CRES.: Let me go and try:

(If only she had obeyed that impulse!)

> I have a kind of self resides with you.
> But an unkind self, that itself will leave,
> To be another's fool. I would be gone!
> Where is my wit? I speak I know not what.
> TRO.: Well know they what they speak that speak so wisely.

A momentary return of her girlhood! How fatal Troilus' slip in choosing such a moment for even the faintest suggestion of praise or flattery. As if at a cue, *his* Cressid vanishes and the self-poised Pandarus' Cressid takes her place:

> CRES.: Perchance, my lord, I show more craft than love,
> And fell so roundly to a large confession,
> To angle for your thoughts. But you are wise,
> Or else you love not, for to be wise and love
> Exceeds man's might; that dwells with gods above.

Later, suffering awakens Troilus to this dichotomy in Cressid's nature, in the scene near Calchas' tent in the last act, when he and Ulysses, eavesdropped on by Thersites, themselves eavesdrop on the love-making of Cressida and Diomedes (who had immediately begun to lay siege to her, it will be remembered, after she was sent, in an exchange of prisoners, to the Greek camp). Sensuality wooed by Brutality, the scene might be called, Woman wooed by War. Incapable of believing the testimony of his senses, Troilus cries, when the lovers go out:

> TRO.: Was Cressid here?
> ULYSS.: I cannot conjure, Trojan.
> TRO.: She was not, sure.
> ULYSS.: Most sure she was.

Tro.: Why, my negation hath no taste of madness.
Ulyss.: Nor mine, my lord. Cressid was here but now.

And we think of Hamlet and Ophelia, as Troilus continues:

Tro.: Let it not be believ'd for womanhood!
  Think, we had mothers; do not give advantage
  To stubborn critics, apt, without a theme,
  For depravation, to square the general sex
  By Cressid's rule: rather think this not Cressid.
Ulyss.: What hath she done, prince, that can soil our mothers?
Tro.: Nothing at all, *unless that this were she.*

(And Thersites, behind, whispers to himself: "Will he swagger himself out on's own eyes?")

Tro.: This she? no, this is Diomed's Cressida.
  If beauty have a soul, this is not she.
  If souls guide vows, if vows be sanctimony,
  If sanctimony be the gods' delight,
  If there be rule in unity itself,
  This is not she. O madness of discourse,
  That cause sets up with and against itself,
  Bi-fold authority, where reason can revolt
  Without perdition, and loss assume all reason
  Without revolt: *this is, and is not, Cressid.*
  Within my soul there doth conduce a fight
  Of this strange nature, that a thing inseparate
  Divides more wider than the sky and earth,
  And yet the spacious breadth of this division
  Admits no orifex for a point as subtle
  As Ariachne's broken woof to enter.

Historical critics complain of those who "modernize" Shakespeare. They had better complain of Shakespeare for modernizing himself, as lines like the preceding, especially those I have italicized, show. In them the classical, and medieval, doctrine of the angelic and diabolic presiders over the destiny of man, and contemporary ideas on the dual character of the unconscious, clasp hands across the centuries. Shakespeare stands between, and combines the virtues of their respective religious and psychological emphases.

  The scene we have been speaking of ends—

   In characters as red as Mars his heart
   Inflam'd with Venus

—by Troilus being drawn through Cressid's sin into a maelstrom of hate, a distracted and hyperbolic dedication of himself to the death of Diomedes.

And whether that my angel be turn'd fiend
Suspect I may, yet not directly tell.

If there is doubt in Shakespeare's, there is no doubt in Troilus' case. The bad angel of Cressida's sensuality has "fired out" the good angel of Troilus' purity, and, from now on, his mood is exactly that rash fury that characterizes Hamlet at the end. Indeed, Thersites, adding, as chorus, his epilogue to the scene on which he has doubly eavesdropped, gives us a clear prophecy (unless it is a reminiscence) of Hamlet in the play scene, as he ties together in words the two main themes that Troilus has just tied in act: "Would I could meet that rogue Diomede! I would croak like a raven." The very raven that bellowed for revenge just as Hamlet's mousetrap began to spring! And it is just here that Thersites puts in his "Lechery, lechery; still wars and lechery; nothing else holds fashion. A burning devil take them!"

IV

And now, with this orientation, let us run swiftly through the action of the play.

After opening scenes in which we are introduced to Troilus, Cressida, and Pandarus, we pass over to the Greek camp and hear the Hellenic chieftains debating why, after seven years' siege, Troy still stands. Agamemnon and Nestor attribute the failure to the gods, who send adversity to men to winnow out the heroes from the weaklings, storms to test seamanship. But Ulysses has a less divine explanation. It is all because we Greeks have quarreled among ourselves, he says. We have failed to observe proper precedence and subordination, proper "degree," as he calls it.

The long and imposing speech in which Ulysses expounds his ideas on order and priority has been widely admired.* It is a powerful defense of

---

* "Troy, yet upon his basis, had been down,
   And the great Hector's sword had lack'd a master,
   But for these instances:
   The specialty of rule hath been neglected;
   And, look, how many Grecian tents do stand
   Hollow upon this plain, so many hollow factions.
   When that the general is not like the hive
   To whom the foragers shall all repair,
   What honey is expected? Degree being vizarded,
   The unworthiest shows as fairly in the mask.
   The heavens themselves, the planets, and this centre
   Observe degree, priority, and place,
   Insisture, course, proportion, season, form,
   Office, and custom, in all line of order;
   And therefore is the glorious planet Sol
   In noble eminence enthron'd and spher'd
   Amidst the other; whose medicinable eye
   Corrects the ill aspects of planets evil,

the feudal idea, and above anything else in Shakespeare it is the stock-in-trade of those who would prove that he was a Tory in temperament and politics. Like everything Ulysses says, it indubitably contains much wisdom, the "universal wolf" passage, for instance, which, a hundred things show, must have come from close to Shakespeare's heart. But it is altogether too easy to pass from such things—as it is from the great speech on the ingratitude of time, with its

> One touch of nature makes the whole world kin,

—to the inference that Ulysses was continuously Shakespeare's mouthpiece in the play. On the contrary, shocking as it will sound to some, he turns out, under analysis, to be more nearly its villain, and the speech on degree, partly in itself but much more in its context, another devastating piece of Shakespearean irony.

Up to a certain point anyone must agree with Ulysses in a general way. Law is indispensable; order—short of the millennium—a *sine qua non* of civilization. Despotism and anarchy, as the History Plays demonstrate, are extremes that meet, but, if it comes to the hard choice, who can doubt that despotism is the better of the two, and, for ruler, even a Richard III preferable to a Jack Cade? But Ulysses means much more than this. His analogy for the social and political order he approves is the solar system with everybody in his appointed place and proper orbit from the center out:

> The primogenitive and due of birth,
> Prerogative of age, crowns, sceptres, laurels.

> And posts, like the commandment of a king,
> Sans check, to good and bad. But when the planets
> In evil mixture to disorder wander,
> What plagues and what portents! what mutiny!
> What raging of the sea! shaking of earth!
> Commotion in the winds! Frights, changes, horrors,
> Divert and crack, rend and deracinate
> The unity and married calm of states
> Quite from their fixure! O, when degree is shak'd,
> Which is the ladder to all high designs,
> The enterprise is sick! How could communities,
> Degrees in schools, and brotherhoods in cities,
> Peaceful commerce from dividable shores,
> The primogenitive and due of birth,
> Prerogative of age, crowns, sceptres, laurels,
> But by degree, stand in authentic place?
> Take but degree away, untune that string,
> And, hark, what discord follows! Each thing meets
> In mere oppugnancy. The bounded waters
> Should lift their bosoms higher than the shores
> And make a sop of all this solid globe.
> Strength should be lord of imbecility,"

etc., as already quoted on p. 6.

The Divine Right of the Status Quo it might be called—the dream of every autocrat since time began, as certainly as its opposite, anarchy, has been his nightmare. Totalitarianism is the fashionable word for it at the moment. What Ulysses does not see, or at any rate does not see fit to admit, is that the extreme he defends is as far from freedom—or nearly so—as the one he quite rightly denounces. To suggest that one of the world's supreme lovers of freedom and individuality is an apologist for any such static system is too preposterous for words. Far from defending it, he is riddling it with holes.

To begin with, down even to such a detail as the touch about the bee-hive, the doctrine is identical with that of that ineffable hypocrite and militarist, the Archbishop of Canterbury in *Henry V*, enough in itself to damn it forever.

In the next place, as he works into his theme, Ulysses as good as admits that this "order," which in theory is so divine, easily degenerates, as in this present predicament of the Greeks, from its centripetal perfection to a centrifugal fever of envy, wherein every inferior is jealous of his superior until the whole body politic is infected:

> The general's disdain'd
> By him one step below, he by the next,
> That next by him beneath,

and so on. Clearly "degree" is not quite so ideal as it appeared.

But most important of all, the grave tone and great length of Ulysses' speech (over a hundred lines interrupted by just four from Nestor and Agamemnon) of themselves put it under grave suspicion, for wisdom in Shakespeare is not in the habit of incarnating herself in long moral harangues or weighty philosophical disquisitions, and those who indulge in them in his plays can, nine times out of ten, be counted on to contradict them in action—if not within about one minute after the speech is over, then in the next scene, or at latest the next act. The King's speech on equality in *All's Well That Ends Well*—as radical in sentiment as Ulysses' on order is reactionary—is a good example. Having proved, with an eloquence worthy of a French Revolutionist or the author of "a man's a man for a' that," that birth and place as such are nothing, the King turns instantly to invoke the power of *his* place to compel Bertram to marry against his wishes. So here with Ulysses. Having proved that any violation of "degree" involves the danger of anarchy, that at that peril everybody must be kept in his place, he proceeds forthwith to hatch a plot for pulling Achilles out of his place—

ULYSS.: The great Achilles, whom opinion crowns
The sinew and the forehand of our host.

While he was theorizing on degree, Ulysses deprecated disdain and envy.
But now listen to him!

What glory our Achilles shares from Hector,
Were he not proud, we all should share with him.
But he already is too insolent.

Ulysses has forgotten his major premise. A few moments ago he was
saying,

And therefore is the glorious planet Sol
In noble eminence enthron'd and spher'd
Amidst the other.

Now he declares,

we were better parch in Afric sun
Than in the pride and salt scorn of his eyes.

The sun, as metaphor, betrays Ulysses as badly as it does Henry V. The
sun is a symbol of the truth. Only those as sincere as the sun should dare
employ it as a figure.

I have a young conception in my brain,

Ulysses cries, when the idea first dawns on him of having Ajax chosen by
lottery instead of Achilles—to whom as chief Greek hero the honor belongs—to meet Hector in single combat. The gusto of the line shows
Ulysses' love of craft and plotting. (And it is a dull ear that does not
catch in it a premonition of a more famous intriguer: "I have 't! It is engender'd!") But imagine a believer in degree resorting to a lottery! No
wonder it is to be a "loaded" lottery.

ULYSS.:   No, make a lottery;
And, *by device*, let blockish Ajax draw
The sort to fight with Hector,

and in an ecstasy of delight, as his "young conception" begins to form
itself in his mind, he concludes:

But, hit or miss,
Our project's life this shape of sense assumes:
Ajax employ'd plucks down Achilles' plumes.

So much, in practice, for keeping everybody in his place. And the "venerable Nestor" whose "experienc'd tongue" had power according to

Ulysses to "knit all the Greekish ears" to it, and who at the beginning of the scene uttered such godlike words about adversity, now, at the end of it, concurs in Ulysses' scheme in these choice terms:

> Two curs shall tame each other; pride alone
> Must tarre the mastiffs on, as 'twere their bone.

Thersites, as usual, supplies the most pertinent comment when he remarks, not on this but on another occasion: "A plague of opinion! a man may wear it on both sides, like a leather jerkin." If that was not Shakespeare's "opinion" too, nothing between the covers of his works is. The combination of psychological insight, cold malice, and artistic gusto with which Ulysses sets out to stir up trouble puts him in a totally different, and lower, camp from perpetrators of crimes of passion, reminding us, in retrospect, of Pandulph with his

> Methinks I see this hurly all on foot:
> ... 'Tis wonderful
> What may be wrought out of their discontent,

and, in prospect, of Iago, with his

> So will I turn her virtue into pitch,
> And out of her own goodness make the net
> That shall enmesh them all.

This is what I meant by suggesting that Ulysses may be the villain of the piece. As a deranger of degree and fomenter of the very anarchy he pretends to hate, he turns out to be an advance agent of his own Universal Wolf. Could irony go further?

How too too well his wiles succeed, the event makes clear. But first a word about certain of the other characters.

V

Achilles is revealed early in the play inactive in his tent, having withdrawn from the fighting against Troy. By general consent, he is the most redoubtable warrior on the Greek side. But what of it, says Agamemnon?—

> A stirring dwarf we do allowance give
> Before a sleeping giant.

Ulysses announces that Achilles will not go to the field tomorrow.

AGAM.: What's his excuse?
ULYSS.:   He doth rely on none.

"You may call it melancholy, if you will favour the man," says Ajax, anticipating Bradley's diagnosis of Hamlet's inaction, "but, by my head, 'tis pride." Ulysses concurs in this amendment, and describes the ailment as a self-inflation that has precipitated a civil war " 'twixt his mental and his active parts."

> My mind is troubled, like a fountain stirr'd;
> And I myself see not the bottom of it,

Achilles himself declares in an accent so unmistakably Hamletian that the couplet could be inserted at a dozen places in the Prince of Denmark's role and deceive everyone but the scholar or close student of the text.

What is the trouble with this melancholy and inactive man? Unless all Shakespearean auspices fail, he must be, as Ulysses suggests, the victim of a divided self, though Ulysses' reason for the division, pride, may be far from getting to the bottom of the matter. And such indeed proves to be the case when, on looking closely, we discover—of all things—that this mighty hero is in the same situation as Romeo! He is in love with a daughter of his enemy, Polyxena, child of Priam, sister of Hector, who is the Achilles of the Trojans. As in the case of Romeo, love puts him out of love with violence:

> What! comes the general to speak with me?
> You know my mind: I'll fight no more 'gainst Troy.

It is like Romeo refusing to fight Tybalt. The different tempers of the two plays make the comparison seem grotesque. Is Shakespeare here burlesquing his own youth and the absurdities of romantic love? There are those who would have us think so. The incident is passed over so swiftly that it is perhaps impossible to be certain what Shakespeare did intend. But the play is so saturated with situations where one touch of nature, if granted its way against the conventions of war, might have brought Greeks and Trojans together that it is hard not to feel that this is one of them. We do not condemn Romeo for preferring Juliet to his hereditary quarrel. Why do we condemn Achilles for preferring Polyxena to the Trojan War? At the very least Shakespeare compels us to ask that question.

> Fall Greeks; fail fame; honour or go or stay;
> My major vow lies here, this I'll obey.

The origin of the Capulet-Montague feud we do not know, but it could have been no more ignominious than the cause of the Trojan War, and even so great a hero as Hector considers that war's continuation an offense against the moral laws of both nature and nations. Over the centuries those impressed into armies have generally been in no position to utter

their convictions on the relative value of love and war. But Hector and
Achilles are great heroes and can speak their minds. The nature of
Achilles' feeling for Polyxena we cannot be sure of, but that it may have
been genuine love can be believed if for no other reason than Achilles'
lines about the human eye, in which Shakespeare endows him with a
poetic perception akin to his own:

> The beauty that is borne here in the face
> The bearer knows not, but commends itself
> To others' eyes; nor doth the eye itself,
> That most pure spirit of sense, behold itself,
> Not going from itself; but eye to eye oppos'd
> Salutes each other with each other's form;
> For speculation turns not to itself,
> Till it hath travell'd and is mirror'd there
> Where it may see itself.

The speaker of those lines was capable of love and was made for something nobler than the vocation of making eyes close forever. Where love
crosses the battle lines there is always a seed of peace. If it was love in this
instance, Ulysses was on guard to see to it that the seed did not germinate,
and the end was to be, not tragedy as in the case of Romeo, but ignominy.

Heat and cold are sometimes extremes that meet. Mercutio's hot blood
was the undoing of Romeo. Ulysses' cold blood is the undoing of Achilles.
And what a saint in comparison Mercutio seems! Ulysses perceives that
Achilles' Achilles heel is pride, and enlisting all the Greek chieftains, and
specifically the unspeakable Ajax, as his tools, he proceeds, if I may use so
odd a metaphor, to lay siege to it. It is exactly as if the dramatic deep-
plotting Hamlet had conspired against the proud and melancholy Hamlet.
And, characteristically, his opening move is a play within a play. He
causes the Greek chieftains to march past Achilles' tent with "negligent
and loose regard." "What mean these fellows?" cries Achilles, taking the
bait. "Know they not Achilles?" And stung by their derision he goes on:

> What, am I poor of late?
> 'Tis certain, greatness, once fall'n out with fortune,
> Must fall out with men too: what the declin'd is
> He shall as soon read in the eyes of others
> As feel in his own fall; for men, like butterflies,
> Show not their mealy wings but to the summer,
> *And not a man, for being simply man,*
> *Hath any honour, but honour for those honours*
> *That are without him, as place, riches, and favour,*
> *Prizes of accident as oft as merit.*

From how much closer to Shakespeare's heart this comes than Ulysses' disquisition on degree a dozen of the *Sonnets* attest, and none more than the 25th:

> Let those who are in favour with their stars
> Of public honour and proud titles boast.

That sonnet is nothing but a paraphrase of Achilles, or more likely, Achilles a paraphrase of it, down even to the companion metaphors of the butterfly and the flower.

> . . . men, like butterflies,
> Show not their mealy wings but to the summer,

says Achilles.

> Great princes' favourites their fair leaves spread
> But as the marigold at the sun's eye,

says Shakespeare. The sonnet tells us just what Shakespeare thought of the relative value of love and "honour":

> Then happy I, that love and am belov'd
> Where I may not remove nor be remov'd.

But Achilles, fatally, thought he was an exception to his own rule:

> But 'tis not so with me;
> Fortune and I are friends,

and this conceit renders him the more susceptible to Ulysses' seductions when the latter, exactly like Hamlet, enters reading a book. The conversation that ensues gives us a hundred and more of the most wonderful lines in Shakespeare. The sincerity and beauty of Achilles' tribute to the human eye—already quoted—seem to "communicate his parts" to Ulysses, whose reply sounds as if it were Achilles himself speaking, with Ulysses' lips, lines that read like a continuation of his own. Then Ulysses relapses for a moment into his crafty self, and, in words that seem to refer only to Ajax, he exposes the mainspring of his own plot against Achilles:

> *How one man eats into another's pride,*
> While pride is fasting in his wantonness!

"I do believe it," cries Achilles, stepping into the trap,

> for they pass'd by me
> As misers do by beggars, neither gave to me
> Good word or look. What, are my deeds forgot?

—whereupon Ulysses launches into his justly famous speech on the vora-
ciousness of time:

> Time hath, my lord, a wallet at his back,
> Wherein he puts alms for oblivion . . .

which, again, might be an amplification of four lines of that same 25th
sonnet:

> The painful warrior famoused for fight,
> After a thousand victories once foil'd,
> Is from the book of honour razed quite,
> And all the rest forgot for which he toil'd.

The speech on time seems like the last word of Ulysses' wisdom. But he
surpasses it a moment later in the one on "the soul of state," which possibly comes closer than anything else in the poet's works to revealing the
secret of Shakespeare's own inspiration. Achilles is filled with consternation on discovering that Ulysses knows all about his love for Polyxena:

> ULYSS.: 'Tis known, Achilles, that you are in love
>   With one of Priam's daughters.
> ACHIL.:   Ha! known!
> ULYSS.: Is that a wonder?

And Ulysses continues in words that *are* a wonder:

> The providence* that's in a watchful state
> Knows almost every grain of Plutus' gold,
> Finds bottom in the uncomprehensive deeps,
> Keeps place with thought, and almost, like the gods,
> Does thoughts unveil in their dumb cradles.
> There is a mystery—with whom relation
> Durst never meddle—in the soul of state;
> Which hath an operation more divine
> Than breath or pen can give expressure to.

The inevitable first reaction to this speech is: "Out of character!" Such
mystic insight seems out of the reach of the crafty Ulysses. But Shakespeare has given too many of his characters *one* such uncharacteristic
speech for us not to know what this one means. Like the apostrophe to
sleep of Henry IV (whom Ulysses in some ways resembles), it is a measure of what this man might have been. How far he is from being it is
shown when, the next moment, he proceeds to use the almost divine wisdom he has just uttered to ensnare the very man who had in a sense inspired it. It is like a change of key in music:

---

* Everyone will see that "providence" signifies foresight, but not everyone that
"state" here means: *a static, perfectly tranquil condition.*

> All the commerce that you have had with Troy
> As perfectly is ours as yours, my lord;
> And better would it fit Achilles much
> To throw down Hector than Polyxena.
> But it must grieve young Pyrrhus now at home,
> When fame shall in our islands sound her trump,
> And all the Greekish girls shall tripping sing,
> "Great Hector's sister did Achilles win,
> But our great Ajax bravely beat down him."
> Farewell, my lord: I as your lover speak.
> The fool slides o'er the ice that you should break.

Exit Ulysses, as the mousetrap springs, the stage direction might have been expanded into, for he leaves Achilles as securely caught in the toils of his pride as Claudius was in those of his guilt. Patroclus adds his word, bidding Achilles rouse himself and let love be shaken from him "like a dewdrop from the lion's mane."

ACHIL.:   Shall Ajax fight with Hector?
PATR.:   Ay, and perhaps receive much honour by him.
ACHIL.:   I see my reputation is at stake;
         My fame is shrewdly gor'd.

Honor, fame, reputation! Like Romeo, like Hal, like Brutus, like Hamlet, Achilles cannot resist, as they in their various ways could not, the power of the fathers, of custom, of renown, of glory, as the case may be. But he has not yet decided. He will send word to the Trojan lords to come to his tent unarmed after the combat between Ajax and Hector:

> I have a woman's longing,
> An appetite that I am sick withal,
> To see great Hector in his weeds of peace,
> To talk with him and to behold his visage,
> Even to my full of view.

Thersites enters and regales the two friends with an account of Ajax' peacock struttings at his new honor as Greek champion, and Thersites and Patroclus put on a little play, "the pageant of Ajax," which reminds us of Falstaff and Hal in the tavern, Patroclus impersonating Thersites and Thersites Ajax. But Achilles' mind is only partly on the fun, for it is just as he goes out that he utters that unforgettable couplet:

> My mind is troubled, like a fountain stirr'd;
> And I myself see not the bottom of it.

Where, earlier in this same scene, did we hear that word "bottom"?

> Finds bottom in the uncomprehensive deeps.

It is one of Shakespeare's incomparable echoes which reveal the uncomprehensive deeps of his characters and which we miss at our peril: the same metaphor, then of a clear, now of a muddied, fountain. It tells us infallibly who and what is troubling Achilles' mind, and how close, here as elsewhere, this play which has been variously called "history," "comedy," and "satire" steers toward tragedy.

"Would the fountain of your mind were clear again," says Thersites, taking up the metaphor as Achilles goes out, "that I might water an ass at it!" We know what sort of man Thersites is. But what sort of man is this Ulysses who

> almost, like the gods,
> Does thoughts unveil

only to use them to tempt like a devil? "All other knowledge is hurtful," says Montaigne, "to him who has not the science of honesty and goodness." Shakespeare might have created Ulysses expressly to bring home that truth. Whoever prostitutes wisdom and knowledge to ends of dissension is a Ulysses.

It is from this man's own lips that we first catch this theme, in the scene before Agamemnon's tent in the first act. The physical champions and their satellites, he complains, do not appreciate the part that the brain, or, as he calls it, wisdom, plays in war:

> They tax our policy, and call it cowardice,
> *Count wisdom as no member of the war,*
> Forestall prescience, and esteem no act
> But that of hand. *The still and mental parts,*
> That do contrive how many hands shall strike
> When fitness calls them on, and know by measure
> Of their observant toil the enemies' weight,—
> Why, this hath not a finger's dignity.
> They call this bed-work, mapp'ry, closet-war;
> So that the ram that batters down the wall,
> For the great swing and rudeness of his poise,
> They place before his hand that made the engine,
> *Or those that with the fineness of their souls*
> By reason guide his execution.

Modern war, it is a truism to remark, is primarily characterized by an immense development of this Ulyssean element. Not just strategy and diplomacy, but science, administration, the harnessing of industry, all the ten thousand activities behind the battle line that brains control, are a development of these "still and mental parts" of which he speaks. And so Ulysses becomes a prophetic symbol. By sheer intellect he hurls Achilles back into the battle. *That which lets loose force is itself a form of force.* Pure intellect, Shakespeare seems to be saying, mind divorced from virtue, no matter how covertly or circuitously, always lends itself, as here, to envy and destruction. Derision, disdain, scorn, contempt, craft, satire, sarcasm, condescension: these are at once its marks and weapons. Ulysses was a master of all of them. . . . Intellect obviously must have arisen from an attempt of the physically weak to outwit or destroy the physically strong. Later, made the slave of higher faculties, it became a servant of unparalleled power and beneficence. But it is always likely to revert and reassert its autonomy. . . . From Pandulph and Richard III on, Shakespeare is full of this idea. Most of his Commodity-servers, all his plotters and politicians, illustrate it in some way. Machiavelli's *The Prince* is their political New Testament. The stage Machiavel is the idea reduced to a type. Ulysses, if we try to place him, might be put about halfway between Henry IV and Iago. He who begins by tracing the Greek failure to factions and quarrels among themselves ends by fomenting just such envy among them.

VI

On the Trojan side we encounter a still more startling situation. If Achilles, the bravest of the Greeks, was not inclined to fight, Hector, the flower of Troy, was even less so. And if Achilles was being pushed into the conflict by the craft of Ulysses, Hector was doing his best to keep his younger brother, Troilus, out of the fray. Such a parallelism and contrast can obviously be the result only of the author's constructive intention.

Among the warriors Shakespeare has drawn in any detail, Hector is the noblest and most heroic. Othello and Antony might be cited to challenge that statement. But Othello as warrior figures in the main only retrospectively and symbolically in the play that bears his name. Long before it is over "Othello's occupation's gone," as is Antony's in another sense before *Antony and Cleopatra* is over. Faulconbridge and Coriolanus are just as brave as Hector, but they lack his "sadness," as Laotse would call it. They move in another and lower world (though Coriolanus ascended from it at the very end). If there were more warriors like Hector, there would be no war. He is as alien, intrinsically, to the military world as Abraham Lincoln was. For the truth about that world, there is no one to go to like a brave but disillusioned soldier. Hector is a warrior who sees through war. The tragedy lies in his failure to live up to his vision.

Strangely—yet on second thought not strangely, but prophetically—the first glimpse we have of him is about the most unattractive one in the whole play. Says Alexander:

> Hector, whose patience
> Is as a virtue fix'd, to-day was moved.
> He chid Andromache and struck his armourer.

In its "dumb cradle" we might find the whole future of Hector in those two lines and a half. Alexander offers as explanation of Hector's unaccustomed mood the fact that Ajax had bettered him in battle the day before. But we need know little of Shakespeare to know that the cause lies deeper than that. Hector "chid Andromache and struck his armourer." Hamlet excoriated Ophelia. Othello struck Desdemona. The causes in all three cases were the same: distress of soul, a tumult in the underworld.

An offer comes from the Greeks via Nestor to end the conflict:

> Deliver Helen, and all damage else . . .
> Shall be struck off.

"Hector, what say you to 't?" asks Priam. And Hector, who almost alone because of his unassailable valor can afford to say it, replies:

> Let Helen go.

Hundreds of the Greeks who have been slain in her defense, he goes on to say, have been just as priceless as Helen. The speech in which he asserts it is just as "democratic" as that of Ulysses on degree was feudal. Who can doubt with which of the two the author came closer to agreeing? But Hector's utterance scandalizes his younger brother Troilus, who chides him for weighing the honor of a king—Priam—"in a scale of common ounces." Helenus, a third brother, here mixes in the discussion on Hector's side, but Troilus has nothing but contempt for the pacifist sentiments of this "brother priest." As Caesar did the Soothsayer, he dismisses him as a dreamer. But he cannot answer Hector in that tone, and when the latter announces tersely:

> Brother, she is not worth what she doth cost
> The holding,

all Troilus can say is,

> What is aught but as 'tis valu'd?

It is Hamlet's "there is nothing either good or bad, but thinking makes it so." The profound words with which Hector replies to his brother's question sound like Shakespeare's own answer to Hamlet's great half-truth, the poet's denial that human thought alone makes the distinction between good and bad.

> But value dwells not in particular will;
> It holds his estimate and dignity

As well wherein 'tis precious of itself
As in the prizer. 'Tis mad idolatry
To make the service greater than the god;
And the will dotes that is inclinable
To what infectiously itself affects,
Without some image of the affected merit.

There, in serious vein, is the justification of Falstaff's soliloquy on honor. There is the eternal distinction between imagination, which actually grasps reality, and idealization, which merely tries to impose itself on it.

The length and lameness of Troilus' reply are the measure of the unanswerableness of Hector's wisdom.

We turn not back the silks upon the merchant,
When we have soil'd them, nor the remainder viands
We do not throw in unrespective sieve,
Because we now are full.

Helen would hardly have been flattered by such an argument for her retention.

O theft most base,
That we have stol'n what we do fear to keep!

the younger brother concludes, letting all the cats out of the bag of war at once! Here, in so many words, in a too expansive moment, one of war's own apologists admits precisely that connection between war and robbery on which, if we are not mistaken, Shakespeare's own *Henry V* is founded.

Cassandra, inspired or mad as you choose to think her, comes in, calling out:

Cry, Trojans, cry! Lend me ten thousand eyes,
And I will fill them with prophetic tears . . .
Cry, Trojans, cry! Practise your eyes with tears!
Troy must not be, nor goodly Ilion stand.
Our firebrand brother, Paris, burns us all.
Cry, Trojans, cry! A Helen and a woe!
Cry, cry! Troy burns, or else let Helen go.

"Our firebrand brother"! The phrase should be revived in our day. But notice that the fire with which Paris burns is not pugnacity but lust (and we think of an earlier firebrand brother, Mercutio, who burned with both), as the scene at the opening of the third act is especially designed to make clear. Its theme is "love, love, nothing but love," love of course in its prostituted sense. Well does the cynically wise Pandarus inquire: "Is love a generation of vipers?" And when he turns to Paris and asks who is on the field of battle today, Paris replies, embarrassed: "Hector, Deiphobus, Helenus, Antenor, and all the gallantry of Troy: I would fain have armed to-day, but my Nell would not have it so." Helen, too, it appears, dissuades from war, as does Cassandra. But for what opposite reasons! And there is clear symbolism when, a retreat being sounded announcing the return of the warriors, Paris begs Helen to *un*arm Hector:

> Sweet Helen, I must woo you
> To help unarm our Hector . . . You shall do more
> Than all the island kings,—disarm great Hector.

It is the Samson and Delilah theme.

But to return to Cassandra. Hector, profoundly moved by her prophetic words and never doubting their authentic source from above, turns to Troilus and asks:

> Now, youthful Troilus, do not these high strains
> Of divination in our sister work
> Some touches of remorse? Or is your blood
> So madly hot that no discourse of reason,
> Nor fear of bad success in a bad cause,
> Can qualify the same?

What far-off echo do these lines start?

> . . . didst thou never hear
> That things ill got had ever bad success?

Henry VI! In those two passages, Shakespeare's supreme peace-lover (among men of political position) and his supreme military hero embrace. Hector and Henry VI. How strange a union! It confirms the conjecture that the significance of Henry VI in Shakespeare's spiritual evolution has been neglected.

Troilus replies that Cassandra is mad, not inspired, and with characteristic romantic logic proves the goodness of their cause by the fact that they are fighting for it!

> Her brain-sick raptures
> Cannot distaste the goodness of a quarrel
> Which hath our several honours all engag'd
> To make it gracious.

This pleases Paris, who, conscious that the world may accuse him of "levity" in precipitating such public turmoil for the sake of his private satisfaction, declares that, if all the power and all the difficulties were his own, he would do the same thing right over again. "Paris," says Priam,

> you speak
> Like one besotted on your sweet delights:
> You have the honey still, but these the gall;
> So to be valiant is no praise at all.

This merited rebuke from his father for his silly utterance stirs Paris to a reply that probably registers the extreme ebb of logic in all Shakespeare. And yet what a searchlight it throws across three-quarters of all the wars of history, and quite particularly over the one that culminated in the Battle of Agincourt. One can fairly see Paris draw himself up to resent Priam's charge of selfishness:

> Sir, I propose not merely to myself
> The pleasures such a beauty brings with it;
> But I would have the soil of her fair rape
> Wip'd off, in honourable keeping her.

So, and not otherwise, did Henry IV and Henry V try in vain to wipe off the soil of Richard II's blood and compensate for the fair rape of his kingdom and that of France by honorably keeping them. More phrases that fit our day. It grows increasingly clear that this play does not deal with Homeric war, or medieval war, or Elizabethan war, but with War.

And then Hector replies to Paris and Troilus—in a speech that is the crisis of the play. It is thirty-one lines long and every one of them is worthy of scrutiny, for they tell, with a kind of finality, how it is that war can continue in a world where all decent men agree in condemning it as a moral horror. They show how little you can end war merely by convincing people that war ought to be ended. They define, as no other words I can remember in Shakespeare do so succinctly (not even Hamlet's speech on blood and judgment which says much the same thing), what constitutes the freedom of the will and what the two chief enemies of that freedom are. They suggest the only sound basis for international law. And then . . .

For what comes then we are utterly unprepared. One of the noblest and wisest, suddenly, without warning, becomes one of the most disappointing speeches in Shakespeare—the last thing we would expect of Hector. The reversal at first seems out of character. Yet it is exactly what we see around us every day, what we ourselves are forever doing, if, like the vast majority, we are reasonably decent, well-meaning persons who defer to the opinions of everybody else, especially of our own class. Why, then, if Hector does what we all do, are we so unready for it? Because art is a magic mirror. In it we have seen Hector's soul, and know, as we knew of Hamlet, that he was created for something better. So were we. "Man will become better," says Chekhov, "only when you make him see what he is like." Here is what Hector said:

> Paris and Troilus, you have both said well,
> And on the cause and question now in hand
> Have gloz'd, but superficially; not much

Unlike young men, whom Aristotle thought
Unfit to hear moral philosophy.
The reasons you allege do more conduce
To the hot passion of distemper'd blood
Than to make up a free determination
'Twixt right and wrong, for pleasure and revenge
Have ears more deaf than adders to the voice
Of any true decision. Nature craves
All dues be render'd to their owners: now,
What nearer debt in all humanity
Than wife is to the husband? If this law
Of nature be corrupted through affection,
And that great minds, of partial indulgence
To their benumbed wills, resist the same,
There is a law in each well-order'd nation
To curb those raging appetites that are
Most disobedient and refractory.
If Helen then be wife to Sparta's king,
As it is known she is, these moral laws
Of nature and of nations speak aloud
To have her back return'd. Thus to persist
In doing wrong extenuates not wrong,
But makes it much more heavy. Hector's opinion
Is this in way of truth; yet ne'ertheless,
My spritely brethren, I propend to you
In resolution to keep Helen still,
For 'tis a cause that hath no mean dependance
Upon our joint and several dignities.

This by way of truth—and yet. "Yet ne'ertheless": seldom can you put your finger on the very syllables that register the turning point of a play. It is what Bernard Shaw calls Heartbreak House—

When he who might
Have lighted up and led his age,
Falls back in night.

From truth to—dignity. From wisdom to—fame. From heroism to—glory. But most of all from one's own soul to—what everybody thinks and does. Once more, "Falstaff on honour" is justified.

No wonder that Troilus exults over the conversion of his brother:

Why, there you touch'd the life of our design.
Were it not glory that we more affected
Than the performance of our heaving spleens,
I would not wish a drop of Trojan blood
Spent more in her defence. But, worthy Hector,

> She is a theme of honour and renown,
> A spur to valiant and magnanimous deeds
> Whose present courage may beat down our foes,
> And fame in time to come canonize us;
> For, I presume, brave Hector would not lose
> So rich advantage of a promis'd glory
> As smiles upon the forehead of this action
> For the wide world's revenue.

Troilus is for war that the poets of the future may not lack materials and themes! It is unkind of Shakespeare, who is reaping the harvest, not to be more sympathetic with the sower of the seed.

> I am yours,
> You valiant offspring of great Priamus,

cries Hector;

> I have a roisting challenge sent amongst
> The dull and factious nobles of the Greeks
> Will strike amazement to their drowsy spirits.

"Have sent"—what a light that past tense sheds over the preceding scene! Here doubtless is the real reason why Hector capitulated. He had already committed himself, and did not have the courage to change his mind. He falls victim to a subtler form of the same weakness that undid Achilles: pride. And he hasn't the excuse that it was a Ulysses who seduced him.

But if Hector fails at the supreme moment, it does not mean that his inner convictions are altered, or that he ceases to make efforts for peace. On the contrary. Especially does he attempt to keep Troilus out of the fighting. It is as if he reasoned: "It is too late for me to change. But my young brother can be different and better." The older generation—not to imply that Hector is quite that to Troilus—can always be divided in this respect into two classes: those who say, "We took it in our day, now let the youngsters take it," and those who, just because they faced it, want to save the younger generation from the same experience. Hector belongs to the latter class. But he has a tough subject in Troilus, who, as we have seen, is infected, despite the anachronism, with the pseudo-chivalric ideal of glory and honor.

In the scene where Hector is to fight Ajax, Ulysses draws a penetrating contrast between the two brothers. He says of Troilus that he is

> Manly as Hector, but more dangerous;
> For Hector in his blaze of wrath subscribes
> To tender objects, but he in heat of action
> Is more vindicative than jealous love.

The encounter between the Trojan and Greek champions confirms Ulysses' account of Hector. "Hector, thou sleep'st; awake thee!" cries the disgusted Troïlus, so casual are his brother's blows; and Ajax declares that he himself is not yet warm. Hector's heart is not in the fight, and, the decision left to him, he calls off the duel on the ground that Ajax is his cousin!

> The obligation of our blood forbids
> A gory emulation 'twixt us twain.

(Ajax was Priam's sister's son.) Here is another crossing of the battle lines! Another "touch of nature" to make the whole world kin. Another seed of peace. "You are as much Trojan as Greek," says Hector in effect to Ajax, "to spill your blood would be to spill my own."

> ... the just gods gainsay
> That any drop thou borrow'dst from thy mother,
> My sacred aunt, should by my mortal sword
> Be drain'd! Let me embrace thee, Ajax.

And even the unutterable Ajax—who throughout the play stands for stupid brute force—is momentarily softened; in words that we never would have believed could come from his conceited and boastful mouth, he meets Hector's fraternal attitude halfway:

> I thank thee, Hector.
> Thou art too gentle and too free a man.
> I came to kill thee, cousin, and bear hence
> A great addition earned in thy death.

Thus does a genuinely peaceful spirit in a courageous man beget peace in utterly unpromising quarters. Think, if Richard II could have met Bolingbroke so. And fancy what Hotspur and Mercutio would have said of Hector's conduct! But Romeo would have approved.

Aeneas calls Hector's attention to the fact that the two hosts drawn up to witness the combat are expecting more than this, as we would say, "for their money." Only a man of unimpeachable physical bravery could risk the unpopular answer Hector makes:

> We'll answer it:
> The issue is embracement. Ajax, farewell.

But Ajax invites him to the Grecian tents, and, taking his hand, Hector goes with him to meet and eat with the "enemy."

Then follows a scene of fraternizing and embracements that might have brought the whole affair to a friendly conclusion, if they could but have realized that there is no guide so divine as the spirit of a good moment. Agamemnon says exactly this without realizing what he is saying:

> What's past and what's to come is strew'd with husks
> And formless ruin of oblivion;
> But *in this extant moment*, faith and troth,
> Strain'd purely from all hollow bias-drawing,
> Bids thee, *with most divine integrity*,
> From heart of very heart, great Hector, welcome.

And of all the tributes in the play to Hector's fairness in fight, and proofs that in his heart of heart he is a lover of life, not of death, that of the aged Nestor is most convincing:

> I have, thou gallant Trojan, seen thee oft . . .
> When thou hast hung thy advanced sword i' th' air,
> Not letting it decline on the declin'd,
> That I have said to some my standers by
> "Lo, Jupiter is yonder dealing—*life!*"

(I add the dash and the italics to stress Nestor's meaning.) This from an enemy! Imagine, after that, mentioning the temper-mad, prisoner-slaying victor of Agincourt on the same day with Hector as an ideal warrior.

To Menelaus, Hector makes the mistake of mentioning Helen, his "*quondam* wife."

MEN.: Name her not now, sir; she's a deadly theme.

Hector quickly begs his pardon, and so it remains, characteristically, for Ulysses to bring the conversation back from fraternity to enmity by declaring that the towers of Troy are destined to "kiss their own feet." Hector answers modestly and unprovocatively, but just then Achilles steps up, and the two greatest warriors in the world confront each other, unvisored, for the first time.

HECT.:   Is this Achilles?
ACHIL.: I am Achilles.

It is another supreme moment. Hector, we feel, would have been willing to carry friendliness to the extreme point of peace. But the poison of injured pride, injected by Ulysses, has been working in Achilles' veins. He thinks of nothing but the recovery of his lost laurels, and surveys Hector only in order to decide in which part of his body he shall destroy him. Achilles' boasts draw boasts from Hector, for which, however, he is instantly sorry:

> You wisest Grecians, pardon me this brag.
> His insolence draws folly from my lips.

The scene ends—the genuine friendliness gone—on the note of enmity only momentarily suspended:

ACHIL.: To-morrow do I meet thee, fell as death,

and the next act opens with Achilles telling Patroclus that they must heat Hector's blood with wine tonight and "feast him to the height." Is Achilles learning craft from his master, Ulysses?

VII

At this point comes the eavesdropping of Troilus on the love-making of Diomedes and Cressida, at which we have already glanced, ending in the disillusioned Troilus' furious vow:

> Not the dreadful spout
> Which shipmen do the hurricano call,
> Constring'd in mass by the almighty sun,
> Shall dizzy with more clamour Neptune's ear
> In his descent than shall my prompted sword
> Falling on Diomed.

This from the man who called himself

> weaker than a woman's tear,
> Tamer than sleep, fonder than ignorance,
> Less valiant than the virgin in the night
> And skilless as unpractis'd infancy.

He was right, for his hurricano speech is not strength. It is weakness turned inside out. It is the "King Cambyses' vein," which in Shakespeare is the invariable mark of bloodlust, the "now could I drink hot blood" mood of Hamlet, the nemesis to which romantic idealization is always destined in the reaction, the "mad idolatry" that makes the service greater than the god. Cressida—like Hamlet's father—was not worthy of the worship bestowed on her.

The scene shifts back to Troy and to an unforgettable picture. Hector is about to leave for what turns out to be his last battle. Andromache is attempting to dissuade him. "Unarm, unarm," she cries. All night she has dreamed ominous dreams. Andromache is as clearly the embodiment of womanly intuition as were Portia and Calphurnia in *Julius Caesar*. Cassandra enters, and she appeals to her. But Hector replies that he has vowed to go.

> The gods are deaf to hot and peevish vows:
> They are polluted offerings,

Cassandra protests, and Andromache confirms her:

> do not count it holy
> To hurt by being just.

You might as well rob in behalf of charity, she adds. But Hector, as if he were quoting Hotspur, replies:

> Life every man holds dear; but the brave man
> Holds honour far more precious-dear than life.

Yet how little Hector's soul is back of his resistance to his wife's and his sister's apprehensions is shown a moment later when Troilus enters and Hector discovers that he too intends to enter the battle. He does his best to dissuade him, readily projecting on his brother the truth he will not admit about himself:

> No, faith, young Troilus; doff thy harness, youth. . . .
> Unarm thee.

Unarm! just what the women have been begging *him* to do.

> TRO.: Brother, you have a vice of mercy in you,
> Which better fits a lion than a man.

Hector wants to know what that vice is, and to be chidden for it. His brother has noticed just what Nestor did.

> TRO.: When many times the captive Grecian falls,
> Even in the fan and wind of your fair sword,
> You bid them rise, and live.
> HECT.: O, 'tis fair play.
> TRO.:   Fool's play, by heaven, Hector.
> HECT.: How now! how now!
> TRO.:   For the love of all the gods,
> Let's leave the hermit pity with our mothers,
> And when we have our armours buckled on,
> The venom'd vengeance ride upon our swords,
> Spur them to ruthful work, rein them from ruth.

An echo, if anything ever was, of Henry V's "Then imitate the action of the tiger." And what does Hector think of this red-blooded doctrine?

> Fie, savage, fie!

is his annihilating comment on it, and everything converges to show that it was Shakespeare's too.

> Troilus, I would not have you fight to-day,

he adds more calmly. "Who should withhold me?" the incorrigible youth replies.

And just then Cassandra, who at Andromache's request has gone to fetch Priam, comes back with him.

> Lay hold upon him, Priam, hold him fast,

she cries to her father of Hector,

> He is thy crutch; now if thou lose thy stay,
> Thou on him leaning, and all Troy on thee,
> Fall all together.

And Priam, taking up all the motifs of the scene, condenses them into one final overwhelming appeal:

> Come, Hector, come, go back.
> Thy wife hath dream'd; thy mother hath had visions;
> Cassandra doth foresee; and I myself
> Am like a prophet suddenly enrapt
> To tell thee that this day is ominous:
> Therefore, come back.

What pages those lines recapitulate! It is like a great allegorical painting in words. Andromache is Love and Womanly Intuition. Hecuba is Motherhood. Cassandra is Divine Prophecy. Priam is Age, Experience, Wisdom— earthly Prophecy. The dreams, visions, and divinations are the Gods, or from the Gods, themselves. And they are arrayed unanimously against war.

And who, or what, are arrayed against *them*? The "faith" and "honour" of a man who dares not break a vow taken in what he himself denounced as "a bad cause." That, and the romantic fury of a disappointed boy, who is bent, not on the welfare of his country, but on personal revenge for the perfidy of a woman he has overidealized.

Hector, not unmindful of the respect due to Priam as both his father and his king, begs his consent to go. (Priam, as father, is here the exact opposite of the Ghost in *Hamlet*. He is Wisdom and Experience. The Ghost was paternal Authority and the force of Tradition.) "O Priam, yield not to him!" cries Cassandra. "Do not, dear father," Andromache beseeches.

> Andromache, I am offended with you.
> Upon the love you bear me, get you in,

Hector chides her. And the laconic, but momentous, stage direction is: "*Exit Andromache,*" even as once it was, "*Exit Portia.*"

> This foolish, dreaming, superstitious girl
> Makes all these bodements,

exclaims Troilus, blaming Cassandra for everything. But the superstitious girl, as if the event were right before her eyes, draws a picture of precisely what is to happen, perhaps but a few hours later, on the plains of Troy:

> And all cry Hector! Hector's dead! O Hector!

Then, seeing her warnings are in vain, the prophetess becomes the sister for a moment as she bids a last good-by:

> Farewell; yet, soft! Hector, I take my leave.
> Thou dost thyself and all our Troy deceive.
> *Exit Cassandra*

VIII

We pass to the battlefield, and the rest can be told in a few sentences. Patroclus is slain. His death affects Achilles as the perfidy of Cressida does Troilus. It arouses him to an unreasoning fury. He encounters Hector on the field. But Hector, perfectly self-controlled as usual, perceiving that Achilles is battle-weary, exhibits that "vice of mercy" that Troilus had rebuked him for, and offers to let Achilles catch his breath:

> Pause, if thou wilt.

But Achilles, construing Hector's fairness as pride, replies:

> I do disdain thy courtesy, proud Trojan.
> Be happy that my arms are out of use;
> My rest and negligence befriends thee now,
> But thou anon shalt hear of me again;
> Till when, go seek thy fortune.

Achilles thereupon departs, refusing to fight, and Hector remarks to himself,

> Fare thee well:
> I would have been much more a fresher man,
> Had I expected thee.

And then Achilles, the once noble Achilles, does what is as uncharacteristic of his former self as Hamlet's murder of Rosencrantz and Guildenstern is of his. He gathers his Myrmidons about him and gives them directions:

> Mark what I say. Attend me where I wheel;
> Strike not a stroke, but keep yourselves in breath;
> And when I have the bloody Hector found,
> Empale him with your weapons round about,
> In fellest manner execute your aims.
> Follow me, sirs, and my proceedings eye;
> It is decreed Hector the great must die.

They find Hector resting, his armor off.

> I am unarm'd; forego this vantage, Greek,

the Trojan cries as he spies them.

> Strike, fellows, strike; this is the man I seek,

is Achilles' answer. They strike him down. And Achilles bids them go forth to proclaim:

> "Achilles hath the mighty Hector slain,"

and, tying Hector's body to his horse's tail, he drags it over the field. Jack Cade, the anarchist, treated his fallen foe in the same way. We think, too, of Aufidius, and of that coward and bully Northumberland who declared that all advantages are fair in war, and "ten to one is no impeach of valour."

> He's dead; and at the murderer's horse's tail,
> In beastly sort, dragg'd through the shameful field.

Troilus, in so reporting Hector's death, does not hesitate to use the right word for the man who brought it about. Coward, murderer, beast: such is the end of the man who once uttered those miraculous lines about the human eye—the once bright Achilles. That end is so ignominious that many critics have rejected the conclusion of this play as not Shakespeare's, the work of another hand.

But why?

It is nothing but a more extreme, and, if you insist, cynical, version of exactly that psychology of callousness and fury that we encounter in varying degrees in Richard II, Henry V, and Hamlet. The twentieth century can testify to the difficulty of keeping war "honorable" and the ease with which it passes into atrocity. Shakespeare understood all that. And though he lets Ulysses slip quietly out of the action of the play, he has made abundantly clear the guilt that is upon his head for the murder of Hector. Those who are responsible for "the still and mental parts" of modern war may well reflect on Ulysses and his contribution to the humiliating catastrophe of this drama.

The perfection with which the end of this play fits its beginning is a further reason against rejecting its final scenes as unShakespearean. Troilus opens *Troilus and Cressida* with these words:

> Call here my varlet; I'll unarm again.
> Why should I war without the walls of Troy,
> That find such cruel battle here within?
> Each Trojan that is master of his heart,
> Let him to field; Troilus, alas! hath none.

He ends it—except for Pandarus' last flick of the tail—with these words:

> . . . thou great-siz'd coward,
> No space of earth shall sunder our two hates.
> *I'll haunt thee like a wicked conscience still,*
> *That mouldeth goblins swift as frenzy's thoughts.*
> Strike a free march to Troy! With comfort go;
> Hope of revenge shall hide our inward woe.

Could the poet have taken a better way than by this link between beginning and end to bring home his forever-reiterated idea that war within eventuates in war without? (And what a comment on *Hamlet* is the couplet I have italicized!)

But the *very* end of the play—again a passage often rejected as not Shakespeare's—is left for Pandarus, whose epilogue-like address to traitors and bawds ties its two parts and themes together in a final fling of the sordidest cynicism.

> Hence, broker-lackey! ignomy and shame
> Pursue thy life, and live aye with thy name!

cries the youth who had once accepted his services gladly. To which Pandarus, left alone, replies:

> A goodly medicine for mine aching bones! O world! world! world! thus is the poor agent despised! O traitors and bawds, how earnestly are you set a-work, and how ill requited! Why should our endeavour be so loved and the performance so loathed? What verse for it? What instance for it? Let me see:
>
> > "Full merrily the humble-bee doth sing,
> > Till he hath lost his honey and his sting;
> > And being once subdu'd in armed tail,
> > Sweet honey and sweet notes together fail."

Traitors and bawds. Honey and stings. Lust and war. (If someone else wrote it, he certainly caught the author's idea.) Did not Hector give fair warning of this in that great speech of his which he himself had not the power to heed?

> . . . for pleasure and revenge
> Have ears more deaf than adders to the voice
> Of any true decision.

The two endings of the play strike just those two notes: Troilus' revenge; Pandarus' pleasure. The aching bones of the profligate; the war-racked frame of the body politic. Readers of *Hamlet* who think the killing of the King at the end was a realization after long delay of Hamlet's divinely appointed duty will have a hard time coming to terms with that great sentence of Hector's.

IX

Matthew Arnold once wrote a little poem, *Palladium*, which deals with part of this same Greek-Trojan material. Its tone and atmosphere are about as far removed from those of *Troilus and Cressida* as anything could be. And yet, if I am not mistaken, Shakespeare's play says, mainly in negative terms, exactly the same thing that the poem says more positively:

> Set where the upper streams of Simois flow
> Was the Palladium, high 'mid rock and wood;
> And Hector was in Ilium, far below,
> And fought, and saw it not—but there it stood!
>
> It stood, and sun and moonshine rain'd their light
> On the pure columns of its glen-built hall.
> Backward and forward roll'd the waves of fight
> Round Troy—but while this stood, Troy could not fall.
>
> So, in its lovely moonlight, lives the soul.
> Mountains surround it, and sweet virgin air;
> Cold plashing, past it, crystal waters roll;
> We visit it by moments, ah, too rare!
>
> We shall renew the battle in the plain
> To-morrow;—red with blood will Xanthus be;
> Hector and Ajax will be there again,
> Helen will come upon the wall to see.
>
> Then we shall rust in shade, or shine in strife,
> And fluctuate 'twixt blind hopes and blind despairs,
> And fancy that we put forth all our life,
> And never know how with the soul it fares.
>
> Still doth the soul, from its lone fastness high,
> Upon our life a ruling effluence send.
> And when it fails, fight as we will, we die;
> And while it lasts, we cannot wholly end.

The defect of the characters of Shakespeare's *Troilus and Cressida* was that they visited the soul by moments, ah, too rare!

Chapter XXV

All's Well That Ends Well

I

There is something not far from unanimity among critics that of the works whose authorship has never been seriously questioned *All's Well That Ends Well* is Shakespeare's least satisfactory play. Whether it was an early one (possibly the lost *Love's Labour's Won* of Meres' list), revised during the so-called dark comedy period, or a product of that period alone, has long been debated. Its style, in places, is loose and juvenile; in other places, compact and mature. It is not difficult to think of it as a work conceived and executed in one spirit and revised in another, or, if never revised, written in the first place in a state of vacillation between romance and realism, or even between satire and romance. There is no record of any contemporary performance, and it may be that the poet himself regarded it lightly.

There are two very different ways of taking *All's Well That Ends Well*, either of which receives both support and contradiction from the text.

II

One way to regard it is as a sort of folk tale. In that case it has a certain kinship with the Patient Griselda story. The poor physician's daughter, Helena, falls in love with the young count, Bertram, out of her sphere.

> It were all one
> That I should love a bright particular star
> And think to wed it, he is so above me.

This bright particular star *is* all his worshiper believes. But the star has been occulted by the clouds of this world, the youth corrupted by bad companionship and social fashion into a quite intolerable snob. It has reached a point indeed where, except for his appearance, there is little resemblance between the girl's idea of what he is and what he has actually become. The drastic character of the change is admitted by Bertram himself near the end when, supposing Helena dead, he tells how as a shy boy he fell in love with Lafeu's daughter, Maudlin, only to desert her when he was mastered by a spirit of contempt and scorn. Through this distorting medium all beauty was warped into hideousness, he now confesses: hence his disdain for the woman he abandoned after the marriage ceremony, whom all others praised and whom he has come to love himself now she is dead.* In a word, just as his soul was about to be born, his bad angel, Parolles, took possession of him.

With the penetration of love, his good angel, Helena, alone sees through from the first to what this perverted youth is under what he has become. By keeping her faith in that vision, in spite of the evidence against it, she brings about a resurrection of himself within himself through the miracle of what seems to him her own literal resurrection. Her sudden appearance in the flesh after being reported dead shocks him back into what he has really been all along.

So summarized, the drama is a struggle between Helena and Parolles for possession of Bertram, and, in mere outline, such a story is credible enough. Who, a hundred times, has not seen some young darling of the gods turned into a worldling in a mere matter of months by bad companions? And who, one time in that hundred, has not seen him retransformed into something like his original image by the love of a devoted woman? That Shakespeare intended it so, one might argue, is rendered the more likely by the similar situation at the end of *Much Ado about Nothing* and the analogous one at the end of *The Winter's Tale*. And then, too, there are the fine lines of Lafeu—one of those key speeches that seem to give us a glimpse into the poet's own mind—wherein it is implied that the smart young intellectuals who think the day of miracles is past are more retrograde than advanced in their thinking.

But if Shakespeare planned it this way, it must be confessed that he managed rather badly. Instead of saturating his play, as he did *The Winter's Tale*, with romantic atmosphere, he has kept it on the whole severely realistic, not to say satiric. Moreover, he has blackened Bertram so utterly that,

---

* The puzzling shift of antecedent of the pronoun whereby the speech which begins about Maudlin (V, iii, 44) ends about Helena, so far from being an example of shiftless composition, is an example of psychological subtlety. It is almost exactly paralleled in the opening scene of *Othello* (I, i, 67), where Iago begins speaking of Brabantio and continues about Othello with nothing but the sense to indicate the change of reference. This seems almost enough in itself to assure a late date for this particular passage.

though we admit the general possibility of miracles, this particular combination of green boy, mettlesome animal, and arrogant young count seems to have placed himself beyond their pale. Even after his eyes are opened to the dastardly character of his boon companion, Parolles, and when we might be expecting some signs of regeneration in himself, his prospective father-in-law, Lafeu, grows so disgusted with him that he says, "I will buy me a son-in-law in a fair . . . I'll none of him." And to make the supposed miracle at the end harder to credit, it is just on its threshold that Bertram touches his moral nadir. When he was trying to win her in Florence, Diana was to him a "titled goddess": he swore vows of eternal fidelity to her and gave her his jealously cherished family ring. Now, confronted by her, he dubs her "a common gamester to the camp," and hopes the King will not think so lowly of his honor as to imagine he could ever have made promises to such a "fond and desperate creature." Cad! It is the word that seems to spring to almost every lip in the attempt to characterize this blackguardly young count with his precious "honor." Dr. Johnson, in words that have been quoted over and over, disposes of Bertram tersely:

I cannot reconcile my heart to Bertram; a man noble without generosity, and young without truth; who marries Helena as a coward, and leaves her as a profligate; when she is dead by his unkindness, sneaks home to a second marriage, is accused by a woman whom he has wronged, defends himself by falsehood, and is dismissed to happiness.

Almost the sole thing in Bertram's favor in this final scene is his blush when confronted by Diana with the ring. That blush seems to indicate that his soul is still alive, and it is conceivable that a rare actor, by suggesting the struggle within the man and his suppressed abhorrence of the very lies he is telling, might make the miracle at the end convincing. But the text is against him. The conclusion is too swift and huddled, and when Bertram suddenly exclaims to the King, on hearing that Helena has fulfilled his prescriptions,

> If she, my liege, can make me know this clearly,
> I'll love her dearly, ever, ever dearly,

the light couplet seems utterly out of keeping with the momentousness of the supposed conversion. And even if an actor could carry this off successfully, he would need a still more miraculous actress in the part of Helena to come to his support.

All through the earlier scenes of the play, up to her marriage with Bertram, Helena fits perfectly the role of the romantic heroine. She wins the love and admiration of everyone worth winning. Her foster-mother, the

Countess of Rousillon, grand lady that she is, treats her like her own child, elicits from her the secret of her love for her son, and is all for the misalliance, as the world will call it.

> . . . a maid too virtuous
> For the contempt of empire,

she pronounces her when Bertram will not accept Helena as his wife. (The genuine aristocrat, as Shakespeare never fails to see, is always a democrat at heart.) The wise and fiery Lafeu is furious at the courtiers who are insensible to Helena's charms, calls them "boys of ice," says if they were sons of his he'd have them whipped or worse, and only wishes he were young enough to have a chance of being chosen by this incomparable girl. The stubborn King, mortally ill as he thinks himself, cannot resist her either, finally consents to let her cure him, and in the election scene is inspired by her to an utterance on the equality of man that would have satisfied Robert Burns himself or the most doctrinaire democrat of the eighteenth century. And Helena justifies these high opinions of her by her own conduct. She keeps secrets that are hard to keep, tells truths that are hard to tell, sees instinctively through the good-for-nothing Parolles yet tolerates him for Bertram's sake, and reveals in general a blend of tenderness and courage, religious fervor and capacity for instant action that is irresistible. "Star" is her favorite word. But hers is a pragmatic astrology.

> Our remedies oft in ourselves do lie
> Which we ascribe to heaven,

she remarks in a soliloquy which anticipates Benjamin Franklin on the subject of God helping those who help themselves. Yet she can also say a little later,

> But most it is presumption in us when
> The help of heaven we count the act of men.

The "contradiction" is really an embrace of opposites and is characteristic of her wisdom. Only (in these earlier scenes) her conversation with Parolles on virginity seems to the modern reader out of key, and there the state of the text permits any who are shocked by its frankness to take refuge, with more plausibility than is usual in such cases, in the explanation that the passage may be an interpolation. All in all the early Helena is so entrancingly drawn as to make us think that Coleridge was only partly, not wholly, out of his head when he described her as "Shakespeare's loveliest creation."

But then something happens.

Renunciation, Emily Dickinson reminds us, is a piercing virtue. And

when Helena, hearing Bertram declare that he cannot love her, turns to
the King and says simply,

> That you are well restor'd, my lord, I'm glad;
> *Let the rest go*,

those four words are her moral peak. It is difficult for the imagination not
to ask what would have happened if Helena had had the courage to remain
at this level and had resolutely refused, even against the King's wishes, to
allow an unwilling bridegroom to go through the empty form of marriage
with her. There is no question that we would have admired her more, or
that, however secretly, Bertram would have also. Might he not have gone
away from such a rejection to dream of the spirited girl who had had the
self-respect both to love and to refuse him?

> Renunciation is the choosing
> Against itself,
> Itself to justify
> Unto itself.

Might he not indeed have grown more and more unable to put her image
out of his heart and have come in time to regret and long for her? If Shakespeare had continued his story along these lines, he would have had to
throw away most of his inherited plot, but he might have saved a multitude of critics the trouble of apologizing for or explaining Helena's subse-
quent conduct.

What happens instead, if not so near the romantic heart's desire, is at
least in accord with the recorded fact that women have been known to act
unpredictably in this matter of marriage. When the King orders Bertram,
willy-nilly, to take Helena as his wife under threat of the loss of royal
favor, the Helena Shakespeare has created hasn't the power, any more than
Bertram, to stand out against him.

A little later, after Bertram has deserted her and gone to the wars,
Helena's sacrificial side again comes out when she decides to become a
pilgrim and exile in order that her husband may return to his native land.
But no sooner is she in disguise and in Florence than Fate suddenly confronts her with an utterly incredible chance to attain her heart's desire and
to fulfil the equally impossible conditions of Bertram's acceptance of her
as his wife: to get his family ring from him, namely, and to become the
mother of his child. Whereupon, as before, the pendulum swings in a less
ascetic direction. She now no longer says, "Let the rest go," but, even more
succinctly, "Let's about it." The acceptance of even such conditions as
Helena accepted in order to effect the consummation of marriage may be

considered a morally less difficult act than the renunciation of love—and human nature is capable of both. Helena at different crises of her career shows herself human in each of these respects. It is significant, however, that on the threshold of her nocturnal assignation with Bertram she calls explicit attention no less than four times in rapid succession to the fact that the device to which she has resorted is lawful. (Lawful, be it noted, not holy.)

> You see it lawful, then ... which, if it speed,
> Is wicked meaning in a lawful deed
> And lawful meaning in a lawful act,
> Where both not sin, and yet a sinful fact.
> *But let's about it.*

And she proceeds to go about this sinful fact and sinful act with what from the point of view of getting things accomplished can only be called commendable dispatch.

It has been pointed out that in all this Helena is merely acting as did a long line of folklore heroines from whom she is obviously descended. Her conduct, we are told, would have been perfectly acceptable to an Elizabethan audience. There is no reason to doubt it. But a work of art must be judged by the impression it makes on us, not on somebody in the past. Otherwise we are ceasing to take it as a work of art and turning it into a historical document (which, just possibly, this play may have become). The question is, then, whether Helena is psychologically all of a piece or whether she is two incompatible women made so by a contradiction between the way Shakespeare originally conceived her and the exigencies of his plot. It is interesting to note in this connection that she acts much as does that other virtuous maid, Isabella, in *Measure for Measure*. They both seem to show that while there are moral pinnacles in human nature there are also lower altitudes, and that right after a pinnacle is the time to expect a less lofty elevation. Even more pertinent to Helena's case than folklore parallels perhaps are those stanzas on Opportunity from *The Rape of Lucrece* which deal with the relation to sin and crime of the chance to commit them, but which also have a general bearing on the relation of opportunity to the lower moral ranges of human nature as distinguished from its rarer summits. What Helena and Isabella might be held to demonstrate is that there can be room inside the same feminine creature for both the religiously idealistic girl and the racial woman. In which case *All's Well That Ends Well* would be decidedly more realistic than romantic.

III

And this brings us to the other very different way in which this play may be taken.

It may be taken as a second and less clandestinely ironical *Two Gentlemen of Verona*, the two gentlemen in this case of course being Bertram and Parolles, two gentlemen of France instead of two gentlemen of Italy, though it is in Italy as it happens that their "gentle" tendencies come to full fruit. From this angle, Parolles, seducer of Bertram, becomes centrally important, and that he was so considered in the stage tradition of the seventeenth century may be indicated by the fact that Charles I in his Second Folio copy of the plays substituted *Monsieur Parolles* for the regular title.

However that may be, there is no doubt that in his low kind Parolles is a masterpiece. Into him Shakespeare seems to have poured something like his full abhorrence for the Renaissance gentleman on the French-Italian model, the spineless creature whose aim in life is to wear what is being worn, to say what is being said, and to do what is being done by those who "move under the influence of the most received star": to be a fashionmonger, in other words, a parrot, a parasite, a flatterer, an echo, a copy-cat, a so-say-I, a fool of time. "The soul of this man is his clothes," says Lafeu of Parolles. And it is, both literally and metaphorically. "I will never trust a man again for keeping his sword clean," says the Second Lord to the same effect, "nor believe he can have everything in him by wearing his apparel neatly."

It may be doubted if there is any other figure in Shakespeare for whom so many other characters in the same play express such unanimously savage scorn. To Helena, Parolles is a notorious liar, a great way fool, solely a coward. To the Countess, a very tainted fellow and full of wickedness. To Diana, a vile rascal, a jackanapes with scarfs. To Mariana, a filthy officer. To the First Lord, this counterfeit lump of ore. To the Second Lord, a most notable coward, an infinite and endless liar, an hourly promise-breaker, the owner of no one good quality. . . . To the Clown, a poor, decayed, ingenious, foolish, rascally knave. To Lafeu . . . but Lafeu seems to have been created for the express purpose of detesting Parolles and cannot so much as come into his presence without giving vent to some fresh denunciation of a creature whose master, he says, is the devil and whom he refuses to recognize as a member of the human race. A fool, a knave, a vagabond and no true traveler, a snipt-taffeta fellow, a red-tailed humble-bee, are a few of the names he calls him; but he sums him up best in the five words: "Thou art a general offence." And it is this general offense whom Bertram has picked as his bosom companion and guiding star. When at last, however, his eyes, too, are opened, he adds his voice to the chorus: "Damnable both-sides rogue," "counterfeit model," "cat," "past-saving slave," "most perfidious slave"—his confession of what a slave of a slave he has been himself.

Of the love-making of this type of gentleman Parolles himself gives a classic account when the King is trying to find out the truth about Bertram and Diana. What was there between them? he asks.

PAR.: So please your majesty, my master hath been an honourable gentle-
man. Tricks he hath had in him, which gentlemen have.
KING: Come, come, to the purpose. Did he love this woman?
PAR.: Faith, sir, he did love her; but how?
KING: How, I pray you?
PAR.: He did love her, sir, as a gentleman loves a woman.
KING: How is that?
PAR.: He loved her, sir, and loved her not.

According to the disillusioned Bertram, the mere telling of the truth is enough to turn Parolles sick, but he seems to have come fairly close to it on this occasion. To Bertram, before she was won, nothing could be too good for Diana in the way of rings and promises. After she is won (as he supposes) she becomes in his eyes a drab anyone might have had at market price. But the poet does not leave it to Parolles to pass the last judgment on this gentlemanly behavior. He passes it himself.

The incident of the drum toward the end of the drama has been held by many to be mere theatrical padding. "The whole Parolles business," say the New Cambridge editors, "can be put into square brackets, and cut out of the story, like a wen, without the smallest detriment to the remaining tissue." On the contrary, the poet uses it most effectively to elucidate his main theme. Here, as so often, the rule holds: it is just when Shakespeare seems to sink lowest that he sheds illumination, as stars are visible by daylight from the shafts of deep mines.

We have noted more than once Shakespeare's belief in the radical identity of offensive war and sexual lust. It is no coincidence that in this play Bertram turns from love and a land at peace to adultery and what is little better than mercenary war.

> Great Mars, I put myself into thy file,

he proclaims as he sets out,

> Make me but like my thoughts, and I shall prove
> A lover of thy drum, hater of love.

Oddly, it is a drum that opens Bertram's eyes to the true nature of Parolles. The same drum opens our eyes, if they need any opening, to the true nature of the man Parolles has corrupted. The parallel is startling.

Through a trick of his companions, devised especially to expose him, Parolles, blindfolded, believing himself with strangers, commits treason (as he supposes) against his friends only to discover when his eyes are uncovered that he has been in the company of his friends all along without knowing it. By a trick of Helena's and Diana's especially contrived to deceive him, Bertram, at night and in the dark, believing himself to be with a "strange" woman, commits adultery (as he supposes) against his wife only to discover in the end that he had been in his wife's company throughout the interview without knowing it. Such a meticulous analogy could not conceivably be anything but a conscious one. Once and for all it identifies Bertram's moral conduct with Parolles': after which nothing further need be said of it.

In Parolles, Shakespeare's wrath against the "gentleman" seems to culminate (unless late in life in Cloten he may be said to have surpassed even Parolles). In Proteus and Valentine, in Don Armado and Tybalt, in Bassanio and Claudio, in Aguecheek and Osric, and in a dozen others, Shakespeare paints various shades of the type, on the whole in a bantering or lightly ironical spirit, though in Hamlet's fierce scorn for Rosencrantz and Guildenstern is felt the sense that under fine manners treachery may ever be lurking. But in the utter abjectness of Parolles, who is willing to do anything in order to live, he goes a step further. Parolles, as corrupter of youth, is a cousin of the Immoral Falstaff, but he is without one ray of the sunshine and good humor that redeem the Immortal Falstaff. He is, rather, a sort of Pistol translated from the realm of bombast and blank verse into that of prose and reality. For him Shakespeare seems to feel something of that deep-seated antipathy that characterizes Kent's feeling for Oswald, Imogen's for Cloten, or Lafeu's for Parolles himself in this very play: a sort of instinctive opposite and correlative of love at first sight. Why?

Why should the merciful and charitable Shakespeare who understood so well

> All pains the immortal spirit must endure,
> All weakness which impairs, all griefs which bow,

have felt for this particular type such mounting and extreme aversion? Was it because in the "gentleman" he sensed the everlasting enemy of man? "I write man," says Lafeu to Parolles, "to which title age cannot bring thee."* The man seeks the realization of his own God-given capacities. The "gentleman" seeks the "good form" his fellows follow. In the mutual imitation of one another that this type practices and on which it thrives lies the destruction, Shakespeare apparently felt, of all that he loved best: freedom, growth, individuality, and, in the end, the very principle of life itself. "No, no, no," cries Lafeu to the Countess, "your son was misled with a snipt-taffeta fellow there, whose villanous saffron would have made

---

* Lafeu held man to be a nobler title than gentleman just as Hamlet held it to be a nobler one than king.

all the unbaked and doughy youth of a nation in his colour." The fate of nothing less than the whole younger generation, and ultimately of the nation, is involved in this gregarious slavery.

Not that imitation is not indispensable. Without it man would have no habits and society no cohesion. It all depends on who is set up to be imitated, toward what color youth aspires. If it is a sickly yellow, a "villanous saffron," all is lost. "When you have children," a young mother wrote the other day, "you are constantly amazed that the world turns out to be such a mess. The children of the world are so bright and learn so fast and are so full of promise, you'd think everything would be perfect by the time they grew up. What goes wrong?" What goes wrong of course is that instead of our making ourselves over in our own and our children's best image, they make themselves over in our worst one, or, more likely, in the image of the crowd, and its ringleaders, with whom they are turned loose to play. Bertram falls under the influence of Parolles. There is much to indicate that when he wrote this play Shakespeare was thinking along the same line as this young mother.

Why otherwise should he have made room for such a full study of Bertram's mother, and, in retrospect, of his father, who is no longer living? The Countess of Rousillon ("the most beautiful old woman's part ever written," Bernard Shaw calls her role) is a genuine lady in the finest meaning of that term, and his father, as pictured by the King, a genuine gentleman with manners and morals depicted in detail for express contrast with those of the younger generation. Bertram, in body and face, is like his father, and his mother in blessing him prays he may be like him in manners and virtue too:

> Be thou blest, Bertram, and succeed thy father
> In manners, as in shape! Thy blood and virtue
> Contend for empire in thee, and thy goodness
> Share with thy birthright!

And the King stresses the point by echoing the Countess:

> Youth, thou bear'st thy father's face.
> Frank nature, rather curious than in haste,
> Hath well compos'd thee. Thy father's moral parts
> Mayst thou inherit too!

To these hopes the fact that Helena loves Bertram seems to give some warrant (though she confesses that she knows no more of him than the sunworshiper does of the sun). But something goes wrong. If the Bertrams, born of such stock and having such parents, go to the dogs, what hope is there for youth less fortunate and less well endowed? Or is Shakespeare hinting that life tends to die off at the top and that it is precisely the high-born and privileged who run the greatest risk of degeneration? "Boys will be boys," say the average father and mother as they doff their parental duties and turn their son over to the spirit of the gang for his upbringing. Are parents of supposedly more responsibility doing the same thing when they send their sons to school or college not to be educated but to make "contacts" with scions of the best families and to assimilate their social code?

> Natural rebellion, done i' the blaze of youth,

says the Countess, contemplating the result in Bertram's case,

> When oil and fire, too strong for reason's force,
> O'erbears it and burns on.

But the waste and tragedy are no less on that account, and Lafeu hits the nail on the head when he says that Bertram did wrong not only to the King, his mother, and Helena,

> but to himself
> The greatest wrong of all,

though the King, for ordering Bertram to marry, must accept his share of blame.

The King is an odd mixture. He remarks truly of himself

> thou mayst see a sunshine and a hail
> In me at once.

Kindly and likable in his moments of relaxation, but stubborn and irascible when opposed, he is a radical democrat in theory but a feudal monarch insisting on his royal prerogatives in practice. " 'Let me not live,' " he quotes Bertram's father as having said,

> 'After my flame lacks oil, to be the snuff
> Of younger spirits, whose apprehensive senses
> All but new things disdain,'

and adds,

> I after him do after him wish too.

Yet when Bertram naturally resents having a wife thrust on him, and shows some spirit, the King, right on the heels of the most equalitarian speech in all Shakespeare, snuffs out that spirit without a qualm. And Bertram, to his shame, tamely submits. Yet in the end the King is forgiving:

> Not one word more of the consumed time.
> Let's take the instant by the forward top;

> For we are old, and on our quick'st decrees
> The inaudible and noiseless foot of time
> Steals ere we can effect them,

unforgettable lines that suggest the distinction between living life in the present like a man and squandering it on the present like a "gentleman," things that look so alike but are such poles apart, a distinction on which so much of this play turns.

And right into the midst of a scene that contains things of this high order comes Diana, bursting with explosive secrets, so bent apparently on bewildering the King with her riddling answers and squeezing the last drops of suspense and irony out of a complicated situation, that we scarcely blame the King for ordering her put in prison. With her the play sags to a level of mere ingenuity and theatricalism that might tempt us to date it as early as *The Comedy of Errors.*

The spectator or reader is left to make what he will of the play's abrupt conclusion. Does it end "well"? Has Bertram awakened to his real self at last? Or is it Helena who is in for the awakening? Those who are disposed to accept the miracle will point to the folklore precedents, to analogies elsewhere in Shakespeare, and to the Elizabethan tendency to believe in extreme conversions of this sort—like Oliver's in *As You Like It;* while those who scent irony will italicize two words of the King's in the couplet with which the play closes:

> All yet *seems* well; and *if* it end so meet,
> The bitter past, more welcome is the sweet.

Possibly Shakespeare intended his play to be an interrogation. Perhaps a hesitation between possibilities was the very effect at which he was aiming. In that case one of the keys to the play would be the wise observation of the First Lord:

> The web of our life is of a mingled yarn, good and ill together: our virtues would be proud, if our faults whipped them not; and our crimes would despair, if they were not cherished by our virtues.

Bertram and Helena both illustrate this truth, and Shakespeare was soon to pursue further this problem of the relation of virtue and vice, in *Measure for Measure.*

Chapter XXVI

Measure for Measure

I

"Would you know a man? Give him power." History sometimes seems little else than an extended comment on that ancient maxim. Our own day has elucidated it on a colossal scale. *Measure for Measure* might have been expressly written to drive home its truth. It is little wonder, then, that the play of Shakespeare's in which the word "authority" occurs more often than in any other should have an extraordinary pertinence for a century in which the word "authoritarian" is on so many lips. The central male figure of the drama is one of the most searching studies ever made of the effect of power upon character.

Measure for Measure, like *Troilus and Cressida*, is closely bound to *Hamlet*. It is as if Shakespeare, having exposed in that masterpiece and the plays that culminated in it the futility of revenge as a method of requiting wrong, asked: what then? How, when men fail to keep the peace, shall their quarrels be settled, their misconduct penalized, without resort to personal violence? To that question the all but universal reply of the wiser part of human experience seems to have been: by law. In place of revenge—justice. Instead of personal retaliation—legal adjudication. "A government of laws and not of men": that is the historic answer of those peoples at least who have some freedom. And there is the imposing body of common and statute law to back it up. Trial by jury. Equality before the law. The advance of civilization that these concepts and conquests register cannot be overestimated. Under their spell men are even tempted to the syllogism:

> Quarrels are settled by law.
> Wars are just larger quarrels.
> Therefore: wars can be settled by law.

Recent history is little more than the story of the world's disillusionment
with regard to this conclusion. The weakness of the syllogism lies in its
major premise. "A government of laws and not of men." It sounds august.
But there never was, there is not, and there never will be, any such thing.
If only laws would construe, administer, and enforce themselves! But until they do, they will rise no nearer justice than the justice in the minds and
hearts of their very human agents and instruments. Those with power may
sedulously inculcate in subjects the illusion that there is a necessary connection between law and justice as the very cement of the state, without
which the political structure would collapse (as well it might); but, philo-
sophically, any mental structure erected on this illusion is built on quick-
sand. Disillusionment on this subject, if it comes at all, usually comes
gradually. We cling to the older and more comforting notion here as we
do to infantile ideas of God. When at last we realize that the blessings of the
law (which cannot be exaggerated) are due to the wisdom and goodness
of man, and its horrors (which also cannot be exaggerated) to his cruelty
and greed, we have grasped the fact that law is just an instrument—no more
good or bad in itself than the stone we use as a hammer or a missile—and we
will never again be guilty of thinking of law and war as opposites, or of
confusing peace with the reign of law. Whether the horrors of war are
greater or less than the horrors of law may be debated. Shelley, for one, put
"legal crime" at the nadir of human baseness. In cowardice, at any rate, it
ranks below open violence. *Measure for Measure* records, possibly, Shakespeare's first full disillusionment on this subject.

> It is the law, not I, condemn your brother.

The entire play might be said to have been written just to italicize that lie.
The angel-villain tries to hide behind it as behind a shield. So-called civilization tries to do the same. But civilization—as Emerson remarked—crowed
too soon.

II

For fourteen years Vienna has suffered from so lax an enforcement of
the laws that the very babies have taken to beating their nurses, and a
visitor from outside the city might actually

> have seen corruption boil and bubble
> Till it o'er-run the stew: laws for all faults,
> But faults so countenanc'd, that the strong statutes
> Stand like the forfeits in a barber's shop,
> As much in mock as mark.

The ruling Duke decides that, with such a reputation for lenity, he is not
the one to rein in a steed that has known no curb. He will delegate his

power to a sterner hand and let justice get a fresh start under a new regime. At least, such seems his motive on the surface. But the Duke is a curious character—"the old fantastical Duke of dark corners"—whether born so or made so by the exigencies of Shakespeare's plot. He is as fond of experimenting on human beings and inquiring into their inner workings as a vivisector is of cutting up guinea pigs. And when he retires not for a trip to Poland, as he gives out, but to return, disguised as a friar, to note the results of his temporary abdication, his motive seems less political and social than psychological. He is really not so much giving up his power as increasing it by retaining it in secret form. The Duke is as introspective as Hamlet, "one that, above all other strifes, contended especially to know himself," and his theatrical instinct also reminds us of the Prince of Denmark, though in his fondness for dazzling his audience he is more like Hal. In spite of his professed love of retirement and hatred of crowds and applause, he is the very reverse of a hermit, and intends (though he doesn't announce the fact in advance and may even be unconscious of it) to burst forth out of the clouds of disguise in full dramatic glory, as he does in the fifth act. His whole plan may be viewed as a sort of play within a play to catch the conscience of his deputy—and of the city. Moreover, he does not intend to miss the performance of his play any more than Hamlet did. The proof that his impulse is melodramatic, or at best psychological, is the fact that he knows at the time he appoints his deputy of a previous act of turpitude on his part. Angelo—for so the deputy is ironically named—deserted the girl to whom he was betrothed when her worldly prospects were wrecked, and slandered her into the bargain to escape the world's censure. He succeeded. His reputation for virtue and austerity is unimpeached. He can be reckoned on to put the screws on all offenders. It is as if the Duke were saying to himself: "Granted that my dispensation has been too lenient; I'll show you what will happen under a paragon of strictness. See how you like it then!" If he had not been more bent on proving his point than on the public welfare, why did he pick out a man whose secret vices he knew? How often have men been given temporary power precisely in order to prove them unworthy of it! Lord Angelo, says the Duke in the first act,

> is precise;
> Stands at a guard with envy; scarce confesses
> That his blood flows, or that his appetite
> Is more to bread than stone: *hence shall we see,*
> *If power change purpose, what our seemers be.*

That last is tolerably explicit. And that there may be no doubt as to what the Duke has in mind, Shakespeare has him again call him "this well-seeming Angelo," when, much later in the play, he reveals his outrageous treatment of Mariana.

III

So Angelo comes to power—ostensibly in association with the kindly and humane but weak-kneed Escalus, who, however, is chiefly a figurehead. The new ruler's hammer comes down first on Claudio, who, under an obsolete blue law, is condemned to death for anticipating the state of marriage with the girl to whom he was betrothed. The judgment is the more reprehensible because the worldly circumstances of the guilty pair demanded a certain concealment, their union was a marriage in fact if not in law, and no question of premeditated infidelity or broken vows was involved. The moral superiority of Claudio to the man who is to judge him is sufficiently pointed. Isabella, Claudio's chaste and virtuous sister, who is about to enter a nunnery, in spite of her reluctance to condone any laxity, intercedes with Angelo on Claudio's behalf. Angelo, at first, will do nothing but repeat "he must die," but as Isabella's beauty mounts with her ardor, the Deputy, who prides himself on being above all such appetites, is suddenly aware of a passion for her, his attitude alters, and he says, with a new sensation at his heart:

> I will bethink me. Come again tomorrow.

> Hark how I'll bribe you;

retorts Isabella, carried beyond discretion by her sense of coming victory.

> How! bribe me?

cries Angelo, startled by a word that fits with deadly accuracy a criminal thought he has not dared confess to himself. We can fairly see him turn on his heel and grow pale.

> Ay, with such gifts that heaven shall share with you,

the innocent Isabella replies. But what other Isabella, or what devil within the innocent one, had put that fatally uncharacteristic and inopportune word "bribe" on her tongue? It is one of those single words on which worlds turn that Shakespeare was growing steadily more fond of.

Isabella returns the next day, and Angelo, after hints that produce as little effect as did Edward IV's on Lady Grey, makes the open shameful proposal that the sister herself be the "bribe" to save her brother. Isabella, spurning the infamous suggestion, cries that she will proclaim him to the world if he does not give her an instant pardon for her brother. But when he reminds her that his impeccable reputation will protect him like a wall, she realizes it is true, and goes to report her failure to Claudio and to prepare him for death.

The scene between brother and sister (on which the disguised Duke eavesdrops) is one of the dramatic and poetic pinnacles of Shakespeare, and we scarcely need to except anything even in *Hamlet* when we say that few scenes in his works elicit from different readers more diametrically opposite reactions. Is Isabella to be admired or despised? Some think her almost divine in her virtue; others almost beneath contempt in her self-righteousness. You could fancy the two parties were talking about two different Isabellas. They are. There are two Isabellas.

Hamlet acquaints us with the psychological proximity of heaven and hell. This play goes on to demonstrate that, despite their polarity, the distance between them can be traversed in just about one-fortieth of the time it took Puck to put a girdle round about the earth.

A pendulum is ascending. It reaches the limit gravity will permit and instantly it is descending. A ball is sailing through the air. It touches the bound interposed by a wall and instantly it is sailing in the opposite direction. And even when the reaction is not instantaneous the same principle holds: everything breeds within itself the seed of its contrary. Human passion is no exception to the rule. At the extremity, it too turns the other way around, upside down, or inside out.

"Why, how now, Claudio!" cries Lucio, meeting his friend under arrest and on his way to jail, "whence comes this restraint?"

> CLAUD.: From too much liberty, my Lucio, liberty:
> As surfeit is the father of much fast,
> So every scope by the immoderate use
> Turns to restraint. Our natures do pursue—
> Like rats that ravin down their proper bane,—
> A thirsty evil, and when we drink we die.

To which Lucio, ever the wit, replies: "I had as lief have the foppery of freedom as the morality of imprisonment." The play is saturated with antitheses like that, and abounds in examples that recall Claudio's rat. There is a woman in it, a bawd and keeper of a brothel, Mistress Overdone, almost the double in marital virtue of Chaucer's Wife of Bath.

> Hath she had any more than one husband?

Escalus inquires of Pompey, her tapster, and the loyal Pompey proudly replies:

> Nine, sir; Overdone by the last.

Overdone! it might be the name of most of the leading characters of the play. Each of them is too something-or-other. And what they do is likewise overdone. Good and evil get inextricably mixed throughout *Measure for Measure*, for virtue is no exception to the rule, and, pushed to the limit, it turns into vice.

Which brings us back to the two Isabellas.

Whatever it may be to an inveterately twentieth-century mind, the question for Shakespeare does not concern Isabella's rejection of Angelo's advances and her refusal to save her brother at such a price. Any one of his greater heroines—Imogen, Cordelia, Desdemona, Rosalind—in the same position would have decided, instantly, as she did. Who will doubt it? The notion that Isabella is just a self-righteous prude guarding her precious chastity simply will not stand up to the text. Lucio's attitude toward her alone is enough to put it out of court. Her presence can sober this jesting "fantastic" and elicit poetry and sincerity from his loose lips:

> I hold you as a thing ensky'd and sainted,
> By your renouncement an immortal spirit,
> And to be talk'd with in sincerity,
> As with a saint.

Prudes do not produce such effects on libertines and jesters.

The question rather concerns what follows. The sister comes to the brother religiously exalted by a consciousness of the righteousness of what she has done—ever a dangerous aftermath of righteousness. The brother catches something of her uplifted mood.

> CLAUD.:   If I must die,
> I will encounter darkness as a bride,
> And hug it in mine arms.
>
> There spake my brother,

the sister, thrilled, replies. And there indeed the noblest Claudio did speak, or Shakespeare would never have put such poetry on his lips. But Isabella, whom we interrupted, has instantly gone on:

> there my father's grave
> Did utter forth a voice. Yes, thou must die.

What a flash of illumination! *Is there a ghost in this play too?*

And when Isabella reveals the terrible price that Angelo has put on his life, Claudio is equal to that too—or he and his sister's spirit are together. Pushed to his limit by that spirit, his instantaneous reaction—it cannot be marked too strongly—is exactly hers:

> O heavens! it cannot be,

and, again,

> Thou shalt not do 't.

If it were my life, Isabella cries, I would throw it down like a pin. And she would have *at that moment*, as Claudio perceives:

> Thanks, dear Isabel.

But Claudio is made of more human stuff than his sister, and, held as she has held him to an extremity of courage and resolution almost beyond his nature, the law of reaction asserts itself and he drops into fear:

> Death is a fearful thing.

And then follows that terrific Dantesque-Miltonic picture of life after death with its "viewless winds" and "thrilling region of thick-ribbed ice" that leaves even Hamlet's similar speculations nowhere—nowhere in appalling power at least. Obscurity made vivid.

> Sweet sister, let me live.

And what does the sweet sister reply?

> O you beast!

Imagine Desdemona saying that! Claudio has said, or done, nothing to deserve such a term. A weak wretch on the threshold of execution, yes. But surely no "beast." What has happened? What always happens. What happened a few seconds before to Claudio himself in another fashion. The overstretched string of Isabella's righteous passion snaps. She has herself dropped from saintliness to beastliness—and projects her own beastliness on her brother. "Isabella—beastly!" her defenders will cry. Why not? There is both beast and saint in every one of us, and whoever will not admit it had better close his Shakespeare once for all, or, rather, open it afresh and learn to change his mind. It is now, not before, that those who have harsh things to say about Isabella may have their innings. Drunk with self-righteousness, she who but a moment ago was offering her life for her brother cries:

> Die, perish! Might but my bending down
> Reprieve thee from thy fate, it should proceed.
> I'll pray a thousand prayers for thy death,
> No word to save thee.

This is religion turned infernal. And it is the worse because of her allusion, in her scene with Angelo, to Christ's atonement:

> Alas, alas!
> Why, all the souls that were were forfeit once;

> And He that might the vantage best have took
> Found out the remedy. How would you be,
> If He, which is the top of judgement, should
> But judge you as you are? O, think on that;
> And mercy then will breathe within your lips,
> Like man new made.

And then, "O you beast!"

What is there to question in this psychology? Is there any human being who cannot confirm it—on however diminished a scale—from his own experience? Who in the midst of making a speech, performing a part, or carrying a point, realizing with delight that it is "coming off," has not paused for a fraction of a second to pat himself on the back, and then—it was indeed all "off" in another sense! The whole thing collapsed, instantly or gradually according to the degree of the complacency.

Commentators have wondered at the pure Isabella's quick acquiescence in the disguised Duke's scheme for having her go back and seem to consent to Angelo's proposal while he arranges to substitute the rejected Mariana, once the Deputy's betrothed, at the rendezvous. You may call the Duke's stratagem vile, shady, or inspired, as you will, and Isabella's reaction to it laudable or damnable. Commendable or not, her conduct is one thing at any rate: credible. It is just the next swing of the pendulum. Conscious, or underconscious, of the fearful injustice she did her brother in that final outburst, she now seeks to set the balance straight. She would not have turned a hand to save him: *therefore*, she will now do anything to save him. Whatever we say, and whatever the Elizabethans said, to the morality of this much debated point, the psychology of it at any rate is sound. Shakespeare's part was done when he showed how a girl made like Isabella would act in those circumstances. And her conduct here coheres perfectly with another bone of contention at the end of the play: her apparent abandonment of getting herself to a nunnery in favor of getting a husband to herself—or at least taking one when offered. Her religious fervor at the outset—with which the ghost of her father plainly had something to do—was "overdone."

And that prospective husband, the Friar—otherwise the Duke! He is tarred with the same brush of excess. He professes to affect retirement and shun publicity. But it is not solitude that he loves. Whatever he was as a ruler, he becomes a moral meddler as a friar, as intoxicated over the human puppet-show whose strings he is pulling as Angelo is in another way over the moral-social drama of which he is manager. He will lie right and left, and even make innocence suffer cruelly (as in his concealing from Isabella the fact that her brother is not dead), merely for the sake of squeezing the last drops of drama or melodrama from the situation. And we must admit that it *is* a situation indeed, a dozen situations in one, in that last act. *Measure for Measure* has been widely criticized as an example of Shakespeare's own too great concession to theatrical effect. The point is in one sense well taken. But the author very shrewdly shifts the responsibility from himself to the Duke by making the man who was guilty of the worst offenses of that sort just the sort of man who would have been guilty of them.* The man who made the great speech beginning:

> Heaven doth with us as we with torches do,
> Not light them for themselves,

had rare insight. It is Shakespeare's own ideal of going forth from ourselves and shining in, and being reflected from, the lives of others. But torches can serve the incendiary as well as the illuminator, and while the Duke did not go quite that far, if we reread the fifth act—with special attention to his part—the verdict will be: "Overdone by the last."

The only way to make the Duke morally acceptable is frankly to take the whole piece as a morality play with the Duke in the role of God, omniscient and unseen, looking down on the world. As has often been pointed out, there is one passage that suggests this specifically:

> O my dread lord,

cries the exposed Angelo, when the Duke at last throws off his disguise,

> I should be guiltier than my guiltiness,
> To think I can be undiscernible,
> *When I perceive your Grace, like power divine,*
> *Hath look'd upon my passes.*

The title of the play—the most "moral" one Shakespeare used—gives some warrant to the suggestion, as does the general tone of forgiveness at the end. But if the Duke is God, he is at first a very lax and later a very interfering God, and both the atmosphere and the characterization of the play are too intensely realistic to make that way out of the difficulty entirely satisfactory. If Shakespeare wants us to take it so, the execution of his intention is not especially successful. But we may at any rate say there is a morality play lurking behind *Measure for Measure*.

---

* He may be compared with Dostoevsky's Kolya in *The Brothers Karamazov*. They must have had similar mothers. Only there, in the great scene of the revelation of the dog's identity, the result is tragic.

IV

And this brings us to the apex of the triangle, or the pyramid, Angelo, for the illumination of whom almost everything in the play seems expressly inserted.

Angelo is one of the clearest demonstrations in literature of the intoxicating nature of power as such. Power means unbounded opportunity, and opportunity acts on the criminal potentialities in man as gravitation does on an apple. Shakespeare wrote his *Rape of Lucrece* around this theme (and came back to it in *Macbeth*), and the stanzas on Opportunity in that poem are the best of glosses on *Measure for Measure*, such lines, to cull out just a few, as

> O Opportunity, thy guilt is great! . . .
> Thou sett'st the wolf where he the lamb may get . . .
> And in thy shady cell, where none may spy him,
> Sits Sin, to seize the souls that wander by him . . .
> Thou blow'st the fire when temperance is thaw'd . . .
> Thou foul abettor! thou notorious bawd!

This is why power as such is so often synonymous with crime. "Power as such," said Emerson, "is not known to the angels." But it was known to Angelo.

Angelo, in spite of his treatment of his betrothed, Mariana, was not an intentional villain or tyrant. His affinities are not with Pandulph and Richard III, but with Edward IV and Claudius. His soliloquy, on his knees,

> When I would pray and think, I think and pray
> To several subjects. Heaven hath my empty words,

looks back to Hamlet's uncle, as his

> Would yet he had liv'd!

when he supposes Claudio is dead at his command looks forward to Macbeth. But his case is in a way worse than theirs, for, supposing himself a mountain of virtue, when the temptation—and with it a sensation he has never experienced—comes, he rolls almost instantly into the abyss. Spiritual pride erects no defenses.

> ANG.:   I have begun,
> And now I give my sensual race the rein.

He loathes himself:

> The tempter or the tempted, who sins most?
> Ha!

Not she; nor doth she tempt: but it is I
That, lying by the violet in the sun,
Do as the carrion does, . . . *Most dangerous*
Is that temptation that doth goad us on
To sin in loving virtue.

In loving Isabella, he thinks he means. But how much profounder the second construction that the sentence bears, which makes it embrace both intending violator and intended victim! Though poles apart, the virtuous maid and the respected head of the state are here identical. Their vulnerable spot is the same: the sin of loving their own virtue.

There are few passages in Shakespeare that give a more inescapable impression of coming from the poet himself than Isabella's great speech to Angelo on power. It is the speech perhaps above any other in his works that seems written to the twentieth century and that the twentieth century should know by heart. The spectacle of

man, proud man,
Dress'd in a little brief authority,

"like an angry ape" playing "fantastic tricks before high heaven" made Shakespeare as well as the angels weep. But her words recoil too perfectly on Isabella's own head not to make them also perfectly in character:

Merciful Heaven!
Thou rather with thy sharp and sulphurous bolt
Split'st the unwedgeable and gnarled oak
Than the soft myrtle.

This shaft is aimed at the man who would make the soft Claudio a public example of the moral austerity of his regime. But how about Isabella herself, who is shortly to launch thunderbolts against the same weakling in the scene where she calls him beast? —not to mention what she is doing at the moment, for Angelo in strength is nearer the myrtle than the oak he considers himself. *Tu quoque!* Shakespeare perceives that spiritual power is quite as open to abuse as political power. The sheer theatrical effectiveness of this astonishing scene can easily blind us to the tangle of moral ironies and boomerangs it involves. This retiring girl, who had fairly to be pushed into the encounter by Lucio, finally standing up with audacity to the first man of the state is thrilling drama. But unfortunately Isabella gets an inkling of that fact herself.

Go to your bosom,

she cautions Angelo,

> Knock there, and ask your heart what it doth know
> That's like my brother's fault.

If only she could have said those lines to herself, substituting for the last one,

> That's like this man's offence,

she never would have let slip from her lips that fatal word that ties some unplumbed sensual element in her own nature to the very corruption of justice and virtue she is condemning.*

But Angelo's blackest act is not his sin of sensuality against Isabella, which he commits in wish and as he thinks in fact. Nor is it even the prostitution of his office that that involves. It is his acceptance of Isabella's sacrifice of herself and his then sending Claudio to death nevertheless. This final infamy —completed in intention though defeated in fact—ranks with John of Lancaster's treachery to the rebels in *II Henry IV*. Nothing worse need be said of it than that.

> Alack! when once our grace we have forgot,
> Nothing goes right,

Angelo cries, in anguish at what he has done. He might just as well have said,

> Alack! when once our power is unbounded,
> Nothing goes right,

for his are the typical sins and crimes of unlimited authority.

"Power is poison."

What power is has never been more tersely summed up than in those three words of Henry Adams in the section of the *Education* in which he analyzes its effect on Presidents of the United States, as he had observed it in Washington.

Power is poison. Its effect on Presidents had been always tragic, chiefly as an almost insane excitement at first, and a worse reaction afterwards; but also because no mind is so well balanced as to bear the strain of seizing unlimited force without habit or knowledge of it; and finding it disputed with him by hungry packs of wolves and hounds whose lives depend on snatching the carrion.... *The effect of unlimited power on limited mind is worth noting in Presidents because it must represent the same process in society, and the power of self-control must have limit somewhere in face of the control of the infinite.*

Shakespeare was saying precisely that, I think, in *Measure for Measure*. If concentration of authority in time of "peace" can let loose such demons

---

* As usual, Dostoevsky confirms Shakespeare's psychology. Compare the great scene between Dounia and Svidrigailov in *Crime and Punishment*, where another virtuous sister intercedes, for another brother who has broken the law, with a man who has power over him.

of Opportunity in those who possess power, and transform their subjects either into pelting petty officers, hungry packs of wolves and hounds, or into their victims, what will the same thing do in time of war? In "peace" such unadulterated authority is at least not "necessary." It is the crowning infamy of war that it does make it essential. Victory demands efficiency, and efficiency calls for undisputed unity of command. War is authority—overdone.

V

The underplot of this play is unsavory. But of its kind it is a masterpiece of the first order, both in itself and in its integration with the main plot and its themes. Mistress Overdone, the keeper of a Viennese brothel, Abhorson, the executioner in a Viennese prison, and Barnardine, a condemned murderer, may be said to be its symbolic triad. A prison is presumably a place where Justice is done. Pompey, Mistress Overdone's tapster, is struck rather by its resemblance to his employer's establishment.

"I am as well acquainted here as I was in our house of profession: one would think it were Mistress Overdone's own house, for here be many of her old customers. First, here's young Master Rash . . ." and foregoing acquaintance with the rest of the inmates whom Pompey goes on to introduce, we are sent back in astonished recognition, by that name "Master Rash," to Hamlet (and his "prais'd be rashness") who first made known to us the idea that the world is a prison. This play carries Hamlet's analogy a step further, and continually suggests the resemblance of the main world, not so much to a prison—though it is that too—as to a house of ill fame, where men and women sell their honors in a dozen senses.

Lucio, for instance, mentions "the sanctimonious pirate, that went to sea with the Ten Commandments, but scraped one out of the table." If this is not an oblique, if a bit blunt, hit at Angelo (on Shakespeare's part of course, not Lucio's), then a cap that fits should never be put on. It was "Thou shalt not steal," of course, that the pirate scraped out. We know which one of the ten Angelo eliminated, if, indeed, it was not half-a-dozen of them. It would be interesting, taking Lucio's hint, to run through the cast and ask which and how many of the Commandments each character discarded. Isabella certainly could close her eyes to the first one. But without taking time for the experiment, one thing is certain. There would be no perfect scores—either way. The man in ermine in this play casts wanton eyes on the same woman whom the libertine looks on as a saint. That is typical of almost everything in it.

" 'Twas never merry world," declares Pompey, comparing his profession with a more respectable one, "since, of two usuries, the merriest was put down, and the worser allowed by order of law a furred gown to keep him warm; and furred with fox and lambskins too, to signify that craft, being richer than innocency, stands for the facing." This might be dismissed as the irresponsible chatter of the barroom, did not the main plot so dreadfully confirm it and Angelo himself confess it in soliloquy:

> Thieves for their robbery have authority
> When judges steal themselves.

If it will help any ultramodern person to understand Pompey's "usuries," read "rackets" in their place.

When the Provost tells this same Pompey, then in prison, that he may earn his freedom if he will act as assistant to the executioner, Shakespeare gives us another of his deadly parallels between the world of law and the world of lawbreakers. Pompey jumps at the chance: "Sir, I have been an unlawful bawd time out of mind; but yet I will be content to be a lawful hangman." But Abhorson, who is proud of his calling, is scandalized at the suggestion: "A bawd, sir? Fie upon him! he will discredit our mystery." To which the Provost replies: "A feather will turn the scale." (Between being bawd and executioner, he means, of course.) As to what Shakespeare thought, we get a hint when we remember the Duke's tribute:

> This is a gentle Provost: seldom when
> The steeled gaoler is the friend of men.

So recklessly does Shakespeare go on heaping up analogies between persons and things of low and those of high estate* that when Elbow, the Constable, who must have been Dogberry's cousin, brings Froth and Pompey before Angelo and Escalus in judicial session, and introduces his prisoners as "two notorious benefactors," we begin to wonder, in the general topsy-turvydom, whether there may not be relative truth in his malapropism. At any rate, the upperworld characters are guilty of far worse moral and mental, if not verbal, confusions. "Which is the wiser here," asks Escalus, "Justice or Iniquity?"†

> And you shall have your bosom on this wretch,

cries the disguised Duke to Isabella, when Angelo's infamy becomes known to him,

> Grace of the Duke, revenges to your heart,
> And general honour.

---

* "The vice is of a great kindred; it is well allied." Lucio, III, ii, 110.
† Notice the echo from *The Merchant of Venice:*
> "Which is the merchant here and which the Jew?"

An odd idea of honor for a supposed friar to impart to a prospective nun: the time-worn notion that it consists in having all your old scores settled. And when he hears that "a most notorious pirate" has just died in prison of a fever, thus supplying a head that can be sent to Angelo in place of Claudio's, he exclaims:

O, 'tis an accident that Heaven provides!

—an equally odd idea of Heaven. But he far exceeds these lapses. At the end of the play, in an atmosphere of general pardon, Lucio, who—unwittingly but not unwittily—has abused the Duke to his face when disguised as a friar, does not escape. The Duke orders him married to the mother of his illegitimate child, and, the ceremony over, whipped and hanged. "I beseech your Highness," Lucio protests, "do not marry me to a whore." And the Duke relents to the extent of remitting the last two but not the first of the three penalties.

The emphasis on this incident at the very end brings to mind the moment when Lucio pulls off the Duke's hood:

DUKE: Thou art the first knave that e'er mad'st a duke . . .
     Come hither, Mariana.
     Say, wast thou e'er contracted to this woman?
ANG.: I was, my lord.
DUKE: Go take her hence, and marry her instantly.

Poor Mariana's willingness, in contrast with Lucio, to marry *her* "knave" makes the parallelism more rather than less pointed.

Measure for Measure—once one gives the underplot its due—fairly bristles with disconcerting analogies and moral paradoxes like this last one. Only a hopelessly complacent person will not be challenged by it. And whoever will be honest with himself will confess, I believe, to a strange cumulative effect that it produces. Barring Escalus and the Provost, who are put in to show that not all judges are harsh nor all jailers hardhearted, we are more in love in the end with the disreputable than with the reputable characters. Overworld and underworld threaten to change places.

Whether *Measure for Measure* was a favorite play of Samuel Butler's I do not know. It ought to have been. In it Shakespeare certainly proves himself a good Butlerian, an adherent to the principle that "every proposition has got a skeleton in its cupboard." Many entries in the *Note-Books* might have been composed to illuminate Shakespeare's play:

God is not so white as he is painted, and he gets on better with the Devil than people think. The Devil is too useful for him to wish him ill and, in like manner, half the Devil's trade would be at an end should any great mishap bring God well down in the world.... The conception of them as the one absolutely void of evil and the other of good is a vulgar notion taken from science whose priests have ever sought to get every idea and every substance pure of all alloy.

God and the Devil are about as four to three. There is enough preponderance of God to make it far safer to be on his side than on the Devil's, but the excess is not so great as his professional *claqueurs* pretend it is.

What is this but the repentant Angelo's

> Let's write good angel on the devil's horn,

slightly expanded?

Quite in conformity with Butler's dicta, I am not sure that honest readers do not find Barnardine, the condemned murderer, the most delectable character in *Measure for Measure*—he who for God knows how long has defied the efforts of the prison authorities to execute him. We like him so well that we do not wish to inquire too curiously into his past. For my part, I am certain the murder he did—if he really did it—was an eminently good-natured one. "Thank you kindly for your attention," he says in effect, when they come to hale him to the gallows, "but I simply cannot be a party to any such proceeding. I am too busy—sleeping." Let him sleep. Let anyone sleep to his heart's content who puts to rout one Abhorson. He has earned his nap.

Like Falstaff, Barnardine tempts the imagination to play around him. No higher tribute can be paid to a character in a play, as none can to a person in life. The fascination he has for us—he, and, in less degree, the rest of the underworld of which he is a member—is partly because these men and women, being sinners, have some tolerance for sin. And some humor, which comes to much the same thing. *Judge not:* they come vastly nearer obeying that injunction (of which *Measure for Measure* sometimes seems a mere amplification) than do their betters. Never will anyone say of them as Escalus said of Angelo: "my brother justice have I found so severe, that he hath forced me to tell him he is indeed Justice." They are not forever riding the moral high horse. They make no pretensions. They mind their own business, bad as it is, instead of telling, or compelling, other people to mind *theirs* or to act in *their* way. It is a relief to find somebody of whom that is true. "Our house of profession." No, Pompey is wrong. It is not the establishment to which he is bawd and tapster, but the main world, that better deserves that name. For everybody with power—save a few Abraham Lincolns—is, *ipso facto*, professing and pretending all day long. "I am convinced, almost instinctively," says Stendhal, "that as soon as he opens his mouth every man in power begins to lie, and so much the more when he writes." It is a strong statement, and Shakespeare would certainly have inserted an "almost" in his version of it, but there are his works, from the History Plays on, to show his substantial agreement with it. Why does Authority always lie? Because it perpetuates itself by lies and thereby saves itself from the trouble of crude force: costumes and parades for the childish, decorations and degrees for the vain and envious, positions for the ambitious, propaganda for the docile and gullible, orders for the goosesteppers, fine words (like "loyalty" and "co-operation") for the foolishly unselfish—to distract, to extort awe, to flatter and gratify inferiority, as the case may be. Dr. Johnson ought to have amended his famous saying. Patriotism is only one of the last refuges of a scoundrel.

Angelo and the Duke, if anyone, ought to know, and in their hearts they agree exactly. Hear them in soliloquy. The identity is not accidental.

ANG.:
> O place, O form,
> How often dost thou with thy case, thy habit,
> Wrench awe from fools and tie the wiser souls
> To thy false seeming!

DUKE:
> O place and greatness! millions of false eyes
> Are stuck upon thee. Volumes of report
> Run with these false and most contrarious quests
> Upon thy doings; thousand escapes of wit
> Make thee the father of their idle dream
> And rack thee in their fancies.

The effect of power on those who do not possess it but wish that they did, Shakespeare concludes, is scarcely better than on those who do.

And here is the deepest reason—is it not?—why we prefer the "populace" in this play to the powers-that-be. The vices of the two ends of "society" turn out under examination to be much alike. But the lower stratum has one virtue to which the possessors and pursuers of power, for all their pretensions, cannot pretend: namely, lack of pretension. Here is a genuine basis for envying the dispossessed. Revolutions by the downtrodden, abortive or successful, to regain their share of power have occurred throughout history. The world awaits a revolution by the powerful to gain relief from the insincerities to which their privileges and position forever condemn them. Thoreau staged a one-man revolution based on a kindred principle. If this is what it implies, *Measure for Measure* may yet be banned by the authorities. . . . But no! it is as safe as the music of Beethoven. "The authorities" will never understand it.

VI

If we do not want a world presided over by a thundering Jove—this play seems to say—and under him a million pelting petty officers and their understudies, and under *them* millions of their victims, we must renounce Power as our god—Power and all his ways. And not just in the political and military worlds, where the evils of autocracy with its inevitable bureaucracy of fawning yes-men, while obvious to all but autocratic or servile eyes, may be more or less "necessary." It is the more insidiously personal bondages to power that should concern us first. Revolution against authority—as Isabella, for all her great speech, did not perceive, and as Barnardine did—begins at home. Let men in sufficient numbers turn into Barnardines, who want to run no one else but will not *be* run by anyone, even to the gallows, and what would be left for the pelting petty officers, and finally for Jove himself, but to follow suit? There would be a revolution indeed. The more we meditate on Barnardine the more he acquires the character of a vast symbol, the key perhaps to all our troubles. Granted, with Hamlet, that the world is a prison. We need not despair with Hamlet. We may growl rather with Barnardine at all intruders on our daydreams, and learn with him that even in a prison life may be lived—independently. Why wait, as modern gospels preach, until we are out of prison before beginning to live? "Now is a time."

Approximately three hundred years before the twentieth century, *Measure for Measure* made clear the truths that it has taken two world wars to burn into the consciousness of our own generation: that Power lives by Authority and that Authority is always backed by two things, the physical force that tears bodies and the mental violence that mutilates brains:

> In every cry of every Man,
> In every Infant's cry of fear,
> In every voice, in every ban,
> The mind-forg'd manacles I hear.

The two—dynamite and propaganda, to use modern terms—are always found together. "By skilful and sustained propaganda," said Hitler, "an entire people can be made to see even heaven as hell and the most miserable life as paradise." Where there is an Angelo on the bench, there will always be an Abhorson in the cellar. And how well Shakespeare liked Abhorson, his name proclaims.

> O, it is excellent
> To have a giant's strength; but it is tyrannous
> To use it like a giant. . . .
> Could great men thunder
> As Jove himself does, Jove would ne'er be quiet;
> For every pelting, petty officer
> Would use his heaven for thunder,
> Nothing but thunder! Merciful Heaven!

Thou rather with thy sharp and sulphurous bolt
Split'st the unwedgeable and gnarled oak
Than the soft myrtle; but man, proud man,
Dress'd in a little brief authority,
Most ignorant of what he's most assur'd,
His glassy essence, like an angry ape,
Plays such fantastic tricks before high heaven
As make the angels weep; who, with our spleens,
Would all themselves laugh mortal.

Chapter XXVII

Othello

I

Hamlet is Shakespeare's supreme interrogation, the culmination of his capacity to ask questions of life. In *Othello* life begins to answer. Not that *Hamlet* contains no answers, but they are not so much expressed as to be inferred. *Othello* speaks more directly. In it the poet's tragic genius moves from its negative to its positive phase and tragedy recovers something of that pre-Euripidean state so eloquently characterized by Nietzsche in his *Birth of Tragedy*. *Romeo and Juliet*, it is true, is always the exception. It is like an overture to the later Tragedies and contains hints and glimpses of what was to come in practically every one of them. But if Juliet is the morning star, Desdemona is the dawn—another morn risen on the mid-noon of *Hamlet*. With her, an almost unbroken line of beings begins to enter the Shakespearean world, with power not so much to solve as to put out of existence the problems which *Hamlet* propounded but to which Hamlet himself had no answer but silence.

The psychological link between *Hamlet* and *Othello* is close. The one grows out of the other as naturally as the blossom from the bud. The obvious tie between the two is that both are plays of revenge. A far subtler and more intimate one is the fact that the motifs of eavesdropping, of pouring poison in the ear ("I'll pour this pestilence into his ear"), and of the mousetrap—the sublimation of which from the literal to the figurative had already gone far in the earlier play—are in the later one carried to the psychological limit. Iago is a sort of super-eavesdropper. His plot is the last word in traps. And the scene in the third act, where he pours his vile story in the waking Othello's ear—accounted by many the most dramatic one in Shakespeare—

makes the corresponding scene where Claudius murders the sleeping King Hamlet, whether as narrated by the Ghost or re-enacted in the dumb show, primitive in comparison. However, these metaphorical similarities and echoes are merely the signs of a more deep-lying organic connection. And here, again, dreams illuminate the poetic mind.

The analogy has already been noted between the successive works of a poet and the successive dreams of a dreamer. On this principle a character with a double personality in an earlier work may appear as two characters in a later one, as the promise of both Julius Caesar and Brutus, for example, may be traced in the man who was, variously, Hal, Prince Henry, and King Henry V. The imaginative energy that created Hamlet did not cease functioning when Hamlet himself expired. There could scarcely be a better example than the Prince of Denmark of the divided, or, we might better say, the dividing man. With the deep conflict within him of masculine and feminine traits, he is, as we noted, a sort of unfulfilled promise of the Platonic man-woman. It is as if the tension between these poles of his nature sought an equilibrium too unstable to be maintained, so that, like a cell that bifurcates, Hamlet in the next world—that is, in *Othello*—divides into Desdemona and Iago.

The idea must of course not be taken too literally nor pressed too far, but, within limits, it can be highly suggestive to those interested in psychic relationships of this sort. (Those who are not, or who consider them fanciful or far-fetched, may ignore this one—the rest of the argument does not depend on it.) Hamlet, it is generally admitted, is the most paradoxical mixture of good and evil. Iago is close to pure evil; Desdemona close to pure good. Hamlet's most endearing traits—his ingenuousness, his modesty, his truthfulness, his freedom, his courage, his love, his sympathetic imagination—are all Desdemona's. His darker and more detestable ones—his suspicion, his coarseness, his sarcastic wit, his critical intellect, his callousness, his cruelty, his sensuality, his savage hatred, his bloodiness, his revenge—are all Iago's. Only in dramatic imagination is the nobler Hamlet akin to Iago. But even there his final prostitution of that gift to evil* ties him exactly to his counterpart who notoriously did the same. What looked like an exception clinches the analogy. And the qualities of Hamlet that neither Desdemona nor Iago inherits—his melancholy, his brooding, his hesitancy, his hysteria—instead of confuting, confirm the contention: for these are the result of the strife between his two selves, and when the two have been split apart the strife naturally ceases. The strife *within* Hamlet is replaced by the strife *between* Iago and Desdemona (for the possession of Othello), or, if one prefers, is replaced by the contrast between them, the

---

* See the chapter on *Hamlet*.

strife in that case being between Iago and that part of Othello that loves Desdemona and has faith in her. Hamlet—not quite able to slough off his atavistic traits and step into the future—divides into his components, one part going up with Desdemona, another down with Iago. (Where still other parts go will be seen later.)

It is Othello and Cassio, standing between the extremes, who in a way inherit and continue the divided nature of Hamlet. In fineness of impulse, in tenderness, in trustfulness, in openness and freedom, both of them are much like Desdemona. Shakespeare had to endow all three with these qualities to make the machinations of Iago credible. If any one of them had been lacking in faith, his plot would have been frustrated. So, in a sense, it is the triad, Othello-Cassio-Desdemona, rather than just Desdemona, with whom Iago is thrown into contrast. But Othello compared with Desdemona is vulnerable, and Cassio compared with her is common clay. Their weaknesses are Iago's opportunity and the source of the dramatic warfare.

II

And there is another bond between *Hamlet* and *Othello*—or more specifically between the Prince of Denmark and Desdemona. Both dramas emerge from a parent-child situation. Hamlet obeys his father. Desdemona disobeys hers. And the more we figure the Father to ourselves as the symbol of Authority and Force, the deeper the significance of the contrast becomes. Romeo, Hal, Brutus, and Hamlet opposed to the Father's will an energy that, viewing them as a group, steadily mounted until in Hamlet a stage of near-equilibrium was reached. Desdemona is the next term of the progression. She successfully defies the Father. It is this seemingly trifling fact that makes *Othello* the turning point of Shakespeare.

Brabantio may seem like a very diluted counterpart of the Ghost, and he is as an emissary of revenge. But his function in the play is in a negative sense the same. Like Capulet or like Portia's father, he would impose his will on the next generation. But Desdemona, unlike Hamlet, will not sacrifice her life or happiness on the altar of Authority, however willing she is to sacrifice both on the altar of Love. She stands for freedom, and her audacity in doing what she thinks right in the face of her father's opposition is sufficient answer to those incredible readers who persist in thinking her weak. We are reminded by contrast of Ophelia, in which case Brabantio falls into Polonius' place, however unfair in other respects the comparison may be. Desdemona is Ophelia choosing the other fork of the road. She is an anti-Ophelia. All we have to ask is what would have happened in *Hamlet* if Hamlet had had her love. She never would have deserted him in his critical hour. "Frailty, thy name is woman." Desdemona is a living contradiction of that indispensable premise of Hamlet's philosophy and action. In her presence his tragedy would have melted into thin air.

The significance in the fact that it is a *woman* who thus refuses to ruin her life by surrender to the Force of the Past—"the tyrant custom," as Othello calls it—cannot be exaggerated, for Desdemona, heralded indeed by Juliet, is the first of a series of Shakespearean women, in tragedy at least, who defy authority in this sense. Man after man has wrestled with this problem of force in vain, for force is traditionally man's method. Now, women begin to attack it not in vain—not in vain, that is, from the tragic viewpoint. The feminine pole of Shakespeare's genius is gaining ascendancy. "Shakespeare led a life of allegory: his works are the comments on it." Desdemona helps us understand that alluring sentence.

III

The audacity of Desdemona's act is at least quadrupled by the fact that the man she marries is a Moor. Which raises the old question:

Is Othello brown or black?

The controversy over this problem has been a long and heated one. Its main result has been to prove once more that learning is the least imaginative thing in the world. The argument has been in part textual: the marshaling on both sides of every passage in the play that seems in any way pertinent to the question of Othello's color; in part historical and ethnological: an attempt to determine whether Shakespeare could himself have been aware of the distinction between Moor and Ethiopian. Two things at any rate are clear: (1) Iago's statements about Othello's appearance cannot be taken at face value; (2) the word "black" is used more than once in the play—even by Desdemona herself—as a synonym for brunette in contrast with "fair" which, when put over against it, stands for blonde. These considerations may or may not be deemed decisive. The scholar who is not convinced one way or the other can still keep his mind open. But the actor and director in the case of a particular production must decide the question once for all. On the stage Othello cannot be both brown and black at the same time, and the decision, in certain places and circumstances, may be a critical one. The reader on the other hand is relatively free. He may visualize Othello more or less to suit himself.

But turn from the world of drama to the world of poetry and we perceive that all this misses the point and begs the question.

What attracted Shakespeare in the first place to this exotic story of a Moor, this blood-and-thunder novella of Cinthio's, so inferior in many ways to anything else he ever used for tragedy? A futile question, it would seem, beyond the fact that the tale had obvious theatrical qualities. Yet perhaps not so futile after all, for in one respect we can answer it with almost as much assurance as if we actually had access to Shakespeare's mind.

The moment he saw that first line, "There was once a Moor in Venice . . . ," how could he have failed to recall *The Jew of Venice*, as the public had apparently insisted on rechristening his own play laid in the same city? The scene the same, the title almost the same, and both stories centering around one alien in the midst of many native Venetians! Nor did the analogy stop there. Everything in *The Merchant of Venice* turns on the contrast between inner and outer, depth and surface, on the gilded that is mistaken for the golden, the precious that is hidden beneath the base. But here, in Cinthio's tale, is a hero with a dark skin caught in the toils of a villain with a fair and honest exterior. The casket theme exactly! the old story over again—with its implicit tragedy now explicit—only with its material symbols transmuted into the very stuff of human life, not gold and lead, but good and evil, light and shadow, black and white. Othello and Iago must have been conceived at the moment that that analogy struck the poet, one black without and white within, the other white without and black within. And to these two a third was inevitably added, Desdemona, white both without and within. These contrasts are obviously the substance and essence of the play, penetrating far under any merely ethnological or theatrical considerations to the heart of the imagination itself* and making even the symbolism of *The Merchant of Venice* crude in comparison. To the imagination, black, not brown, represents the shadow, evil, death. On the level of poetry that settles it beyond appeal. Othello is black.

This contrast scheme of light and dark sets everything in perspective. In a sense it predetermines the characterization.

> I saw Othello's visage in his mind,

says Desdemona, and instantly we are convinced that though the two are alien in race they are akin in spirit. Throughout, she seems unconscious of his color and under the influence of her love he too forgets it. The symbolism demands that Desdemona's own visage, both without and within, be a shining white. And, symbolism or no symbolism, that is exactly what Shakespeare makes it. Which is why her role is beyond the reach of any

---

* All this is remarkably confirmed by a dream of a young theological student that Jung records. The dreamer saw a magician dressed wholly in black who, he nevertheless knew, was the white magician. Presently the figure was joined by another, the black magician, dressed wholly in white. It was obviously at the moment Cinthio's tale activated, as the psychologists say, the same ancestral images in Shakespeare's mind that Othello and Iago were conceived. There could scarcely be better proof that he who takes *Othello* as just "theater," just realism, or even as just drama, is missing something.

Another confirmation of this imagery is to be found in Blake's "The Little Black Boy" with its line: "And I am black, but O! my soul is white."

actress. Innocence cannot be imitated. Only some Desdemona-like woman from some region uncontaminated by anything theatrical might be Desdemona momentarily on the stage, as a child becomes what he plays.

Just the opposite is true of Iago. Only a consummate actor can render him. I wonder if anyone ever has—ever has succeeded, I mean, in making him convincingly "honest" not just to Othello, Cassio, and Desdemona, but even, in its presence, to the audience that is in the secret. That would be the test. That would make everything credible. Iago is a snake—but a snake under a flower. On the surface he must not fascinate like a snake. He must charm like a flower. What wisdom he utters, and into what depravity it turns on his lips! Take his metaphor of the garden: "Our bodies are our gardens, to the which our wills are gardeners. . . . If the balance of our lives had not one scale of reason to poise another of sensuality, the blood and baseness of our natures would conduct us to most preposterous conclusions"—like the conclusion of this play! What is that but Hamlet's speech on blood and judgment translated, significantly, from poetry into prose? But one was spoken to Horatio, the other to Roderigo. One in profound affection, the other in murderous contempt. How diametrical ideas become that are practically identical!

Iago keeps reminding us of Othello's color just as Desdemona causes us to forget it. To him Othello is "an old black ram," or worse. He loses no opportunity to keep him conscious of his supposed inferiority and he makes the most of the unnatural character of his union with Desdemona. The degree to which the other characters are scandalized by the marriage is a measure of their own blindness or depravity, or both. Brabantio is scandalized by it out of family pride: he wants to marry his daughter to one of the "wealthy curled darlings of our nation." Roderigo, one of those very darlings, is scandalized by it because of envy: he wants Desdemona for himself, and to him Othello is a "thick-lips." Emilia refers to the marriage as Desdemona's "most filthy bargain." (The phrase reveals her vulgar quality, but it was uttered under a tragic misunderstanding and on the brink of incredible loyalty, so we forgive it.) The Duke of Venice, on the other hand, a man of character and insight, approves the match:

> Noble signior,
> If virtue no delighted beauty lack,
> Your son-in-law is far more fair than black.

And as for Cassio, he seems scarcely more conscious of anything alien in Othello than Desdemona herself. To the end, in spite of everything, Othello remains to him just "dear general."

These characters, it is interesting to note, all conform, if less extremely, to the pattern of light and shade of the three main figures. Like those in *The Merchant of Venice* they are all one thing without, another within. Emilia: common clay concealing a capacity for devotion almost divine. Roderigo: the fine young gentleman rotten at the core. Bianca: the courtesan who falls in love. Brabantio: the unrelenting father, who, nevertheless, dies of a broken heart. Cassio: the profligate with a pure heart, the drunkard who comes through true as steel. All this cannot be chance.

IV

Iago's jealousy of Cassio is real enough, but it is the occasion rather than the cause of his plot against Othello; and the other reasons he assigns for his hatred in the course of the play are not so much motives as symptoms of a deeply underlying condition. The psychology of Iago is that of the slave-with-brains who aspires to power yet remains at heart a slave.

> We cannot all be masters, nor all masters
> Cannot be truly follow'd.

"Some cogging cozening slave," says Emilia, describing the as yet hypothetical and unidentified villain who is actually her husband. "O cursed, cursed slave!" cries Othello, at the end, to that part of himself that Iago had corrupted. We are led to conjecture that some situation or event early in Iago's life that produced a profound sense of injustice or inferiority, and instigated a revolt against it, could alone have produced so twisted a nature, as in the case of Emily Brontë's Heathcliff or Dostoevsky's Smerdyakov, figures spiritually akin to Shakespeare's villain. It would be consumingly interesting to have a peep into Iago's childhood, as we have into theirs. It must have been full of power-fantasies like those that Dostoevsky describes in *A Raw Youth*. "The secret consciousness of power is more insupportably delightful than open domination." "I don't know," the Raw Youth declares, "whether the spider perhaps does not hate the fly he has marked and is snaring. Dear little fly! It seems to me that the victim is loved, or at least may be loved. Here I love my enemy; I am delighted, for instance, that she is so beautiful." Compare this with Iago's words on Desdemona:

> Now, I do love her too;
> Not out of absolute lust, though peradventure
> I stand accountant for as great a sin,
> But partly led to diet my revenge,

or his,

> So will I turn her virtue into pitch,
> And out of her own goodness make the net
> That shall enmesh them all.

Iago is a spider whose web is spun out of his brain. (Though that is by no means all he is.) Whatever he began by being, however human the motives that at first led him on, he ends by being an image of Death revenging itself on Life through destruction. Why does a small boy knock down, in pure wantonness, the tower of blocks his younger brother has so slowly and laboriously built up? Iago is like that:

> If Cassio do remain,
> He hath a daily beauty in his life
> That makes me ugly.

These are the most consciously self-revealing words he speaks. Ugliness cannot tolerate beauty. Death cannot tolerate life.

> That that likes not me
> Pleases me best.

If you are defeated, change the rules of the game, call defeat success (as if to get the fewest runs in baseball were the object), and then you win! Drag down the good—it is so much easier than rising. Define darkness as light.

Shakespeare's archvillain had many Shakespearean forerunners: the melodramatic Richard III, the casuistical Pandulph, the sly and crafty Ulysses. But they all fade before him. He is perhaps the most terrific indictment of pure intellect in the literature of the world—"pure intellect," which, as Emerson said, "is the pure devil." "Think, and die," as Enobarbus puts it, though he may not have realized all he was packing into three words. The intellect, as all the prophets have divined, should be the servant of the soul. Performing that function it is indispensable. There can scarcely be too much of it. Indeed, the primacy in the world of art of men like Beethoven, Michelangelo, and Shakespeare himself is that their imaginations are held in check by their critical power. But the moment the intellect sets up a claim of sovereignty for itself, it is the slave in revolt, the torchbearer turned incendiary, Lucifer fallen. Iago is a moral pyromaniac.

I wonder, if he had been of more limited intelligence, whether he might not have been, literally, a pyromaniac. He exhibits a dozen traits of that type of criminal, including a secret joy in being on the scene of the conflagration he has kindled. Shakespeare himself hints as much in the speech in which, of all in the play barring the soliloquies, Iago most fully reveals himself for what he is. It is in the opening scene, while his plot, if conceived, is still unconscious. And he is boasting to his dupe, Roderigo. He is off guard. But first we must recall the conscious revelation that leads up to the unconscious one:

For when my outward action doth demonstrate
The native act and figure of my heart
In compliment extern, 'tis not long after
But I will wear my heart upon my sleeve
For daws to peck at: I am not what I am.

How characteristic of Shakespeare that in his very next speech Iago should place his heart squarely on his sleeve, and put into words, and still more into tone, precisely what he is.

Rod.: What a full fortune does the thick-lips owe,
    If he can carry't thus!
Iago: Call up her father:
    Rouse him, make after him, poison his delight,
    Proclaim him in the streets, incense her kinsmen,
    And, though he in a fertile climate dwell,
    Plague him with flies; though that his joy be joy,
    Yet throw such changes of vexation on 't,
    As it may lose some colour.
Rod.: Here is her father's house; I'll call aloud.
Iago: Do, with like timorous accent and dire yell
    As when, by night and negligence, the fire
    Is spied in populous cities.

Poison! Plague! Fire! Never again, unless to himself, do we hear Iago speak with such gusto. The bewildering shift in antecedents of the pronouns ("Rouse him, make after him"), the first referring to Brabantio, the second to Othello, is intentional on Shakespeare's part, revealing in a flash that Iago's hatred of Othello is already an obsession. For these few seconds, before he puts on his perpetual mask and cloak, Iago stands before us naked.

But if he is a moral pyromaniac, it is *only* morally that he is mad, and, whatever may be said of the fires he kindles in others, the fire in his own veins is an icy fire. "Now could I drink hot blood," cried Hamlet. Iago goes fathoms lower than that. "For I am nothing if not critical," he observes calmly, as he scrutinizes Desdemona's beauty on the threshold of her destruction; and as he begins to weave the web that is to enmesh her, he cries:

By the mass, 'tis morning;
Pleasure and action make the hours seem short.

Hot revenge is a fearful thing. But its devastation has bounds, because its passion reveals its secret, makes it act prematurely, mars its aim, and soon burns it out. Cold revenge is incredibly more awful. For it can conceal, it can calculate, it can lie in wait; it can control itself, it can coil and strike without warning at the crucial moment. Cold revenge is the union of intellect and hate—the most annihilating of all alliances. Dante was right in making his nethermost hell of ice.

V

The deliberate placing of the highest intellectual gifts and achievements at the service of the lowest human instincts is a phenomenon with which the twentieth century is acquainted on a scale never previously attained. And whether the instinct be fear (the main defensive one) or revenge, greed, cruelty, thirst to possess more power or to assert power already possessed (the main offensive ones) makes little difference in the end, so readily do they pass into one another.

It is no recent discovery that brain as well as brawn is essential to the efficient fighter. The Trojan Horse is the perennial symbol of that truth, and it is appropriate that Shakespeare put on the lips of Ulysses an enco-mium on the "still and mental parts" of war. But it remained for war in our time to effect the total mobilization of those still and mental parts. The ideological warfare that precedes and precipitates the physical conflict (*cold war* as it has significantly come to be called); the propaganda that prepares and unifies public opinion; the conscription, in a dozen spheres, of the na-tion's brains; the organization of what is revealingly known as the *intelli-gence* service; but most of all the practical absorption of science into the military effort: these things, apart from the knowledge and skill required for the actual fighting, permit us to define modern war, once it is begun, as an unreserved dedication of the human intellect to death and destruction.

But that is exactly what Iago is—an unreserved dedication of intellect to death and destruction. To the extent that this is true, Iago is an incarnation of the spirit of modern war.

This does not mean that those who participate in modern war are Iagos. The scientist calmly conducting his experiment in a clean laboratory with-out an iota of hate in his heart bears no resemblance to Shakespeare's Italian fiend. But there may be hate, and there will almost certainly be fear, in the heart of the man who months later and thousands of miles away utilizes the results of that experiment on the fighting front (not to imply for a moment that there may not be heroism in it also). Nobody wants war. No individual does, that is, or very few. But that great Composite Personality which is the nation is driven into it nevertheless against the wishes of the thousands of individuals who make it up. It is within that Personality, not generally within the individual, that the union of intellect with animal instincts takes place, the prostitution especially of man's supreme intellectual achievement, modern science, to the most destructive of his ancestral practices. It is something within this Composite Personality that is like Iago, and, like him, it did not foresee when it set out to make war efficient that it was playing with the possibility of its own extinction. The uniqueness of Iago, like the uniqueness of modern war, does not lie in the spirit of destruction. That has always been common enough. It lies in the genius he dedicates to destructive ends. Modern war would not recognize itself in the portraits of Shakespeare's classical and feudal fighters, in Hector and Hotspur, in Faulconbridge and Coriolanus, or in Othello himself. But let it look in the glass and it will behold Iago. In him Shakespeare reveals, with the clarity of nightmare, that unrestrained intellect, instead of being the opposite of force, and an antidote for it, as much of the modern world thinks, *is* force functioning on another plane. It is the immoral equivalent of war, and as certain to lead to it in due season as Iago's machinations were to lead to death. "All other knowledge is hurtful," says Montaigne, "to him who has not the science of honesty and goodness."

VI

To those who forget Emerson's wise observation that "perpetual modernness is the measure of merit in any work of art" all this will be an unpardonable digression from the play. To them it will be allegorizing *Othello*, reading into it what could never have entered Shakespeare's head. On the contrary, it is in this case demonstrable from the text that Shakespeare definitely intended precisely this equation between Iago and War, though, naturally, he could not have foreseen how the changes in the conduct of war between his time and ours were to sharpen and point the analogy. It is a perfect example of the nature of poetic foresight as distinguished from the popular conception of prophecy.

The opening of every one of Shakespeare's greatest Tragedies, as certainly as a Wagnerian overture, sounds the central theme or themes of the play. *Othello*, taking its cue from *Troilus and Cressida*, begins with a contrast between the physical and the mental parts of war. Iago, who is to prove himself such a master of intrigue, is cursing Othello to Roderigo for preferring Cassio as his lieutenant, with his "bookish theoric," "mere prattle, without practice," to himself with his active service in the field. However little we may suspect his sincerity at a first reading, the subject of his introductory speech portends a play in some sense about war as infallibly as their respective openings indicate that *Hamlet* will concern itself with ghosts, *Macbeth* with the nature of evil, and *King Lear* with the relations of the generations.

I doubt whether many people think of *Othello* as a play about war. But it is, even literally. Three of its four main characters are warriors. And the fourth is a warrior's wife, herself referred to by her husband at the climax of his joy as "my fair warrior." Even Cassio, whom Iago so despised, was considered worthy by the home government of taking Othello's place in Cyprus. Furthermore, the war between the Venetians and the Turks, which is the background and occasion of the action, is as indispensable to the plot and the "moral" as the feud between the Capulets and the Montagues is to *Romeo and Juliet*. It is obvious in the earlier case that if you drop out the feud the play falls to pieces. It is not so obvious, but it is just as true, that if you drop out the war from *Othello* it falls to pieces. The more closely one examines the analogy between the two plays in this respect the more impressive it becomes.

War is the royal occupation. Othello is a follower and master of it. Yet, before the play is over, "Othello's occupation's gone." Why and how it went it is vital for us to see, for in these days war is the world's occupation.

The Turk in this play, until he disappears beneath the waves, is consistently represented as the Enemy. At the beginning, his fleet is reported as bearing down on Cyprus, then on Rhodes, then again on Cyprus. The Venetians set out to head him off—or to be on hand when he appears. A terrific storm arises. The Turks are all drowned. The Venetians arrive safe in Cyprus.

All this at first sight seems of no intrinsic interest. It is mere machinery, mere scenery against which the domestic drama is to be enacted. Unless we are on guard, we skip it mentally in the reading. But we do so at our peril, for the "scenery" in Shakespearean tragedy is part of the action, and never more so, not even in *King Lear*, than here. "Be what cannot be skipped." The war in *Othello* conforms to that Emersonian injunction.

Reread the play with sharp attention to the parts in which war figures, pondering particularly every allusion to the Turks—there are many of them—and it is inescapable that what Shakespeare is bent on is an insinuation into the underconsciousness of the reader of an analogy between Iago and the Turk. Indeed, in one passage Iago openly makes the identification himself. Desdemona has dubbed him "slanderer" for his strictures upon women. "Nay, it is true," retorts Iago, "or else I am a Turk." But it is not true. And so he is a Turk.

The end crowns the whole, and Othello confirms the capital nature of the analogy in those last words that set the seal on his lips and create the metaphor he acts out in death:

> And say besides, that in Aleppo once,
> Where a malignant and a turban'd Turk
> Beat a Venetian and traduc'd the state,
> I took by the throat the circumcised dog,
> And smote him—thus.

Whereupon he stabs himself, as if he would reach down with his dagger to that Turk-Iago within himself that enabled the other Iago to beat and traduce him.

The speech in which the analogy is first set up is one of those seemingly casual, unnecessarily digressive ones that a stage director can be counted on to abbreviate or cut out. As we have repeatedly noticed, it is into such passages, when attention is suspended, that Shakespeare loves to insert his most valuable clues. So here. A sailor enters and announces that the Turkish preparation makes for Rhodes. Incredible, says a Senator, that they should not take Cyprus first, which is both easier to capture and more useful to them. The expedition to Rhodes must be a blind.

> FIRST SEN.:   This cannot be,
> By no assay of reason; 'tis a pageant,
> To keep us in false gaze. When we consider
> The importancy of Cyprus to the Turk,
> And let ourselves again but understand
> That, as it more concerns the Turk than Rhodes,
> So may he with more facile question bear it,
> For that it stands not in such warlike brace,
> But altogether lacks the abilities
> That Rhodes is dress'd in; if we make thought of this,
> We must not think the Turk is so unskilful
> To leave that latest which concerns him first,
> Neglecting an attempt of ease and gain
> To wake and wage a danger profitless.

It would be prosaic to put the analogy on all fours. But who can miss it? The Turk is apparently taking one course that under cover of it he may take an entirely different one. Iago is about to do the same. "A pageant To keep us in false gaze." What better description could we ask of his plot? And the last four lines of the passage quoted—do they not fit Iago as well as they do the Turk? Indeed we are almost tempted to go on and seek analogies for Cyprus and Rhodes in Iago's story. But that would be to force what is thrown out as a suggestion rather than intended for an exact comparison. What is beyond doubt is that the passage is prophetic of the plot against Othello, and, in the light of the doom that overcame the Turks, of its ultimate spiritual defeat and of Iago's submergence under the waves of a final silence.

With this hint, the storm scene at the beginning of Act II takes on undreamed-of meanings.

When, following the tempest that has imperiled them all and engulfed the Turks, Othello at last arrives in Cyprus, he is shaken to the depths of his nature by the experience of stepping, as it were, from the embrace of death to the embrace of Desdemona. The piercing beauty of the words he speaks to her is stamped with that individual quality which Shakespeare somehow imparts to the speech of all his lovers, revealing his belief that every true love between man and woman is unique. "O my fair warrior!"—note the word, for it is Shakespeare's as well as Othello's—the Moor exclaims, as he catches sight of his wife. "My dear Othello!" she replies. And, as he takes her in his arms, he goes on:

> It gives me wonder great as my content
> To see you here before me. O my soul's joy!
> If after every tempest come such calms,
> May the winds blow till they have waken'd death!
> And let the labouring bark climb hills of seas
> Olympus-high, and duck again as low
> As hell's from heaven! If it were now to die,
> 'Twere now to be most happy; for, I fear,
> My soul hath her content so absolute
> That not another comfort like to this
> Succeeds in unknown fate.

At a first reading we enter into Othello's wonder and joy, a content so absolute that we, like him, cannot imagine it augmented; and we feel that undertone of sadness that accompanies all supreme felicity and beauty—enhanced in this instance by our knowledge of the plot against them. When, however, having finished the play, we reread these lines, we suddenly realize that Othello has prayed in them for exactly what the future was to bring him: a storm as much more terrific than the tumult of wind and wave through which he has just passed as the ocean of human emotion is more treacherous than any Mediterranean—a storm whose crest and trough should literally touch heaven and hell.

> Wash me in steep-down gulfs of liquid fire!

he was to pray later, when the full fury of that storm burst on him. But little, now, does he envisage any such tragic answer to his prayer, and, having uttered it, he kisses Desdemona and exclaims contradictorily:

> And this, and this, the greatest discords be
> That e'er our hearts shall make!

Whereupon Turk-Iago mutters to himself,

> O, you are well tun'd now!
> But I'll set down the pegs that make this music,
> As honest as I am.

To this unoverheard diabolic comment on the situation, Othello, utterly forgetting his prayer of the instant before for a vaster war of the elements, unwittingly replies:

> our wars are done, the Turks are drown'd.
> ... I prithee, good Iago. ...

This, to put it mildly, is premature. There is one war that is not done, one Turk that is not drowned, though he is destined before long to go down in a tempest of his own raising. Prayers are always answered, but not always in the way or in the sense that we intend.

Thus does Shakespeare tie Iago with the Turk—and so with the Enemy, and so with War. The connection is too often reiterated to be coincidence. It is too clearly contrived to be unconscious. It is plainly intentional.

So much for the first two readings of this scene. (To something else in it to be discovered only by a third or later reading I will return before I am done.)

VII

Desdemona is one of those touchstones in which Shakespeare's plays abound. Ask a group of people whether Desdemona is a weak or a strong character, and they characterize themselves by their answers. There are those who would dilute her away into a foolish and timid girl who makes a precipitate and unfortunate misalliance with a foreigner much older than herself. That is to pay scant attention to the picture Shakespeare gives of her as she was before the shadow of tragedy touched her, the girl her father referred to as "perfection." She was nearer perfection than he suspected. He never dreamed what audacity there was under her quietness and stillness. Desdemona was not absorbed merely in household duties. She loved company, could be witty, could dance, play, and sing. But her world was not bounded by these things either, and if she could do fine needlework, be sure she could dream over it too. As her response to Othello's tales of his adventures shows, she was in love with danger. It takes your shy ones to be bold. And when she says, as he reports,

> she wish'd
> That heaven had made her such a man,

whatever she meant by it and however Othello took it, Shakespeare plainly contrived that Delphic line as a preparation for Othello's own "O my fair warrior!" There was a boy within this girl, a man's courage at the heart of this maiden whose very motion blushed at herself. Desdemona is merely an extreme example of that union of feminine and masculine qualities that Shakespeare plainly held essential for either the perfect man or the perfect woman.

It is extraordinary (and especially to be noted for future reference) that Iago gives the best full-length description of Desdemona in the play. In the interlude at Cyprus before Othello's entrance after the storm, Desdemona asks Iago how he would praise a woman so deserving that malice itself would have to admit her merit. Malice itself of course is Iago and the deserving woman Desdemona. She naturally does not recognize either of these facts; he recognizes them both. And this is his description of the ideal woman he knows her to be:

> She that was ever fair and never proud,
> Had tongue at will and yet was never loud,
> Never lack'd gold and yet went never gay,
> Fled from her wish and yet said, "Now I may,"
> She that being anger'd, her revenge being nigh,
> Bade her wrong stay and her displeasure fly,
> She that in wisdom never was so frail
> To change the cod's head for the salmon's tail,
> She that could think and ne'er disclose her mind,
> See suitors following and not look behind,
> She was a wight, if ever such wight were,—

and as Iago pauses, Desdemona asks, as he hoped she would, "To do what?"

> To suckle fools and chronicle small beer.
>
> O most lame and impotent conclusion!

she exclaims, never guessing what Iago has been up to. His picture reveals with what completeness he can appraise both truth and beauty, and then revert—as he does the next second in an aside, "with as little a web as this will I ensnare as great a fly as Cassio"—to the spider. Desdemona may be evaluated, she will never be caught—in either sense—by the intellect.

"At some thoughts," says Dostoevsky, "one stands perplexed, especially at the sight of men's sin, and wonders whether one should use force or humble love. Always decide to use humble love. If you resolve on that once for all, you may subdue the whole world. Loving humility is marvelously strong, the strongest of all things and there is nothing else like it." It would be impertinent to say that Desdemona believed that. She was it— and it is superfluous to believe what we are. Desdemona a strong or weak character? Under her spell, one is tempted to assert that she is the strongest character in all Shakespeare. Who can contend with her for that eminence? Only the transformed Cordelia. But Desdemona did not have to be transformed. While blows, physical, mental, and spiritual, rained on her head, she held to her faith in goodness and to the end helped answer her own prayer:

> Heaven me such uses send,
> Not to pick bad from bad, but by bad mend.

"O my fair warrior!" Othello was right. "The divine Desdemona." Cassio did not exaggerate.

And it is precisely one of her divinest acts that, curiously, is most often set down to her discredit: the dropping of the handkerchief. "That is a fault," says Othello in the next scene, when he asks his wife to lend him the handkerchief and she cannot produce it, and many readers agree that it was a fault, not noticing that Shakespeare has been careful to show that, so far as Desdemona is concerned, the loss of the handkerchief was not only not a fault, but actually a virtue of an angelic order. Indeed, there is a sense in which Desdemona tells no lie when she denies that the handkerchief is lost. Things are lost through carelessness or genuine accident—and the dropping of the handkerchief came about through neither of these. The truth, as contrasted with the fact, of the matter is that neither Desdemona, nor accident, nor Fate, dropped the handkerchief. Othello dropped it.

DES.:	How now, my dear Othello!
	Your dinner, and the generous islanders
	By you invited, do attend your presence.
OTH.:	I am to blame.
DES.:	Why do you speak so faintly?
	Are you not well?
OTH.:	I have a pain upon my forehead here.
DES.:	Faith, that's with watching; 'twill away again:
	Let me but bind it hard, within this hour
	It will be well.
OTH.:	Your napkin is too little:
	Let it alone. Come, I'll go in with you.
DES.:	I am very sorry that you are not well.

And Othello and Desdemona go out as Emilia picks up the handkerchief.

It is vital here to visualize what has happened. The stage business is left to the actors and director, but surely there is only one right way of arranging it. Othello, his mind full of the terrible doubts Iago has poured into it, explains his embarrassed manner and faint voice as due to headache, as, indeed, they may well be. Desdemona takes out her handkerchief and starts to bind his forehead. At the moment, he cannot bear this act of affection with its physical contact from the woman he has begun to doubt, and with a gesture of impatience—"Let it alone"—he pushes her hand away, causing the handkerchief to drop, the "it," of course, referring not to the handkerchief, as it is often taken to, but to the forehead. Now if Desdemona had loved Othello less, had been less genuinely pained by his pain, or had valued a mere token of love above love itself, she would naturally have noticed the fall of the handkerchief and would, however unconsciously, have stooped and picked it up. But every fiber of her soul and body, conscious and unconscious, is so totally devoted to Othello that the handkerchief for the moment ceases to exist. The slightest deflection of her eye in its direction as it dropped would have been a subtraction from the infinity of her love—just as the movement of Othello's hand when he pushed her hand away measured his distrust of that love, gave the villain his unique opportunity, and sealed his own doom forever. Is there anything in all the drama of the world, I wonder, to equal this in its own kind? The moment when Romeo thrust his rapier between Tybalt and Mercutio is similar. But that was a rapier, the moment was patently critical, and the act, however impulsive, was a conscious one. This, on the other hand, is only a handkerchief, the situation the most ordinary, and the act one that almost anybody might be guilty of any day in his life. "Trifles light as air." Was there ever a better demonstration that everything may depend on anything? "Who can control his fate?" asks Othello when it is too late. And there have been those who think that Shakespeare is asking the same question. But in that case he is answering: Othello for one could have controlled his—and Romeo for another—if, like Desdemona's and Juliet's, their bounty had been as boundless as the sea, their love as deep. This is not fate. This is freedom.

But if the hero foredooms himself by causing the handkerchief to drop, the villain does as much for himself just twenty-seven lines further on when he snatches the handkerchief from his wife's hand. Emilia, as the event proves, was Iago's oversight. "It is in just such stupid things," says Dostoevsky (without any allusion to *Othello* of course), "that clever people are most easily caught. The more cunning a man is the less he suspects that he will be caught in a simple thing." But long before his wife turns the handkerchief against him, Iago uses it with bloody effect on Othello. When, on top of his account of Cassio's revelation in his sleep, he tells him that that very day he saw Cassio wipe his beard with it, Othello is finally convinced:

> Now do I see 'tis true. Look here, Iago;
> All my fond love thus do I blow to heaven.
> 'Tis gone.

Arise, black vengeance, from the hollow hell!
Yield up, O love, thy crown and hearted throne
To tyrannous hate! Swell, bosom, with thy fraught,
For 'tis of aspics' tongues! . . .
O, blood, blood, blood!

In the next scene where Othello demands the handkerchief and Desdemona persists in turning the subject back to Cassio—"the handkerchief," "Cassio"; "the handkerchief," "Cassio"—she is generally blamed, first, for lying, and, second, for an utterly unforgivable lack of sense and tact. But it is Othello, not Desdemona, who really lies about the handkerchief in this scene! For the express, if not conscious, purpose of frightening his wife, he invents a fabulous story of the handkerchief's origin and magical properties, the falsity of which Shakespeare is careful to bring out by having him give a true account of it at the end of the play. Desdemona is naturally awed, and like a scared child evades her husband's questions. Her "guilt" is venial compared with his. And it is precisely her utter innocence that permits her insistence about Cassio. A guilty woman would have sensed at once that she must keep clear of so dangerous a subject. But to Desdemona a chance to help another is a command to do so instantly and utterly. Truth and compassion are rare. Tact and worldliness are common. Only those who think that the transformation of a childlike and loving woman into a discreet and worldly one is a moral ascent can wish that Desdemona had acted otherwise than she did in this distressing scene. If she exhibits a deficiency of common sense, she shows an abundance of a sense utterly uncommon. If it had been a younger daughter entreating a father to forgive an older sister who had fallen out of his favor, and not allowing herself to be put off, we would have nothing but admiration for her. We should have nothing but admiration for Desdemona's persistence in behalf of Cassio.

Desdemona's "lie" about the handkerchief is not the only one that is charged against her. There is also what is generally known as her dying lie in the last words that she speaks:

EMIL.: O, who hath done this deed?
DES.: Nobody; I myself. Farewell!
      Commend me to my kind lord. O, farewell!

"Truth sits upon the lips of dying men." Dostoevsky thought it worth while to write a novel of a thousand pages to bring home the truth that sat upon the lips of the dying Desdemona. The central doctrine of Father Zossima in *The Brothers Karamazov* is that each is "to blame for everyone and for all things." The plot of the novel was conceived to illustrate and prove that paradox. There is hardly one of its pages that has no bearing on it. Desdemona expressed it more briefly: "I myself." Into those two words she put the whole mystery of the atonement. And this is what the world chooses to call a lie.

VIII

If, so far, we have said more about Desdemona and Iago than about the one who gives the title to the play, it is because he cannot be understood without first understanding them. They are the poles between which he moves. At the opening of the story, before Iago begins to enmesh him, he seems as simple and noble as Desdemona herself, and, however black without, is rightly described as white within, made so partly by her love. But when the poison begins to work, when that simplicity and nobility begin to be contaminated, then Othello becomes an alternation of mighty opposites, not gray, but black-and-white—the poet-barbarian, the hero-murderer, the paragon of self-control gone mad, the harmonious nature to whom chaos comes again. Taking the whole play into account, he is equally susceptible, almost, to the influence of Desdemona and to that of Iago. First Desdemona wins him; then Iago; then Desdemona, dead, wins him back. There is the plot reduced to a dozen words. Though he kills her, she saves him. Perhaps that is Shakespeare's unconscious prophecy of the destiny of a mankind that in so many ways resembles Othello.

There is no other among his supreme plays against the plot and the psychology of which so many objections have been brought as against *Othello*, and they are leveled primarily against the conduct of its hero. The improbabilities of *King Lear* are another and more venial matter because of its remote and semimythical setting and atmosphere. *Othello* is domestic, it is said, and should submit to more exacting tests. A real Othello would have gone to his wife for an explanation. (And, incidentally, a real Desdemona would have found a chance to explain.) In answer, his defenders are compelled to plead his age, his brief acquaintance with his wife, his ignorance of Venetian society and consequent self-distrust and willingness to accept Iago's account of its habits.

This much is true at any rate: Othello regarded Desdemona's love for him as a dream too beautiful to be true. Hence, when it is suggested to him that it is not true, this is in a sense nothing but what he has been ready to believe all along. What wonder that it is easy for him to dismiss his happiness as an illusion! "Desdemona love *me!* Impossible!" When we waken from a dream we do not go about searching for material evidence that it was not a dream after all. Neither does Othello. It is the best things in him, his love, his imagination, his lack of suspicion, his modesty, that give Iago his chance. But such considerations will not silence the doubters.

Apparently only some parallel incident from real life would convince them that a man of Othello's temperament could act as Othello is represented as acting in this play. Such an incident, it would seem, would be rather difficult to produce. And yet, strangely, it can be produced. Under the title of *A Practical Joke*, Dostoevsky's wife relates a domestic incident which occurred in the spring of 1876. If it had been expressly written to prove, a fortiori, the truth of the psychology of *Othello*, it could scarcely have been improved, as anyone who reads it will be bound to agree. It runs as follows:

On 18th May, 1876, an incident took place which I recall almost with terror. This is how it happened. A new novel by Mme. Sophie Smirnov entitled *The Strong Character* was running as a serial then in *The Otechestvennya Zapiski*. Fiodor was on friendly terms with Sophie Smirnov and valued her talent very highly. He was interested in her latest work, and asked me to get him the numbers of the monthly as they appeared. I chose those few days, when my husband had a rest from his work on *The Journal of an Author*, and brought him the numbers of *The Otechestvennya Zapiski*. But as journals are lent by the libraries only for two or three days, I urged my husband to read the journal quickly so as to avoid paying a fine at the library. So it was also with the April number. Fiodor read the novel and spoke to me of how our dear Sophie (whom I, too, valued very highly) had succeeded in creating a certain male character in the novel. That evening my husband went out to some gathering, and after seeing the children to bed, I began reading the novel. In it, by the way, was published an anonymous letter, sent by the villain to the hero, which ran as follows:

"Dear Sir, Noblest Peter Ivanovich,

As I am a perfect stranger to you, but take an interest in your feelings, I venture to address these lines to you. Your nobility is sufficiently well-known to me, and my heart is pained at the idea, that despite all your nobility, a certain person, who is very close to you, is so basely deceiving you. Having gone away with your blessing to a place four hundred miles off, she, like a delighted dove spreading its wings and soaring upwards, has no mind to return to the marital home. You have let her go to your own as well as to her ruin, into the claws of a man who terrifies her, but who fascinates her by his flattering addresses. He has stolen her heart, and there are no eyes more beautiful to her than his. Even her little children are loathsome to her, if she gets no loving word from him. If you want to know who this fellow the villain is, I must not reveal his name, but look for yourself among those who frequent your house, and beware of dark men. When you see the dark man, who loves haunting your doors, have a good look at him. It is now a long time since that fellow has crossed your path, and you are the only one who does not notice it.

Nothing but your nobility compels me to reveal this secret to you. And if

you don't trust me, then have a look at the locket which your wife wears round her neck, and see whose portrait she wears in that locket near her heart.
                                                                    YOUR EVER UNKNOWN WELL-WISHER."

I must say here that lately I had been in the best of moods; my husband had had no epileptic fits for a long time, our children were perfectly well, our debts were gradually being paid, and the success of *The Journal of an Author* was marked. All this strengthened my characteristic cheerfulness, and under the influence of the anonymous letter, just read, a playful idea flashed across my mind—to copy that letter (changing the name and striking out certain lines) and to send it by post to Fiodor. It seemed to me that, as he had only yesterday read that letter in Mme. Smirnov's novel, he would guess at once that it was a joke, and we should have some fun. There also occurred another idea to me, that my husband might take the letter seriously. In that case I was interested to see how he would regard it: whether he would show it to me, or throw it away into the waste-paper basket. As usual with me, I had no sooner thought of the idea than I put it into execution. At first I wanted to write the letter in my own handwriting; but as I had been copying for Fiodor every day, and my handwriting was too familiar to him, I resolved to cover up my joke and began copying out the letter in a rounder handwriting than mine. But it turned out to be a hard job, and I spoilt several sheets before I managed to write the whole letter in a uniform hand. Next morning I posted it, and in the afternoon it was delivered to us together with other letters.

That day Fiodor was out later than usual, and returned only at five o'clock and, not wanting to keep the children waiting for their dinner, he just changed and came straight into the dining room, without looking at his letters. The dinner passed off merrily and noisily. Fiodor was in a good mood; he talked a good deal and laughed, as he answered the children's questions. After dinner, with the usual cup of tea in his hand, he went into his study. I went into the nursery, and in about ten minutes' time I entered the study to see the effect which my anonymous letter had produced.

I sat down in my usual seat by the writing table, and purposely asked Fiodor something to which he had to give an answer. But he kept a gloomy silence, and paced the room with heavy steps. I saw he was upset, and instantly I felt sorry. To break the silence I asked him: "Why are you so gloomy, Fedya?"

Fiodor gave me an angry look, walked across the room a couple of times and came to a stop just facing me.

"You wear a locket?" he asked in a choking voice.

"I do."

"Show it to me."

"What for? You have seen it many times."

"Show—me—the locket!" Fiodor shouted at the top of his voice.

I realised that my joke had gone too far, and in order to reassure him I began undoing the collar of my dress. But I had no time to take the locket out. Fiodor could not restrain the anger which had seized him. He quickly rushed to me and caught my chain with all his strength. It was a thin chain which he himself had bought for me in Venice. It broke instantly, and the locket remained in my husband's hand. He quickly swept round the table and with his head bent down, he began opening the locket. Not knowing where to press the spring, he fussed over it for a long time. I saw how his hands trembled, and the locket nearly slipped from them on to the table. I was very sorry for him and terribly angry with myself. I began to speak in a friendly tone, and proposed to open the locket for him; but Fiodor with an angry nod of his head refused my help. At last my husband opened the locket and found there—on one side the portrait of our little daughter, on the other—his own portrait. He was absolutely confused, and kept on looking at the portrait in silence.

"Well, now, have you found it?" I asked him. "Fedya, you silly, how could you believe an anonymous letter?"

Fiodor instantly turned his face to me. "How do you know of the letter?"

"How? I myself sent it you!"

"What do you mean; you sent it me? It is incredible!"

"I'll prove it to you at once."

I went to the other table on which lay the copy of *The Otechestvennya Zapiski*, and got out several sheets of paper, on which I had practised my changed handwriting.

Fiodor raised his hands in astonishment. "And did you yourself compose the letter?"

"Not at all. I simply copied it from Sophie's novel. Surely you read it yesterday? I thought you would guess at once."

"Well, how could I remember! Anonymous letters are always in that style. I simply can't understand why you sent it me?"

"I just wanted to have a lark," I explained.

"How could you play such a joke? I have been in anguish for the last half hour."

"How could I know that you would be such an Othello, and get into such a rage without giving yourself time for a moment's thought?"

"One does not think in such cases. Ah, well, it is clear that you have never experienced real love and real jealousy."

"As for real love, I experience it even now, and as for my not knowing 'real jealousy,' it is your own fault. Why aren't you unfaithful to me?" I laughed, wishing to divert his mood. "Please, be unfaithful to me. Even then I would be kinder than you are. I would not touch you, but I would scratch out her eyes, the villainess. . . ."

"Well, you are laughing, Anechka," Fiodor began apologetically. "But think what a misfortune might have happened: indeed, in my anger I could have strangled you. I may indeed say: God has taken pity on our little ones. And suppose I had not found those portraits, a grain of doubt as to your faithfulness would have remained in my mind for ever, and would have tortured me all my life. I implore you, do not play with such things: in a rage I am not responsible for my actions."

During the conversation I felt a slight awkwardness in moving my neck. I passed my handkerchief over it, and there was a line of blood on it. Evidently the chain in being wrenched off by force had scratched my skin. Seeing blood on my handkerchief, my husband was in despair.

"My God," he exclaimed, "what have I done? Anechka, my dear, forgive me. I have wounded you. Does it pain you, tell me, does it pain you very much?"

I began to reassure him that there was no "wound," but just a mere scratch which would disappear by the morning. Fiodor was seriously upset, and, above all, was ashamed of his fit of anger. The whole evening was given up to his apologies and expressions of sympathy and tenderness. And I, too, was boundlessly happy that my absurd joke had ended so happily. I sincerely repented of having made Fiodor suffer, and I promised myself never again to play such a joke, having learnt from this experience to what a furious, almost irresponsible state my dear husband was capable of being reduced in moments of jealousy.

I still preserve the locket and the anonymous letter (of 18th May, 1876).

Here, then, is another case of an older and experienced man married to a younger wife, hardly able to believe, as other documents attest,* that his happiness is real. This man, moreover, is by general consent one of the profoundest students of human nature that ever lived, especially of its roots in the unconscious. Yet, caught in the grip of ancestral jealousy, his wisdom vanishes as if it had never existed and he becomes as helpless as a child. It would be tedious to point out all the parallels between this narrative and *Othello* (the mention of which in the narrative is itself significant) down even to such a detail as the strangling. The same readiness of a profoundly loving nature to believe the worst, the same precipitate rage and failure to give any opportunity to explain, the same centering of everything on a token of love, with the other ending only perhaps because Anna was able to produce the locket as Desdemona was not able to produce its counterpart, the handkerchief. And the startling thing is that it all happened in this later case without an Iago—the Russian Desdemona being her own Iago. Then how much more easily with him! The fact that Dostoevsky and Othello, too, were both prone to epileptic attacks is of more than passing interest, as is the antipodal reversal of emotion in the two men when the truth appears. All in all, the irrational and inundating character of jealousy has seldom been better set forth than in this incident, not even in Leontes in *The Winter's Tale*, whom it also helps us understand. I can testify from many experiments with this anecdote that it ends for good and all the doubts of those who until they heard it

* It is of interest that Dostoevsky proposed to this woman through the medium of an invented story, just as Othello wooed Desdemona through stories into which a considerable element of unconscious invention undoubtedly entered.

thought that in *Othello* Shakespeare had for once slipped up in his knowledge of human nature or, worse, had sacrificed that knowledge to theatrical effect.

IX

Though the main stumbling block to readers of *Othello* is an incapacity to realize what jealousy can be when aroused in a nature not easily jealous, there are other sources of trouble, numerous specific moments in the play where a failure to notice some "tremendous trifle" in the text is the source of grave misunderstanding. Three of them may be mentioned.

1. In the scene, staged by Iago, where Othello oversees Cassio talking with Bianca, supposedly of Desdemona, and catches fragments of their conversation, it is frequently held that the Moor is too readily duped. This sort of thing is all right on the stage, but it couldn't happen in life. Such objectors have forgotten that Othello has but a moment before emerged from an epileptic fit and is in no condition to exercise his critical faculty.

2. When Othello, near the end, declares that Cassio has admitted his guilt, he is usually taken to be speaking in general of the circumstantial case against him and, more particularly, of Iago's loathsome account of Cassio's confession to him. But he means far more than this. In the darkness and confusion Othello mistakes the voice of the wounded Roderigo—"O, villain that I am!"—for Cassio's. He hears what he fears. He thinks he has heard Cassio with his dying words admit his guilt. "It is e'en so," Othello assents. What more convincing evidence could he ask for? Fail to take that "O, villain that I am!" into account, and the mistake based on it, and the whole character of Othello's act in killing Desdemona is altered. The point is a capital one. Many must have detected it. Yet of hundreds of readers of the play I have questioned I have yet to find the first one who noticed it for himself. Even when asked to find the passage in which Othello hears with his own ears "Cassio's" confession, few, even with the text before them, can locate it.

3. And then the classic question: How could Desdemona speak after she had been strangled? Medical authority has been marshaled on both sides of this question. But Shakespeare was seeking poetical, rather than physiological or anatomical truth (not that the former violates the latter). What happens at this point should be plain—and there is an old stage tradition, it is said, to support it. Othello has failed to stifle his wife, and, perceiving signs of life, does not again try to do what he has attempted in vain, but stabs her at the words "So, so." Not only does this make understandable her speaking again before death: the irony, the contrasts, and

the symbolism agree in demanding what it is natural anyway for Othello to have done in the circumstances. His earlier,

> Yet I'll not shed her blood,
> Nor scar that whiter skin of hers than snow,

makes the inference almost irresistible that he will and does shed her blood, that he will and does scar that skin. Blood, throughout Shakespeare as throughout poetry, is the symbol of passion, of the instinctive as against the rational life. It is needed here to make visible Othello's descent from the judicial and sacrificial mood in which he enters his wife's chamber—

> It is the cause, it is the cause, my soul,

—to the fury at the last when he denies his victim even a moment for one prayer. The linking of Desdemona with snow at this point is a confirmation of the symbolic color scheme of the play and effects a final fearful contrast with the red for which Othello has now come to stand. Moreover, Shakespeare seems to have specifically prepared for the moment when Othello stabs Desdemona by the moment when he strikes her. In retrospect the earlier scene seems like a rehearsal of the later. They are the two most nearly unendurable moments in the play. The sharpness of the contrast depends on Othello's finally doing with a knife what he had already done with his hand.

X

Nowhere else in a single pair of characters, not even in *King Lear*, does Shakespeare more squarely confront the diabolic and the divine than in Iago and Desdemona.

> . . . do but see his vice;
> 'Tis to *her* virtue a just equinox.

With a change of one word, Iago himself expresses it for us perfectly.

One might expect that in order to make the most of this contrast the two would be brought into frequent contact in the course of the play. But they are not. They are never alone together, and only twice are there what might be called dialogues between them. Near the quay at Cyprus, partly to hide her fears about Othello in the storm, Desdemona indulges in light banter with Iago and, as we saw, he draws the ideal portrait which clandestinely is a picture of herself and which he brings to a "lame and impotent conclusion." No more is needed to show his sensitiveness to moral beauty. Why did Shakespeare take the trouble to demonstrate it so convincingly? What becomes of it during the rest of the play? It is almost wholly repressed. That it is capable of rising above the surface, however, is proved by that extraordinary exclamation near the end,

If Cassio do remain,
He hath a daily beauty in his life
That makes me ugly.

But if the daily beauty in Cassio's life makes Iago ugly, how about the hour-ly, the momentary beauty in Desdemona's? What does that do to him? The poet, if I am not mistaken, dedicates the one highly dramatic scene in which the two talk with each other to bringing that out.

It comes just after the fearful "brothel" scene in which Othello has flung all the evil he imagines straight in his wife's face. On his exit, Desdemona, stunned, sinks into a state beyond the relief of tears. She ominously bids Emilia lay her wedding sheets on her bed and summon to comfort her in her distress—of all people on earth—the very one who has caused it! At the nadir of her despair she will consult Iago on what she can do to win her lord again. Iago comes, and we have as psychologically interesting a scene as there is in the play. Desdemona's condition of semi-somnolence, just pre-ceding it, is the correlative and opposite of Othello's epileptic seizure. In each case a scene with Iago follows. The same thing that Iago does to Othello in the earlier one is done to him, in a reversed sense, in the later one. Here, if ever, in this interview between the villain and the heroine, we have a chance to study the effect on each other of something close to pure evil and pure good. By way of mediation, Emilia, who is a paradoxical mixture of the two, is also present.

The effect of evil on good may be dismissed in a word by saying that good here not only does not resist evil, it is unaware of its presence. It acts as if it did not exist—which is another way of saying that it treats the evil man as if he were good.

Does evil reciprocate and treat good as if it did not exist? It does not. It cannot. Evil is forever uneasy in the presence of good, and it is significant to begin with that Desdemona and Emilia in this scene each speak almost twice as many words as does the usually voluble Iago. But the quality as well as the quantity of his utterances is altered.

Do not weep, do not weep. Alas the day!

I pray you be content.

Go in, and weep not; all things shall be well.

In their simplicity and sympathy the words sound utterly unlike anything else in Iago's role. "Exactly!" it will be said. "Here the man's histrionic powers are at their acme. He can feign even pity and compassion perfectly. Here he sinks to his lowest point—pretending to comfort the one he is about to destroy. These, if any were ever shed, are crocodile tears." Of course they are crocodile tears. Short of throwing up his whole plot, Iago is compelled to go on acting. But what taught this crocodile-Iago to simulate sympathy so consummately? What if not the very buried sympathy that Desdemona's presence had activated in him? The words that crocodile-Iago needs for his part are the very ones that a genuinely sympathetic Iago might have spoken. It is as if an inner prompter handed them to him at a moment when he was at a loss for the next words in his role. Who is that Inner Prompter? An unconscious as well as a conscious Iago are present in this scene exactly as there were two Shylocks to offer to Antonio in one breath, as it were, the loan without interest and the bloody bond. The parallel is startling. To feign goodness successfully it is not enough that we should have had experience with goodness in the past; we must retain potential goodness. Otherwise the counterfeit will be crude. Iago's is so true it could be passed for genuine coin. It was the unconscious Iago that made it so.

Whatever unique thing, good or bad, any individual may have made out of his inherited qualities, there underneath, however deep down, the human nature into which he was born is bound to survive in its general composite trend and upshot as incarnated in the lives of all his ancestors, a mingled web of light and dark. Only let that individual be taken off guard, suddenly confronted with some circumstance or person alien to the world to which he has conditioned himself, and that fundamental human nature will reassert itself. The situation here is precisely that. Unless Shakespeare is contravening his seemingly universal practice and is making Iago a pure abstraction, the rule is bound not to fail. It does not fail. And this scene is inserted, I believe, to show that it does not fail.

Imagine any man calloused by bitterness and cruelty. If a child, especially a beautiful child, were without warning to throw her arms about his neck, nestle up to him confidingly, and speak words of piercing loveliness, is it conceivable that he would not be moved? No matter how he might try to hide it or deny it to himself, that remnant of goodness in him that nothing can eradicate would respond. Dostoevsky chose precisely this situation for the crisis of the first of his great masterpieces, *Crime and Punishment*. It is at the moment when the little girl Polenka throws her arms about the murderer Raskolnikov and kisses him that he is reborn. He reverts a moment later, as might be expected, to his most devastating power-fantasies. But the seed has been sown. Long afterward it comes to fruit. *Mutatis mutandis*, Shakespeare, if I am not mistaken, gives us the same situation here, if with the other outcome. We never see Iago repentant as we do Raskolnikov, but the effect of his brief interview with Desdemona shakes him to the foundation.

From the moment he enters he is scarcely recognizable as the same man we have known under the name of Iago, and except for three sharp sen-

tences he speaks to his wife which make the difference the more conspicuous, the man who addresses Desdemona remains unrecognizable throughout the scene. If anyone ignorant of the story were to read it by itself, he
would be utterly bewildered. One Iago is so tender and sympathetic, the
other so coarse and ill-tempered.* But we who have read the play, if we have
been attentive, will recall certain passages from Iago's own role that throw
light on this moment of it, for Shakespeare is nothing if not preparatory.
First, we remember his penetrating description of the moral beauty of the
woman into whose intimate presence he now comes for the first time since
the occasion near the quay when he uttered it. He stressed then, particularly, her power to subdue all feeling of anger or revenge, precisely the emotions that almost any woman would have given unrestrained vent to after
being struck and insulted by her husband as Desdemona had been just before
this very meeting. "She is of so free, so kind, so apt, so blessed a disposition,
that she holds it a vice in her goodness not to do more than she is requested."
That sentence, too, might well come to mind. And those strange words in
soliloquy:

> Now, I do love her too,
> Not out of absolute lust,

and, finally, the words to Roderigo, "as, they say, base men being in love
have then a nobility in their natures more than is native to them," which
puts in a nutshell the very truth on which we are now insisting: that no matter how wicked a man may become, the nobility that is an inevitable part of
his inheritance will be there underneath ready to appear under the right
conditions. Are the conditions right for the appearance of the nobility in
this base man? They obviously are, whether he knows it or not.

At the end of their interview Desdemona kneels. It is left to the actress
and to our imaginations to decide whether she kneels just to heaven or to
Iago also, whom she is beseeching to go to her lord on her behalf. If, as I
believe, it should be to Iago too, we have a counterpart of the famous scene
where the sainted Father Zossima kneels to the potential parricide, Dmitri
Karamazov, in Dostoevsky's novel. (And if we want to press the parallel
we may even believe that something deep in Desdemona's unconscious
mind saw into the future and was seeking less a reconciliation between

---

* When Emilia suggests that some cozening slave is the author of this slander, Iago
turns it off with a "Fie, there is no such man." Whereupon Desdemona exclaims,

> "If any such there be, Heaven pardon him."
> "A halter pardon him! and hell gnaw his bones!"

cries Emilia. Our emotional responses to these two lines measure the respective
amounts of Desdemona and Emilia there are in our own natures. Emilia is the Gratiano
—on an immensely higher plane—of this scene. She is a safety valve for the crowd's
feelings.

herself and her lord than one between Iago and Othello, of any breach between whom she is of course at the moment unaware.) It is noteworthy that Desdemona's final words in this interview are practically a paraphrase of Shakespeare's own confession of faith about love in the 116th sonnet, culminating, in her case, in the lines:

> Unkindness may do much;
> And his unkindness may defeat my life,
> But never taint my love.

If anything was capable of it, this longest and in many respects loveliest speech in the role of the laconic Desdemona, from which these words come, must have moved Iago to the depths, imparting a meaning he had never dreamed of to his, "Now I do love her too." If it did shake him, it is the supreme tribute to her in the entire play: even Iago could not escape the effect of her presence. That the whole interview did move him profoundly Shakespeare all but proves, where it is his habit to prove such things, in the little scene that immediately follows—in that and in the rest of the play.

When Desdemona goes out, Roderigo enters, and in the first part of what ensues we see Iago for the first time at his wit's end, unable to devise anything by way of answer to Roderigo's importunities. In his brief and stalling replies to his dupe's reiterated complaints Shakespeare is plainly registering the profound and disturbing effect that Desdemona—and incidentally Emilia—has just had on him. She has sapped his power. In thirty-four lines of text, these are Iago's speeches—Roderigo says all the rest:

> What in the contrary?
> Will you hear me, Roderigo?
> You charge me most unjustly.
> Well; go to; very well.
> Very well.
> You have said now.

Is this Iago? To paraphrase Lodovico's words about Othello: Is this the resourceful nature that obstacles could not daunt? He resembles himself as little as Falstaff does himself at the moment of his rejection, or as Falstaff resembles that other Falstaff who creeps into the basket of foul linen in the home of Mistress Ford. It is no answer to say that Iago, before the scene is over, does partly recover his wits. How came he to lose them? And such wits as he does recover resemble those of some common ruffian rather than those of the archpsychologist that Iago was at his intellectual best. The expedient he recommends to Roderigo is the desperate one of knocking out Cassio's brains. It is not coincidence, but more nearly cause and effect, that from the presence of Desdemona he steps immediately to this fatal mistake.

The man has himself received a death blow. For the first time in his life he has encountered a force more powerful than his own diabolic nature. What has happened to him he doubtless does not understand. He is intelligent, but not intelligent enough for that. Never again in the play do we find him perfectly poised and sure of himself as he had been previously. He almost hesitates about Cassio's death. The final reason he gives for it, the daily beauty of Cassio's life, shows that the beauty of Desdemona has given him a mortal (or perhaps we should say an immortal) wound. He would have been incapable of offering that highly uncharacteristic reason before he had that fatal interview. He is defeated. From his first false step he goes on to another and another until he sinks into that final terrific silence that is but a prelude to the silence of death. The Turk to whom he is compared went down under the waters of the Mediterranean. He goes down under the same element in its symbolic sense.

XI

Into what element did Desdemona pass at death?

Our imaginations cannot help asking that question, however idle it may seem. If Iago went down under water, Desdemona might well have been lifted into air. If his end was silence, hers should be harmony. If he descended to hell, she should have ascended to heaven, or, as we are more prone to say today, if he reverted to the unconscious, she must have been transformed into spirit. Water, silence, hell; air, harmony, heaven: that is what the symbols seem to call for. But this is the merest fancy unless there is warrant for it in the text. These are castles in the air unless there is a Shakespearean foundation to put under them.

We have noted over and over Shakespeare's habit of concealing, in what seem like brief digressions or superfluous scenes, clues to the over- and undermeanings of his plays—as in the garden scene in *Richard II*, the dawn passage in *Julius Caesar*, or the one in *Hamlet* where the Prince teases Polonius about the cloud.

If readers of *Othello* were asked to select the most supererogatory passage in the play, they would probably be unanimous, unless some forgot its very existence, in picking the opening of Act III where Cassio comes in with some musicians who are prepared to play but are peremptorily dismissed by the Clown (for there *is* a clown in *Othello*):

CLOWN: Then put up your pipes in your bag, for I'll away. Go; vanish into air, away! (*Exeunt Musicians*)

This brief overture to what is admittedly one of the greatest acts Shakespeare ever wrote is a tolerably obvious allegory of that sudden interruption of the music of Othello's love which is to be the subject of the act—a fact that in itself justifies us, apart from its very inconsequentiality, in searching it for other clues.

The passage emphasizes the fact that it is upon wind instruments that the musicians are prepared to play, and the Clown himself plays on that idea when he tells them to "vanish into air." Vanish into your proper element, he might have said. The other thing stressed is the idea of inaudible music:

CLOWN: But, masters, here's money for you: and the general so likes your music, that he desires you, for love's sake, to make no more noise with it.

FIRST MUS.: Well, sir, we will not.

CLOWN: If you have any music that may not be heard, to't again: but, as they say, to hear music the general does not greatly care.

FIRST MUS.: .We have none such, sir.

This sounds like the idlest fooling, and on the surface it is just that. But when we remember Keats's

> Heard melodies are sweet, but those unheard
>   Are sweeter; therefore, ye soft pipes, play on;
> Not to the sensual ear, but, more endear'd,
>   Pipe to the spirit ditties of no tone,

we see that, so far from mere fooling, this idea of inaudible music is the idea of poetry itself brought down by the Clown to the level of burlesque and parody. The quintessence of a poem is precisely its music that may not be heard. May not, notice, not cannot.

Where, audible or inaudible, is there music in Othello? Where, especially, if anywhere, is there wind music?

We think immediately of the storm off Cyprus. There the gale roared until Montano cried, "The wind hath spoke aloud." There it tossed water on the very stars, bringing a chaos of the elements that forecasts the chaos that "is come again" in Othello's soul when Iago loosens the moral hurricane that parts the Moor from his wife more violently than ever the physical tempest did. The Turks go down in the first storm. Turk-Iago goes down in the second one. Othello and Desdemona were parted by the first storm, but were reunited after it. They were parted by the second one. Was there a Second Cyprus?

If Shakespeare carries his symbolism through with Iago, is it inconceivable that he may have done the same with Desdemona and Othello? Here, if anywhere, it would be natural to seek the poetry of this poem, the music in this play that may not be heard.

A scientist gets his hypothesis from he does not always know where. He subjects it to the test of facts, and accepts it or rejects it accordingly. So it should be with the interpretation of a work of literary art. Where a suggested reading comes from is not the important question. The important question is whether it can pass the test of the text. If not, however alluring, it must be dismissed.

Let us look at the storm scene for a *third* time.

A Sea-port in Cyprus. An open place near the quay. (Cyprus, remember, is an island, and we know what an island came to mean to Shakespeare near the end of his life.)

Three figures with wind-blown garments and spray-spattered hair are gazing out over mountainous waves toward a misty horizon:

> What from the cape can you discern at sea?
>
> Nothing at all: it is a high-wrought flood.
> I cannot, 'twixt the heaven and the main,
> Descry a sail.
>
> Methinks the wind hath spoke aloud at land;
> A fuller blast ne'er shook our battlements.
> If it hath ruffian'd so upon the sea,
> What ribs of oak, when mountains melt on them,
> Can hold the mortise? What shall we hear of this?
>
> A segregation of the Turkish fleet.
> For do but stand upon the foaming shore,
> The chidden billow seems to pelt the clouds;
> The wind-shak'd surge, with high and monstrous mane,
> Seems to cast water on the burning Bear
> And quench the guards of the ever-fixed pole:
> I never did like molestation view
> On the enchafed flood.

A storm that assaults heaven itself! Which storm is this? The storm in which the Turks went down, or the storm for which Othello prayed?—

> May the winds blow till they have waken'd death!
> And let the labouring bark climb hills of seas
> Olympus-high, and duck again as low
> As hell's from heaven!

—a storm that did indeed awaken death and duck as low as hell:

> Whip me, ye devils, . . .
> Blow me about in winds! roast me in sulphur!
> Wash me in steep-down gulfs of liquid fire!

What place in the story have we reached? On which side of death are we?

And now, suddenly, there is a fourth speaker on the shore. "Our wars are done." A ship has made port, he announces, bringing one Michael Cassio. The Turks are drowned. And while that thought, the messenger declares, comforts Cassio,

> yet he looks sadly
> And prays the Moor be safe, for they were parted
> With foul and violent tempest.

And like an echo from some remote region of

> old, unhappy, far-off things,
> And battles long ago,

we hear a voice saying,

> Dear general, I never gave you cause.

But the confusion—or is it the clarity?—increases. Here is Cassio himself! And as he joins the others on the shore, he cries,

> O, let the heavens
> Give him defence against the elements,
> For I have lost him on a dangerous sea.

You have indeed, Cassio, and on a vaster sea than any Mediterranean. "Is he well shipp'd?" a voice inquires.

> CAS.: His bark is stoutly timber'd, and his pilot
> Of very expert and approv'd allowance;
> Therefore my hopes, not surfeited to death,
> Stand in bold cure.

In spite of all, Cassio has kept faith. And now there is a sudden cry within, "A sail, a sail, a sail!"

> The town is empty; on the brow o' the sea
> Stand ranks of people, and they cry, "A sail!"

We see them gazing out with tense faces over the gray oncoming waves. But who are they? Whom are they awaiting? What town have they left empty? And for a second we remember another unidentified little town that was left similarly desolate:

> What little town by river or sea shore,
>   Or mountain-built with peaceful citadel,
>   Is emptied of this folk, this pious morn?
> And, little town, thy streets for evermore
>   Will silent be; and not a soul to tell
>   Why thou art desolate, can e'er return.

Perhaps these watchers for a sail, likewise, will never return to their homes.
But the ship is in. And whom has it brought?

> Tempests themselves, high seas, and howling winds,
> The gutter'd rocks and congregated sands,
> Traitors ensteep'd to clog the guiltless keel,
> As having sense of beauty, do omit
> Their mortal natures, letting go safely by
> The divine Desdemona.

Desdemona? Then she escaped the traitors? She survived the storm? It cannot be. But it is—for here she is herself:

> O, behold,
> The riches of the ship is come on shore! . . .
> Hail to thee, lady! and the grace of heaven,
> Before, behind thee, and on every hand,
> Enwheel thee round!

Heaven again? We were told it was Cyprus. But wherever she is she acknowledges the welcome. Her brow, however, shows she is troubled.

DES.: What tidings can you tell me of my lord?
CAS.: He is not yet arriv'd. . . .
DES.: O! but I fear—How lost you company?
CAS.: The great contention of the sea and skies
Parted our fellowship.

Will her fears, this time, be justified?
Again there is a cry: "But hark! a sail" that is echoed from within. "A sail, a sail!"

Again it cannot be. But again it is. Othello has come to port. There is an interlude. Then he enters and takes Desdemona in his arms:

> O my fair warrior!
>
> My dear Othello!
>
> It gives me wonder great as my content
> To see you here before me. O my soul's joy!
> If after every tempest come such calms. . . .

And in a kind of divine confusion we ask:
After which storm?

This is what I have long been in the habit of calling *The Sixth Act of Othello*. Here is music played on the wind instruments of the storm, which, like the storm itself, reaches the stars. Here, as surely as music is harmony, is music that may not be heard. Here is form that, like the form of Keats's urn, does

> tease us out of thought
> As doth eternity.

Like a face in the embers, it is there for those who see it, not there for those who do not.

Bradley speaks of *Othello* as having less cosmic sweep than the other Tragedies. "We seem to be aware in it," he says, "of a certain limitation, a partial suppression of that element in Shakespeare's mind which unites him with the mystical poets and with the great musicians and philosophers." It is true that the atmosphere of *Othello* is more realistic and "modern" than that of the other Tragedies. But that is precisely what makes such effects as his use of the storm in this play the more miraculous. It is the virtue of *Othello* that—like the poetry of Emily Dickinson—it synthesizes the domestic and the cosmic.

"But you have forgotten one thing," someone can be counted on to object just here. "Iago, too, survived the storm off Cyprus. It was he, indeed, under whose conduct Desdemona came safely through!" And the tone of triumph implies, "What can you say to that?"

How fortunate that there are prose and reason in the world to keep the poetry straight! Why not go even further and point out that this whole play is obviously rubbish because all the Italians in it speak English?

But the objection about Iago is overruled even on its own premise. The Turk goes down. And if Desdemona reaches heaven after the Second Storm, it is partly because of the very tempest through which Iago led her. Here Shakespeare plumbs the very depths of evil. There were two Iagos: the one who went down, and the "good Iago" whom Desdemona trusted and who drew the picture of her on the quay.

Here, if ever, we see the difference between logic and imagination, between factual and poetical truth. To the intellect this diagram is what it is, no more, no less:

But the eye inevitably supplements it by drawing two lines parallel to the right-hand sides of the inner figure, completing the outer one. To the reason, the fact that Othello and Desdemona were parted by a physical tempest, then reunited, then parted by a moral one, sets up no presumption whatever that they will again be reunited. The opposite assumption is just as logical, and probably even more convincing to the intellect, which is skeptical by nature. But, to the imagination, what may be called the transcendental reunion of Othello and Desdemona is as irresistible as the completion of the geometrical diagram is to the eye. For, as Blake is continually reminding us, imagination is more analogous to sensation than to thought. Imagination is spiritual sensation—"That most pure spirit of sense." It is its own evidence.

> Beauty itself doth of itself persuade,

says Shakespeare in *Lucrece*. As Longinus saw, long ago, it does not convince by logic, it takes captive. What happens after death is strictly an unknown quantity to reason. But as certainly as the value of x in an equation can be calculated if the other quantities are known, so certainly can the imagination "calculate" the unknown factors in life from the known ones. Poetry is the art of spiritual mensuration. Its validity or lack of validity can be referred to no standard outside itself and us. It depends solely on its impact on our imaginations. So with such creations of the Imagination as heaven and hell. Whether they are true or not is the most important thing in the world. Whether or not they exist is a senseless question. "He who has never hoped shall never receive what he has never hoped for."

XII

Whoever is content to see Iago go down under water with the Turks and does not "hope," in this high Heracleitean sense, to behold Desdemona "vanish into air" or catch a glimpse of her in heaven will be compelled to admit at any rate that she is alive after death, on earth, both within the play and without it. Cassio, near the end, tells how, in a letter found in the slain Roderigo's pocket, there is a revelation of Iago's original plan to have Roderigo brave Cassio upon the watch after Iago has made him drunk.

> . . . even but now he spake,

says Cassio, wondering as if at a miracle,

> After long seeming dead.

But if Roderigo spoke after death, Desdemona not only spoke but, in the words of Wordsworth's great sonnet, lived, and acted, and served the future hour. That which acts is actual, and it is Desdemona who effects the final transformation in Othello that imparts to his last words their preternatural calm. In that last speech he describes himself as one who

> Like the base Judean, threw a pearl away
> Richer than all his tribe.

It is strange that nearly all editors have preferred to this reading of the Folio that of the Quarto,

> Like the base Indian, threw a pearl away ...

in the face of Othello's "I kiss'd thee ere I kill'd thee" a moment later, which is as clear an identification of the murderer-Othello with Judas as could be asked. (The Othello who *now* kisses her is another man.)

Who the pearl was the base Judean threw away all the world knows, final proof, were it needed, that just as the poet ties Iago and war together in this play, so he links Desdemona with the spirit that brings war to an end. "*Solitudinem faciunt, pacem appellant*," cried Tacitus, compressing into one of the compactest sentences ever written the fatal error we make in confusing *the end of war* and *what ends war*. At the end of war, if there is not a "solitude," then there is a truce, a fresh balance of power, or an imposed reign of order ("order," the counterfeit of peace) which holds until the old conflict breaks out anew. And meanwhile men go on seeking some law, or formula, or system that will end the rule of Mars. Only the simple way, that is at once the easiest and the hardest, is not tried. "Here you are teaching all the time," says a character in Chekhov, "fathoming the depths of the ocean, dividing the weak from the strong, writing books and challenging to duels—and everything remains as it is; but, behold! some feeble old man will mutter just one word with a holy spirit, ... and everything will be topsy-turvy, and in Europe not one stone will be left standing upon another." One word with a holy spirit. It was such a word that Desdemona spoke. She *is* what the greatest sages from Laotse to Tolstoy have taught. She shows that to be is better than to act, for through whoever is the gods themselves act.

The secret of social and political strife, of conflict between nations, is only that of individual and domestic strife writ large. War and peace, says *Othello*, confirming *Hamlet* and carrying the thought from its negative to its positive phase, are states of the soul. War in the military sense is the outer manifestation of war in the psychological sense pre-existing in the inner worlds of its fomenters and participants. That is not saying that outer conditions have nothing to do with the production of war. But it is only as those conditions first produce a military state of the soul that they secondly produce war in its more generally accepted sense. And, no matter how adverse, they do not necessarily produce a military state of the soul, as Desdemona shows; on the contrary, as Iago shows, that state is a most potent producer of those very conditions. It was to demonstrate this double truth that Dostoevsky wrote *Crime and Punishment*. *Othello* demonstrates it even more compactly.

Chapter XXVIII

Macbeth

Men are probably nearer to the essential truth in their superstitions than in their science.—Thoreau.

I

In spite of the intimate links between *Hamlet* and *Othello*, if there were no
external evidence to the contrary a case could be made for the view that
Macbeth was the tragedy to come next after *Hamlet*, just as a case can be
made for the view that *Macbeth* preceded rather than followed *King Lear*.
In the former instance I have conformed to the nearly unanimous opinion
of scholars. In the latter, more doubtful one I reverse the more generally
accepted sequence and take up *Macbeth* before *King Lear*.

Macbeth and *King Lear* were so nearly contemporary that the question
of their exact dates is not of overwhelming importance. It is psychological
development, not chronology, that counts. And the two are not the same.
We frequently go back in going forward. There are eddies in the stream.
Ascent and descent are not continuous. We may go down temporarily in
climbing a mountain. The child often resembles a grandparent more than
he does either father or mother, and there is a similar alternation of generations in the world of art. Because one work is full of echoes of another
does not prove that it must have immediately succeeded it. The likeness of
Macbeth to *Hamlet* is no obstacle to the belief that *Othello* came between
them, nor that of *King Lear* to *Othello* to the possibility that *Macbeth* may
have intervened.

But somehow the idea that *King Lear* was written before *Macbeth* seems
to involve more than this. It is a bit like thinking that *The Brothers Karamazov* was written before *Crime and Punishment*. The analogy is not a casual

one. *Macbeth*, like *Crime and Punishment*, is a study of evil through a study of murder. Each is its author's most rapid, concentrated, terrific, and possibly sublime work. Each is a prolonged nightmare lifted into the realm of art. *King Lear* and *The Brothers Karamazov* are also studies of evil; but if they sound no lower depths, they do climb to greater heights than *Macbeth* and *Crime and Punishment*. All four fight through again the old war between light and darkness. But in *Macbeth* and *Crime and Punishment* we have "night's predominance," as Shakespeare phrases it, and the light is that of a star or two in the blackness, while in *King Lear* and *The Brothers Karamazov* the stars are morning stars and there is dawn on the horizon. I know how preposterous this will sound to those who consider *King Lear* the pessimistic masterpiece of the ages.

II

If it be true that all art aspires to the state of music, the opening of *Macbeth* approximates perfection. The contention of the elements and the battles of men are the themes of the Witches' colloquy. But their lines are more overture than scene, and the drama has a second opening in the account given by the wounded Sergeant of Macbeth's conquest of the rebels. The passage is like a smear of blood across the first page of the play. The double opening defines precisely what we are to expect: a work dedicated not to the supernatural nor to blood but to the relation between the two. (The modern reader who is afraid of the word "supernatural" may substitute "unconscious.") Passion means originally the capacity to be affected by external agents. In this sense *Macbeth* is a play about human passion.

It is significant that the Witches choose for their fatal encounter with Macbeth not the hour of battle but the moment

When the hurlyburly's done.

War plows the soil. Who wins is not what counts. It is what seeds are planted

When the battle's lost and won

that determines the future. Only that future can determine who did win. The phrase might well be written lost-and-won. Already in *Much Ado about Nothing* and *All's Well That Ends Well* (not to mention the Histories) Shakespeare had touched on the aftereffects of war on character. Men who have been valiant on the battlefield can come home to act like cads or criminals in time of peace.

The account of Macbeth's disemboweling of Macdonwald is one of the goriest things in Shakespeare. "Fie, savage, fie!" we are tempted to cry, remembering Hector. But

> O valiant cousin! worthy gentleman!

is the way Duncan greets the bloody story. As a concordance will show, Bernard Shaw himself takes no greater delight than the gentle Shakespeare in using the word "gentleman"* with devastating sarcasm.

> Let each man render me his bloody hand . . .
> Gentlemen all,

says Antony to the assassins of Caesar, conscious of his irony as Duncan was not.

> . . . this dead butcher and his fiend-like queen

is the way Malcolm, with the finality of an epitaph, sums up this worthy gentleman and his wife in the last speech of the play. It is fitting that it should open with an example of his butchery. Macbeth, murderer of Duncan, and Macbeth, tyrant of Scotland, are implicit in Macbeth, slaughterer of Macdonwald. Yet there was a time, we feel, when Macbeth may have been gentle.

The opening scene and the closing act of *Macbeth* are given to war; the rest of the first act and the second to murder; the third and fourth to tyranny—with further murder. The play leaves us with the feeling that offensive war, crime, and tyranny are merely different faces of the same monster. Tyranny is just war catching its breath. Under it the preponderance of power is so markedly on one side that open violence is no longer necessary. The Enemy is now the subjects. If the fragmentary passages describing Scotland under Macbeth are assembled, they read like a documented account of life in the countries subjugated by the "strong" men of the twentieth century. With its remote setting and ancient superstitions, *Macbeth* to a superficial mind may seem dated. On the contrary few of Shakespeare's plays speak more directly to our time.

III

How did Shakespeare have the audacity to center a tragedy around a murderer and tyrant, a man so different in his appeal to our sympathies from a Romeo, a Brutus, or a Hamlet? He had done something of the sort before in *Richard III*, but Richard is more nearly a melodramatic and theatrical than a strictly tragic success. Doubts remain in many minds whether such a creature could ever have existed. But Macbeth is at bottom any man

---

* See the chapter on *The Two Gentlemen of Verona* in Volume I.

of noble intentions who gives way to his appetites. And who at one time or another has not been that man? Who, looking back over his life, cannot perceive some moral catastrophe that he escaped by inches? Or did not escape. *Macbeth* reveals how close we who thought ourselves safe may be to the precipice. Few readers, however, feel any such kinship with Macbeth as they do with Hamlet. We do not expect to be tempted to murder; but we do know what it is to have a divided soul. Yet Hamlet and Macbeth are imaginative brothers. The difference is that Macbeth begins more or less where Hamlet left off.

> Now might I do it pat, now he is praying,

says the latter, meditating the death of the King,

> And now I'll do 't. And so he goes to heaven;
> And so am I reveng'd. *That would be scann'd.*
>
> Strange things I have in head, that will to hand,
> Which must be acted *ere they may be scann'd,*

says Macbeth, plotting the destruction of the Macduffs. The two couplets seem written to match each other. Yet Hamlet had to go down only a corridor or so from the praying King to commit a deed, the killing of Polonius, of which Macbeth's couplet is a perfect characterization.

> My strange and self-abuse,

says Macbeth, unstrung at the sight of Banquo's ghost,

> Is the initiate fear that wants hard use:
> We are yet but young in deed.

Deeds, he divines, are the only opiates for fears, but their defect as a remedy is the fact that the dose must be increased with an alarming rapidity.

> O, from this time forth,

cried Hamlet, shamed at the sight of the efficient Fortinbras,

> My thoughts be bloody, or be nothing worth!

The Macbeth-in-Hamlet meant *deeds*, but there was enough of the original Hamlet still left in him to keep it "thoughts." But bloody thoughts are the seed of bloody deeds, and Macbeth, with the very accent of the Fortinbras soliloquy, says, without Hamlet's equivocation,

> from this moment
> The very firstlings of my heart shall be
> The firstlings of my hand.

The harvest of this creed is of course a complete atrophy of heart.

> The time has been my senses would have cool'd
> To hear a night-shriek,

he says when that atrophy has overtaken him,

> and my fell of hair
> Would at a dismal treatise rouse and stir
> As life were in 't.

That is Macbeth gazing back, as it were, into his Hamletian past ("Angels and ministers of grace defend us!"), quite as Hamlet looks forward into his Macbethian future. In that sense the rest was not silence.

Hamlet is to Macbeth somewhat as the Ghost is to the Witches. Revenge, or ambition, in its inception may have a lofty, even a majestic countenance; but when it has "coupled hell" and become crime, it grows increasingly foul and sordid. We love and admire Hamlet so much at the beginning that we tend to forget that he is as hot-blooded as the earlier Macbeth when he kills Polonius and the King, cold-blooded as the later Macbeth or Iago when he sends Rosencrantz and Guildenstern to death. If in *Othello* we can trace fragments of a divided Hamlet transmigrated into Desdemona and Iago, in *Macbeth* an undivided Hamlet keeps straight onward and downward in Macbeth himself. The murderer of Duncan inherits Hamlet's sensibility, his nervous irritability, his hysterical passion, his extraordinary gifts of visualization and imaginative expression; and under the instigating influence of his wife the "rashness" and "indiscretion" of the later Hamlet are progressively translated into a succession of mad acts.

It is this perhaps that explains the main technical peculiarity of *Macbeth*, its brevity. It is so short that not a few have thought that what has come down to us is just the abbreviated stage version of a much longer play. As it stands, it has no "beginning" in the Aristotelian sense, scarcely even a "middle." It is mostly "end." The hero has already been tempted before the opening of the action. We do not know how long he has been turning the murder over in his mind before he broaches the matter to his wife, in a decisive scene which is recapitulated in half a dozen lines near the end of Act I and which occurred before Macbeth encountered the Weird Sisters. This is exactly the way Dostoevsky manages it in *Crime and Punishment*, where Raskolnikov is represented as having lain for days on his bed "thinking" before the story actually opens, and we learn only retrospectively of his meeting the previous winter with the officer and student in the tavern who echo his innermost guilty thoughts and consolidate his fatal impulse precisely as the Weird Sisters do Macbeth's. If the novelist abstains from

attempting a detailed account of the period when the crime was being in-
cubated, is it any wonder that the dramatist does, especially when he has
already accomplished something resembling this seemingly impossible dramatic representation of inaction in the first two acts of *Hamlet?* Why repeat it? When we consider *Macbeth* as a separate work of art, what its
author did or didn't do in another work has of course nothing to do with it.
But when we consider the plays, and especially the Tragedies, as chapters
of a greater whole, it has everything to do with it. What may be a disad-
vantage, or even a flaw, from the point of view of the man witnessing *Macbeth* for the first time in the theater may be anything but that to a reader
of all the Tragedies in order. And the truth of the statement is in no wise
diminished if we hold that Shakespeare himself was largely unconscious
of the psychic relationship of his plays.

Viewed in the context of his other works, *Macbeth* is Shakespeare's Descent into Hell. And since it is his *Inferno*, it is appropriate that the terres-
trial and celestial parts of his universe should figure in it slightly.

Explorations of the underworld have been an unfailing feature of the
world's supreme poetry. From the Greek myths and Homer, to go no
farther back or further afield, through the Greek dramatists and the theo-
logical-religious visions of Dante and Milton, on to the symbolic poems
and prophecies of Blake and the psychological-religious novels of Dostoevsky, we meet wide variations on a theme that remains basically the same.
All versions of it, we are at last in a position to recognize, are attempts to
represent the psychic as distinguished from the physical world. The difference in nomenclature should not blind us to the identity of subject. We
could salvage vast tracts of what is held to be the obsolete wisdom of the
world if we would recognize that fact. Wisdom does not become obsolete.

IV

Yet there is a historical criticism which thinks Shakespeare was pandering
to the superstitions of his audience in *Macbeth* and following a stage tradition rather than life in his study of the criminal nature. Professor Stoll,
for instance, in his *Shakespeare Studies* devotes a long chapter, "The Criminals," to proving that Shakespeare's tragic evildoers are not "the real thing."
If we seek the real thing we will find it rather, he says, in what science has
discovered about the criminal, and what realistic literature, following in its
footsteps, has portrayed, in the last century or two. "Men are neither good
nor evil," says Professor Stoll, quoting Balzac. "In Nature," he goes on (no
longer quoting), "the good and the bad, the healthy and the degenerate,
are inextricably interwoven, are one. It was quite another atmosphere that
Shakespeare breathed, an atmosphere charged with the dualism of the

Middle Ages and earlier times. Good and evil then were as the poles asunder." "The web of our life is of a mingled yarn, good and ill together"; says Shakespeare, "our virtues would be proud, if our faults whipped them not; and our crimes would despair, if they were not cherished by our virtues." Professor Stoll's idea of the modern attitude exactly, down to the very metaphor! It is a Lord in *All's Well That Ends Well* speaking, but there is *Measure for Measure* with its "write good angel on the devil's horn" to show how completely Shakespeare agreed with him. And not one of his greater plays—including even *King Lear*, in which good and evil are indeed fiercely contrasted—but shows the same. Yet it was "quite another atmosphere that Shakespeare breathed." In that case, he did not make his plays out of the surrounding atmosphere.

Professor Stoll cites numerous near-contemporary examples (in which jockeys, gypsies, horse thieves, and pirates figure) to prove not merely the unrepentant but the carefree mood of the "real" criminal after his crime, in contrast with that of the Elizabethan stage offender. "After the crime they go on a lark, play cards with the family, or take a nap," he tells us. "How shallow and obsequious of us," he continues, "to bow to Shakespeare and almost all the choice and master spirits in drama and fiction up to the present age, in their opinion that though there is joy in our hearts when we engage in works of justice and mercy there is no joy in the heart of the miser as he hoards or in the heart of the murderer as he kills! Do we do good because, despite all, we love it, but they evil because they hate it? We ourselves know better." How almost all the choice and master spirits in drama and fiction up to our own more enlightened age happened to agree in their common blindness to notorious fact in this matter is not explained, but among the more modern and less deluded authorities that are cited against Aeschylus, Shakespeare, and Molière are such men as Sudermann, Pinero, and Henry Arthur Jones. Tolstoy is cited too, but he, as Professor Stoll admits, slipped back into the classic error in *The Power of Darkness*.

However that may be, I see no evidence that Shakespeare was unacquainted with either the lighthearted or the callous type of criminal. Autolycus is as carefree a pickpocket as anyone could ask for. Pistol, granted the caricature in his case, is admirably true to the supposedly "modern" criminal type; while it would be hard in all the literature of the nineteenth and twentieth centuries to match the self-possessed Barnardine in *Measure for Measure*, who, as we have seen, coolly upsets all plans for his execution by simply refusing to accommodate the prison authorities. And if anyone thinks these instances edge too near to farce, there are John of Lancaster, who commits his supreme treachery without an inkling, apparently, of its depravity, and Cloten, who goes to his most unspeakable crime in precisely the spirit which Professor Stoll so exhaustively documents. Iago says his plotting gives him so much pleasure that he forgets the passage of time, and even Hamlet—Iago-Hamlet—murders Polonius almost casually, refers to his corpse as if it were a sack of meal, and later comes home from his callous dispatch to death of his old schoolfellows, Rosencrantz and Guildenstern, to exchange quibbles, however gravely, with the gravediggers—without a single apparent touch of remorse. The Duke of Cornwall, it is plainly hinted, did not intend to let his turning of the aged King Lear into the storm interfere in the slightest degree with a comfortable evening indoors at home. And the list could easily be extended. The discovery that criminals—many of them—can be carefree before, during, and after the crime may be one of the glories of scientific criminology but it would have been no news to Shakespeare.

Professor Stoll's modern instances are unassailable as far as they go, but what he fails to note is exactly what Shakespeare is so careful to observe: that there are criminals and criminals. As usual, he will not be seduced into too easy generalization or classification, and, instead of presenting us with a "criminal type," gives us every variety of offender against the law. His hired assassins, even when they speak only a few lines, are individualized, and, when there are several of them together, one is often of the carefree sort while one will hesitate and tremble. Professor Stoll's admission in passing that in *comedy* the earlier drama approximates what he calls the facts about the criminal nature is fatal to his argument. For in that case the practice in tragedy of Shakespeare and the other choice and master spirits was obviously not the result of ignorance but of something distinctive about the *tragic* criminal.

What that something is, the difference between Macbeth and Lady Macbeth makes plain, for the husband, not the wife, is the truly tragic figure, and the play is rightly entitled *Macbeth*, not *The Macbeths*. Professor Stoll's own criminological data suggest just this distinction. He quotes penological authorities to show that the sleep of criminals is not disturbed by uneasy dreams and that signs of repentance, remorse, or despair are seldom to be detected in them. In one group of four hundred murderers such signs were found in only three, and in another group of seven hundred criminals only 3.4 per cent "showed signs of repentance or appeared at all moved in recounting their misdeeds." That that exceptional 3.4 per cent were specimens of what Nietzsche calls the "pale criminal" and included probably the only ones capable of exciting tragic interest Professor Stoll does *not* go on to say. Imaginative literature is not criminology, and, except incidentally or for purposes of contrast, has no interest in portraying primitive, brutal, or moronic types. When rich or noble natures display atavistic traits or slip back into atavistic conduct, as do Hamlet and Othello, those traits begin to assume tragic interest, for tragedy has to do with men possessing the capacity to become gods who, momentarily at least, become devils. The normal man has little in common with these murderers of Professor Stoll's who slay their victims as unconcernedly as an old hand in a slaughterhouse kills cattle. But the normal man, in his lesser degree, *is* Orestes, Macbeth, and Raskolnikov. Such characters tell us, not how the ordinary run of criminals react, but how Aeschylus and Shakespeare and Dostoevsky would have felt, if they had themselves fallen into crime. They are the 3 per cent of the 3 per cent.

Professor Stoll derides especially the idea that criminals are obsessed with the horror of their deeds before they commit them: "Who sins thus, against the grain?" Or immediately after: "Instead of hearing, like the Scottish thane and the English king, ominous voices," real criminals, he tells us, are likely, after a murder, to fall asleep on the spot, or at least to sleep better afterward. And he cites Raskolnikov in *Crime and Punishment* as one of his examples—a most unfortunate one for his argument, for if ever a man was depicted as both sinning against the grain and being punished *instantly* for his deed it is Raskolnikov. Turn to the text. In the first chapter the murderer-to-be characterizes the crime he is to commit—which he can bring himself to refer to only as *that*—as hideous, loathsome, filthy, and disgusting, two of the four adjectives being identically Macbeth's. ("Temptations," says Professor Stoll, "are not hideous but beautiful." If he had said "fascinating," we could have agreed.) Yet Raskolnikov goes out to do the deed drawn by a power over which he *now* has no control—just as Macbeth was marshaled by the air-drawn dagger. And when does Dostoevsky show his murderer sleeping "better" after the murder? He goes home from it to one fearful nightmare after another, to sleep

> In the affliction of these terrible dreams
> That shake us nightly,

and to say, in effect, exactly as Shakespeare makes Macbeth say:

> Better be with the dead,
> Whom we, to gain our peace, have sent to peace,
> Than on the torture of the mind to lie
> In restless ecstasy.

"Crime and punishment," says Emerson, "grow out of one stem. . . . All infractions of love and equity in our social relations are speedily punished. They are punished by fear. . . . Commit a crime, and the earth is made of glass. Commit a crime, and it seems as if a coat of snow fell on the ground, such as reveals in the woods the track of every partridge and fox and squirrel and mole." Was Emerson, too, an Elizabethan? On the contrary, like Shakespeare and Dostoevsky, he was not a "fool of time."

Shakespeare's play and Dostoevsky's novel are both dedicated to the proof of Emerson's proposition. Different as are the literary traditions from which they stem, opposite in many respects as are the techniques of drama and fiction, point by point, detail by detail, Shakespeare's and Dostoevsky's treatments of the criminal heart and mind correspond. It is one of the most impressive analogies in all literature: an overwhelming demonstration that genius is independent of time. "Psychologically he was for the age correct," says Professor Stoll of Shakespeare. As if the soul altered from age to age, and was busy, about A.D. 1600, conforming to the conventions of the Elizabethan stage! "In that day when men still believed in diabolical possession," he begins. As if Job and Aeschylus, Dante and the Gospels were obsolete! The fact that the ignorant of all ages have believed in diabolical possession in a superstitious sense is no reason for blinding our eyes to the fact that the imaginative geniuses of all ages have also believed in it in another and profounder sense. And so, too, of the prodigies in the sky and elsewhere that accompany murder in Shakespeare and the Elizabethan drama. "Through it all," says Professor Stoll, "runs the notion that the moment of sin and the manner of the sinner are something prodigious and beyond the bounds of nature, as indeed they appear to be in the person of many a famous actor who saws the air in old paintings and prints." Professor Stoll in that sentence comes perilously close to saying that the moment of sin is *not* prodigious. The possibility that these supposedly astronomical and other portents may be psychical rather than physical phenomena—waking nightmares projected on shapes of the natural world that seem expressly molded to receive them—he does not appear to have taken into account. (Not to suggest thereby that they are just subjective.)

V

Deeds of violence that come exclusively out of the brute in man have no tragic significance and take their place in human memory with the convulsions of nature and the struggle to survive of the lower orders of life. But when a man of imagination—by which I mean a man in whom the image of God is distinct—stoops to crime, instantly transcendental powers rush to the scene as if fearful lest this single deed shift the moral center of gravity of the universe, as a finger may tip an immense boulder that is in delicate equilibrium. Macbeth and Lady Macbeth (as she was at the outset) seem created to stress this distinction. "A little water clears us of this deed," is her reaction to the murder of Duncan.

Will all great Neptune's ocean wash this blood
Clean from my hand? No, this my hand will rather
The multitudinous seas incarnadine,
Making the green one red,

is his. One wonders whether the supremacy of the moral imagination over the material universe was ever more tremendously expressed than in those four lines. In them, space is, as it were, forever put in its place. When Lady Macbeth, in the end, attains the same insight that is Macbeth's instantly—"all the perfumes of Arabia will not sweeten this little hand"—she does not pass, it is to be noted, to the second part of the generalization. It is this defect in imagination that makes her, if a more pathetic, a less tragic figure than her husband.

The medieval mind, in the tradition of mythology, represented the tragic conflict, which our irreligious age is likely to think of as just a strife between opposing impulses, as a struggle between devils and angels for the possession of man's soul. Devils and angels are out of fashion. But it is not the nomenclature that counts, and the soundness of the ancient conception is being confirmed, under another terminology, in the researches of psychology into the unconscious mind.

Now the unconscious, whatever else or more it may be, is an accumulation of the human and prehuman psychic tendencies of life on the planet, and the unconscious of any individual is a reservoir that contains latently the experience of all his ancestors. This potential inheritance is naturally an inextricable mixture of good and evil. Hence whenever the threshold of consciousness is sufficiently lowered to permit an influx of the unconscious, a terrific tension arises between forces pulling the individual in different or opposite directions. Samuel Butler has given classic expression to this struggle in *Life and Habit*:

It is one against legion when a creature tries to differ from his own past selves. He must yield or die if he wants to differ widely, so as to lack natural instincts, such as hunger or thirst, or not to gratify them. . . . His past selves are living in unruly hordes within him at this moment and overmastering him. "Do this, this, this, which we too have done, and found our profit in it," cry the souls of his forefathers within him. Faint are the far ones, coming and going as the sound of bells wafted on to a high mountain; loud and clear are the near ones, urgent as an alarm of fire. "Withhold," cry some. "Go on boldly," cry others. "Me, me, me, revert hitherward, my descendant," shouts one as it were from some high vantage-ground over the heads of the clamorous multitude. "Nay, but me, me, me," echoes another; and our former selves fight within us and wrangle for our possession. Have we not here what is commonly called an *internal tumult,* when dead pleasures and pains tug within us hither and thither? Then may the battle be decided by what people are pleased to call our own experience. Our own indeed!

This passage makes clear why an unmediated polarity is a distinguishing mark of the unconscious and suggests a biological reason for the Delphic character of all true oracles. Every sentence, declares Thoreau, has two sides: "One faces the world, but the other is infinite and confronts the gods." An oracular utterance is merely an extreme form of such a sentence, an incarnation in microcosmic form of the duality Butler depicts. In choosing between its worldly or infernal and its unworldly or celestial meaning, the individual without realizing it recruits an army, the good or bad impulses and acts of millions who have gone before him. Dreams too—many of them—have this ambiguous character and without violence to their imagery can often be taken in contradictory senses. And tragic irony always can. But so hidden may be the second meaning that it requires the future to reveal it, as it may take a second or several readings to uncover it in the printed play.

VI

From end to end, *Macbeth* is packed with these Delphic effects as is no other work of Shakespeare's: words, acts, and situations which may be interpreted or taken in two ways at the peril of the chooser and which in the aggregate produce an overwhelming conviction that behind the visible world lies another world, immeasurably wider and deeper, on its relation to which human destiny turns. As a face now reveals and now conceals the life behind it, so the visible world now hides this other world as does a wall, now opens on it as does a door. In either case it is *there*—there not as a matter of philosophical speculation or of theological tradition or hypothesis, but there as a matter of psychic fact.

Scholars who dismiss the supernatural element in *Macbeth* as stage convention or condescension to popular superstition stamp themselves as hopelessly insensitive not merely to poetry but to sincerity. Not only the plot and characters of the play, which are up to a certain point the author's inventions, but its music, imagery, and atmosphere—effects only partly under his conscious control—unite in giving the impression of mighty and inscrutable forces behind human life. Only one convinced of the reality of these forces could conceivably have imparted such an overwhelming sense of their presence. Neither could a mere stage contrivance have exercised the influence *Macbeth* has over the imaginations of later poets: Milton, Blake, the Keats of *Hyperion*, Emily Brontë, to name no others. Each sees the poet's vocation, as Shakespeare did in *Macbeth*, as an attempt to reclaim a dark region of the soul. "Shine inward," is the blind Milton's prayer to Celestial Light, ". . . there plant eyes." "To open the immortal Eyes of Man inwards," says Blake, is his great task. "To see as a god sees," cries Keats,

> and take the depth
> Of things as nimbly as the outward eye
> Can size and shape pervade.

Macbeth is a milestone in man's exploration of precisely this "depth of things" which our age calls the unconscious. The very phrase "depth psychology" has been used to differentiate the psychology of the unconscious from shallower attempts to understand the mind.

The more obviously Janus-like passages in *Macbeth*, where the surface meaning is contradicted from below, have often been pointed out. The double intention of the three prophecies concerning the invulnerability of Macduff, Birnam Wood, and the progeny of Banquo no one could miss. These, to be sure, have their theatrical aspect. But they have universal undertones and overtones. Many examples of dramatic irony in the play, too, are familiar: Macbeth's "Fail not our feast," with Banquo's prophetic reply, "My lord, I will not"; the entrance of Macbeth the moment after Duncan has asserted that treachery cannot be read in the face; the appearance of Lady Macbeth just as Macbeth is lamenting his lack of a spur to the murder; Macbeth's words to the murderer outside the window concerning the blood of Banquo that stains his face:

> 'Tis better thee without than he within,

a line that fairly gleams and undulates with protean meanings. Following one another in uninterrupted succession these things ultimately produce the conviction that there is something deep in life with power to reverse all its surface indications, as if its undercurrent set in just the opposite direction from the movement on its surface.

Take the famous knocking in the scene following the murder of Duncan.

> I hear a knocking
> At the south entry,

says Lady Macbeth. "Here's a knocking, indeed!" exclaims the Porter (who has been carousing till the second cock) and goes on to fancy himself the porter of hell gate.

> Whence is that knocking?
> How is 't with me, when every noise appalls me?

cries Macbeth. It is the same knocking—Macduff and Lennox come to arouse the Porter at the gate—but the sound might just as well be in three separate universes for all it has in common to the three listeners. Lady Macbeth hears it with her senses only; the Porter (dragged out of a dream perhaps) with a slightly drunken comic fancy; Macbeth with the tragic imagination. The sensitive reader hears it differently with each. How shall the man in the theater hear it? Here is a poetical effect beyond the capacity of the stage.

And yet it might be managed better there than it generally is. At such performances of the play at least as I remember, the knocking is heard from the first as a clearly audible noise. This is an obvious mistake. What Macbeth hears is not Macduff and Lennox trying to awaken the Porter, but all the powers of hell and heaven knocking simultaneously at his heart. If the auditor is to feel it with Macbeth, he must hear it with him. His ear and heart, that is, must detect it before his mind. He must hear the sound in Macbeth's listening attitude, in the awe on his face, before the physical sound reaches his ear. He, like Macbeth, must be in doubt as to whether he has heard or only imagined. And so the stage sound should begin below the auditory threshold and mount in a gradual crescendo until it becomes indubitably the pounding at the gate, which, with the dissipation of doubt, brings Macbeth back to earth.

> Wake Duncan with thy knocking! I would thou couldst!

He is at the gate of hell indeed. But still outside. Repentance is yet possible. The cue for the Porter's speech, which follows immediately, is as perfect as if it had been given by thought-transference. And yet the authenticity of the Porter scene has been doubted!

"Is the king stirring, worthy thane?" Macduff inquires when the gate has finally been opened and after Macbeth has returned. "Not yet," replies Macbeth, and what a shudder the future reads into those two words!

"This is the door," says Macbeth. Four words, this time, instead of two, and as ordinary ones as there are in the language. Yet, as Macbeth utters them, they seem whispered back at him in a voice no longer his own, from the very bottom of the universe. How shall an actor get this effect? He cannot. It transcends the theater as certainly as it does not transcend the imagination of the sensitive reader.

Does Lady Macbeth faint, or only pretend to faint, following the discovery of the murder? The point has been much debated. Everything she says or does in this scene is necessarily pretense. She is compelled by the situation to ape the symptoms of fear. But the acting by her body of an assumed fear is the surest way of opening a channel to the genuine fear she is trying to hide. As in the case of Hamlet's antic disposition, the counterfeit on the surface elicits the true from below.

I will not do 't,

cries Coriolanus when his mother begs him to go through the motions of
obeisance to the people,

> Lest I surcease to honour mine own truth,
> And by my body's action teach my mind
> A most inherent baseness.

The psychology here is the same, except that Lady Macbeth does what
Coriolanus declares he will not do. Feinting becomes fainting. By sheer
will power (plus a stimulant) Lady Macbeth has held the unconscious out.
Now its inundation begins. The end is the sleepwalking scene—and suicide.

At the beginning of the third act Macbeth plans the murder of Banquo.
He tries to convince the two cutthroats he has picked for the deed that
their ill fortunes in the past were not due to him, as they thought, but to
Banquo. His mind is so confused, however, that not only can he not keep
track of the passage of time ("Was it not yesterday we spoke together?"),
but he mixes hopelessly these men's supposed grievances against Banquo
in the past with his own fears of him at present and in the future:

> Are you so gospell'd
> To pray for this good man and *for his issue*,
> Whose heavy hand hath bow'd you to the grave
> *And beggar'd yours for ever?*

It is the descendants of Banquo, not the children of the murderers, he is
worrying over. And so of the fierce passage about the dogs that follows.
Again, it is of himself, not of them, he is speaking, unawares.

> What beast was 't, then,
> That made you break this enterprise to me?

Lady Macbeth had asked long before. At last Macbeth realizes that he is
indeed slipping below even "the worst rank of manhood" to a bestial level
of "demi-wolves" and "hounds." Of insects, even! as the most horrifying,
and yet pathetic, line in the play reveals in the next scene:

> O, full of scorpions is my mind, dear wife!

And so, when he cries to the two he is suborning, "Your spirits shine
through you," we know the spirits he glimpses behind them are the same
"black agents" to which he has sold himself. Indeed, so closely does he
identify himself with these men and the deed they are to commit for him
that he tells them no less than four times in a dozen lines that he will be
with them presently again: "I will advise you"; "[I will] acquaint you";
"I'll come to you anon"; "I'll call upon you straight."

As the third scene of the third act opens, a third murderer has just joined the other two where they wait at twilight to waylay the unsuspecting Banquo and Fleance. The next twenty-two lines make one of the most eerie passages in Shakespeare. Who is this Third Murderer? Macbeth himself? As all students of the play know, this explanation of the mystery was suggested long ago, and the idea gains a certain plausibility when we notice that Macbeth has prepared what might well serve as an alibi to cover a secret absence from the palace.

> Let every man be master of his time
> Till seven at night,

he declares to his lords, just after Banquo leaves for his ride,

> to make society
> The sweeter welcome, we will keep ourself
> Till supper-time alone; while then, God be with you!

and the point has added force when we recall that Portia (Bassanio's Portia) and Imogen covered absences from home that they did not wish noted, in just the same way. How easily, too, Macbeth could have hidden his identity —with darkness and fear to help him further to disguise disguise.

> Come, seeling night,
> Scarf up the tender eye of pitiful day,
> And with thy bloody and invisible hand
> Cancel and tear to pieces that great bond
> Which keeps me pale!

"That great bond" is generally taken as referring to the promise of the Weird Sisters to Banquo, but it might also at the same time refer to the great bond of light which by day holds all good things in harmony but keeps pale the criminal who fears it until night tears it to pieces.

But I do not intend to defend the view that Macbeth was the Third Murderer—or that he was not.* I wish rather to call attention to a remarkable fact concerning the response of readers to this question. Over the years I have called the attention of hundreds to it, most of whom had never heard of it before. It seems to exercise a peculiar fascination and to set even ordinarily casual readers to scanning the text with the minutest attention. And to what conclusion do they come? With a small group no one can predict. But with numbers sufficient to permit the law of averages to apply, the results have an almost scientific consistency. After allowing for a small minority that remains in doubt, about half are convinced that Macbeth was

---

* Those interested may find the main arguments pro and con summarized in the Variorum Edition.

the Third Murderer and the other half are either unconvinced or frankly think the hypothesis far-fetched or absurd.

But if the idea that Macbeth was the Third Murderer never entered Shakespeare's head, by what autonomous action of language does the text take on a meaning to the contrary that convinces nearly half of the play's readers? And not only convinces them, but, on the whole, convinces them for the same reasons. That without any basis hundreds should be deluded *in the same way* is unthinkable. But why, then, it will be asked, did not Shakespeare make his intention plain?—a question that reveals a peculiar insensitivity to poetry. What the poet wanted, evidently, was not to make a bald identification of the two men but to produce precisely the effect which as a matter of fact the text does produce on sensitive but unanalytic readers, the feeling, namely, that there is something strange and spectral about the Third Murderer as, unexpected and unannounced, he appears at this remote spot where

> The west yet glimmers with some streaks of day.

Utter darkness is imminent. Now is the time when the last streaks of day in Macbeth's nature are about to fade out forever—and here is the place. Whether he is present or absent in the flesh, it is here and now that he steps through the door above which is written "Abandon all hope, ye who enter." The author must convince us that virtually, if not literally, it is Macbeth who commits the murder. By letting us unconsciously see things simultaneously from two angles, he creates, as sight with two eyes does in the physical world, the true illusion of another dimension, in this case an illusion that annihilates space.

Macbeth's body—who knows?—may have been shut up in his chamber at the palace. But where was the man himself—his ambition, his fear, his straining inner vision, his will? They were so utterly with the hired instruments of that will that we can almost imagine them capable of incarnating themselves in a spectral body and projecting themselves as an apparition to the other two. And who killed Banquo? Is it the cat's paw that pulls the chestnuts from the fire, or he who holds the cat and guides the paw? So here. And we must be made to feel it—whatever we think. It is the poet's duty to bring the spirit of Macbeth to life on the scene. He does.*

How he does it is worth pausing a moment to notice—in so far as anything so subtle can be analyzed—for it reveals in miniature the secret of his power over our imaginations throughout the play.

* He does something similar in the scene where Hamlet visits Ophelia in her closet. See my article, "In Ophelia's Closet," in the *Yale Review*, Vol. XXXV, No. 3 (Spring, 1946). These interpretations tend to confirm each other.

The Third Murderer speaks six times. All but one of his speeches—and that one is but two lines and a half—are brief, one of one word only, and one of two. And every one of these speeches either has something in it to remind us of Macbeth, or might have been spoken by him, or both.

1. When the First Murderer, disturbed, asks who bade him join them, his Delphic answer is:

Macbeth.

2. He is the first to hear the approaching Banquo:

Hark! I hear horses.

The horse, *that on which we ride*, as we have noted elsewhere, is one of the oldest symbols of the unconscious, and that this very symbol is in a highly activated state in Macbeth's mind Shakespeare has been careful to note from his "pity, like a naked new-born babe, striding the blast," and "heaven's cherubin, hors'd upon the sightless couriers of the air" onward. Later, when messengers bring word of Macduff's flight to England, Macbeth's imaginative ear evidently catches the galloping of their horses before it rises above the threshold of consciousness and he translates it into supernatural terms:

MACB.: Saw you the weird sisters?
LENNOX: No, my lord.
MACB.: Came they not by you?
LENNOX: No, indeed, my lord.
MACB.: Infected be the air whereon they ride,
       And damn'd all those that trust them! I did hear
       The galloping of horse: who was 't came by?
LENNOX: 'Tis two or three, my lord, that bring you word
       Macduff is fled to England.

The Weird Sisters could not have been far off, either, when Banquo was murdered. It is interesting, to say the least, that it is the Third Murderer who first hears the horses. Whoever he is, he is like Macbeth in being sensitive to sound. He and Macbeth, it might be said, hear ear to ear.

3. The Third Murderer's next speech is his longest. To the First Murderer's "His horses go about," he replies:

          Almost a mile; but he does usually—
          So all men do—from hence to the palace gate
          Make it their walk.

Dashes, in place of the more usual commas, help bring out what is plainly a slip of the tongue on the Third Murderer's part. He has begun to reveal what in the circumstances is a suspicious familiarity with Banquo's habits, when, realizing his mistake, he hurriedly tries to cover it with his plainly parenthetical "so all men do" and his consequently necessary substitution of "their" for "his." But Macbeth does much the same thing just before the murder of Duncan is discovered:

LEN.:   Goes the king hence today?
MACB.:   He does—he did appoint so.

"He does usually—so all men do." "He does—he did appoint so." Such an echo sounds almost as if it came from the same voice. Only someone like Macbeth in combined impulsiveness and quick repentance of impulsiveness could have spoken the Third Murderer's words.

4. The fourth speech confirms the third:

> 'Tis he.

He is the first to recognize Banquo.

5. "Who did strike out the light?" Who *did?* Is it possible that one of the cutthroats is quite willing to kill a man but balks at the murder of a child? We do not know. But it does not need the King's "Give me some light!" in *Hamlet* or Othello's

> Put out the light, and then put out the light,

to make us aware of a second meaning in this simple question. It was the question that Macbeth must never have ceased to ask himself as he went on down into utter darkness.

6. "There's but one down; the son is fled." The Third Murderer is more perturbed than the others at the escape of Fleance. When at the beginning of the next scene Macbeth learns from the First Murderer of the death of the father and the flight of the son, he cries:

> Then comes my fit again. I had else been perfect,
> Whole as the marble, founded as the rock,
> As broad and general as the casing air:
> But now I am cabin'd, cribb'd, confin'd, bound in
> To saucy doubts and fears.

It is mainly on this speech that those who hold absurd the idea that Macbeth was the Third Murderer rest their case, proof, they say, that the news of Fleance's escape came to him as a surprise. But others think the lines have the same marks of insincerity combined with unconscious truth as those in which Macbeth pretended to be surprised and horrified at the death of Duncan.

All this about the Third Murderer will be particularly abhorrent to "realists," who would bring everything to the bar of the senses, and logicians, whose fundamental axiom is that a thing cannot both be and not be at the same time.* One wonders if they never had a dream in which one of the actors both was and was not a character from so-called "real" life. Anything that can happen in a dream can happen in poetry. Indeed this scene in which Banquo dies seems one of the most remarkable confirmations in Shakespeare of Nietzsche's main thesis in *The Birth of Tragedy*, that dreams and the drama come out of a common root. When an audience gathers in a theater, they come, if the play is worthy of the theater's great tradition, not to behold a transcript of the same old daylight life, but to dream together. In his bed a man dreaming is cut off from all social life. In the theater he is dreaming one dream with his fellows.

VII

From his encounter with the ghost of Banquo at the banquet, Macbeth, too deep in blood to turn back, repairs at the beginning of Act IV to the Witches' cavern, bent on extorting the truth about the future, however bad, from these "filthy hags," as he calls them in self-torture. Which raises the question we have intentionally postponed: Who are the Weird Sisters? The Fates? Just three old women? Or something between the two?

Their own reference to "our masters" would rule out the idea that they are The Fates or The Norns, if nothing else did. Bradley declares without qualification: "There is not a syllable in *Macbeth* to imply that they are anything but women." But certainly almost every syllable of the play that has to do with them implies that, whatever they are, they are in intimate contact with that dark Underworld with the existence of which the play is centrally concerned. "In accordance with the popular ideas," Bradley goes on to say, "they have received from evil spirits certain supernatural powers," to control the weather, for example, to become invisible, to foresee the future, and so on. So when we behold them actually doing these things in the play it makes little difference whether we consider them supernatural beings themselves or women who have sold their souls to supernatural beings. The impression in either case is the same: that of demi-creatures, agents and procurers of those powers that, when men's wills falter, pull them down out of their freedom as the earth does the body of a bird whose wings have failed.

At the outset there is something mysterious and wonderful about the

---

* This suggests a very real dilemma in the theater where obviously the actor who plays Macbeth either must or must not play the Third Murderer. More proof perhaps that Shakespeare transcends the stage. Yet something of the effect that the reader gets can surely be suggested in the acted scene, which should be a challenge to a stage director of poetic perception.

Witches, but they grow progressively more noisome and disgusting as Macbeth yields to them. Such is ever the relation of temptation to sin. The poet has shown us various earlier stages of moral disintegration in Henry IV, Henry V, Brutus, Hamlet, and others. Here is the same thing carried immeasurably further. It is as if man's integrity, once having begun to split up, tends to divide further and further, like the process of organic growth reversed. The Witches, representing this process, resemble fragments of those who, having taken and failed the human test, would revenge themselves on those who are trying to pass it by dragging them back to chaos. "They met me in the day of success"! It is easier to fall than to fly, to destroy than to create, to become like matter than to become like light. Whoever enlists on the side of destruction becomes in that sense an agent of fate.

The ingredients of the Witches' caldron confirm this conception of them. Those ingredients are things that in mythology and superstition, in the old natural philosophy and in our own ancestral consciousness, are associated with the darkest and cruelest elements of human nature: things voracious like the shark, sinister like the bat, poisonous like the adder, or ravenous like the wolf—and of these only fragments, preferably their most noxious or loathsome parts, the tooth, the scale, the sting, the maw, the gall, the entrails. To this predominantly animal brew are added a few vegetable elements, like hemlock and yew, suggestive of death and the grave, and a few reputedly subhuman ones from Turk or Tartar. A baboon's blood cools the whole.

Here Shakespeare is merely reiterating in intensified symbolic form what he has said from the beginning about unregulated appetite and passion. Here, recompounded into a sort of infernal quintessence, is the worst in the spirits of such men as Cardinal Pandulph and Cardinal Beaufort, of Don John and John of Lancaster, of Thersites and Iago. It is as if human nature, which never developed a special gland for the secretion of venom, tends when it degenerates to turn every organ—hand, lip, and brain—into such a gland. The whole body exudes malice and spite of life. The Witches are embodiments of this death-force. Women? Of course—and who has not seen and turned away in horror from just this malevolence in some shrunken old crone? And yet not women—under-women who have regressed beyond the distinctions of sex.

> You should be women,
> And yet your beards forbid me to interpret
> That you are so.

How fitting, after man has done his utmost through war to bring disorder, that the cause of still further dissipation toward chaos should pass, when war closes, into the hands of these wizened hags, the natural representatives of the metaphysically female role of matter in the universe! Earth we think of as clean and beautiful, but spirit gone back to matter is, in all senses, another matter. It is then something miasmic and rotten. "Lilies that fester smell far worse than weeds." It is not just the battlefield covered with things torn and mangled. It is the battlefield after the stench and the putrefaction have set in. The Witches in *Macbeth* are perhaps the completest antitypes to peace in Shakespeare.

The play presents explicitly the relation of Macbeth to the Witches. It leaves implicit Lady Macbeth's relation to them, which is all the more interesting on that account. They do not need to accost her on any blasted heath. She herself invites them into her heart.

> Hie thee hither,

she cries to her husband when she has read his letter,

> That I may pour my spirits in thine ear.

But who are her spirits? We do not have to wait long to know. A messenger enters with word that "the King comes here to-night." Whereupon Lady Macbeth, in a passage that is the very prophecy and counterpart of the caldron scene, summons her spirits, the murdering ministers that wait on nature's mischief—a very definition of the Weird Sisters—calling on them to unsex her, to cram her with cruelty from top to toe, to turn her milk to gall. That ought to be enough. But Shakespeare makes the connection even more concrete. In planning the murder of Duncan, it is Lady Macbeth who, Circe-like, suggests that Duncan's chamberlains be transformed to beasts by wine and the guilt for the King's death laid at their door:

> When in *swinish* sleep
> Their drenched natures lie as in a death,
> What cannot you and I perform upon
> The unguarded Duncan?

It is this cowardly stratagem which finally convinces Macbeth that the enterprise is safe, and which leads, when the murder is discovered, to the unpremeditated death of the chamberlains at Macbeth's hands.

First Witch: Where hast thou been, sister?
Second Witch: Killing *swine*.

The Second Witch and Lady Macbeth are about the same business. Who can question who poured the suggestion into Lady Macbeth's ear, and helped Macbeth to execute it later? It is the Adam and Eve story over again, with the Witches in the role of the Serpent. Yet these same Witches are powerless over those who do not meet them halfway:

THIRD WITCH: Sister, where thou?
FIRST WITCH: A sailor's wife had chestnuts in her lap,
And munch'd, and munch'd, and munch'd. "Give me," quoth I.
"Aroint thee, witch!" the rump-fed ronyon cries.

The Witch is impotent under the exorcism, and swears to try her luck in revenge on the woman's sailor husband. So little, Shakespeare thus makes plain, is there any fatalism involved in the proximity of the Weird Sisters where a resolute will resists. Fire is hot. And fire is fascinating to a child. If the child goes too near the fire, he will be burned. We may call it fate if we will. It is in that conditional sense only that there is any fatalism in *Macbeth*.

VIII

The end of the story is mainly an account of how these two once human beings pass into that subhuman realm of disintegration where the Witches are at home. One is pushed into the abyss as it were by her memories. The other leaps into it fanatically, as if embracing it. Her fall is primarily pitiful; his, fearful.

Because, before the deed, Lady Macbeth suffered from defect of imagination and excess of propensity to act, her punishment, in compensation, takes the form of being pursued, as by furies, by her memories, by the facts of the past. "How easy is it, then!" she had said. "What's done cannot be undone," she says now. Formerly she scorned her husband for his moments of abstraction:

> Be not lost
> So poorly in your thoughts.

Now she is not only lost but buried in her own, abstracted to the point of somnambulism.

> Come, thick night,
> And pall thee in the dunnest smoke of hell,

she had prayed on the verge of the first murder. "Hell is murky!" she mutters in the sleepwalking scene. Her prayer is answered. She is there. She has a light with her continually in a vain attempt to shut out the images that follow one another in perpetual succession. The blood runs from the old man's body unendingly. She washes her hands over and over. Such a circle is madness. Lady Macbeth is caught in it. She prefers death.

Because Macbeth saw the horror in advance and shrank from action, yet let himself be enticed on into it, only to wish his crime undone the moment he had committed it, his punishment takes the form of a fury of deeds. He meets anywhere, in full daylight, the specters that at first came to him only by twilight or at night. If hers is a retrospective and nocturnal, his is a diurnal and dramatic nightmare. If she is transported to an underworld, he transforms his own life into hell. It becomes an alternation of fear and fury. His perpetual reassurance to himself that he cannot know fear is a measure of the fear he feels. As his hand once dyed the world red, his heart now paints it a sickly white. "Cream-fac'd loon! . . . lily-liver'd boy . . . linen cheeks . . . whey-face." These are not so much descriptions of what he sees as projections of what he feels. "Hang those that talk of fear" might be his command for his own death. Now he would have his armor put on, now pulled off. The two moods follow each other with lightning-like rapidity.

> I pull in resolution.
> . . . Arm, arm, and out! . . .
> I 'gin to be aweary of the sun,
> . . . Blow, wind! come, wrack!
> At least we'll die with harness on our back.

These oscillations in less than a dozen lines. And between the fear and the fury, moments of blank apathy culminating, when Lady Macbeth's death is announced, in the famous

> To-morrow, and to-morrow, and to-morrow . . .

the *ne plus ultra* in English words of the meaninglessness of life—

> a tale
> Told by an idiot, full of sound and fury,
> Signifying nothing.

This is Hamlet's sterile promontory, his foul and pestilent congregation of vapors, his quintessence of dust, carried to their nadir. The kingdom Macbeth's ambition has conquered turns out to be a limbo of blank idiocy.

Of Macbeth's physical bravery at the end too much has been made, for it is mainly desperation. There are other things that help him retain our sympathy more than that.

> They have tied me to a stake; I cannot fly,
> But, bear-like, I must fight the course.

That might well be the memory of some bear-baiting Shakespeare witnessed as a boy. And another touch pierces even deeper. When Macduff finally confronts the object of his revenge, crying, "Turn, hell-hound, turn!" Macbeth exclaims:

Of all men else I have avoided thee.
But get thee back; my soul is too much charg'd
With blood of thine already.

It is his sole confession of remorse. But like one star in the blackness it is the brighter on that account.

IX

The fourth act of *Macbeth* has been accused of sagging. It has even been pronounced "tedious." After the concentration of the first three acts on the two central characters, a fourth act which omits both of them except for its first scene is bound to fall off somewhat in interest. Yet the long passage in which Malcolm tests Macduff, to make certain that he is not a hidden agent of Macbeth, is just one more variation of the mousetrap situation in *Hamlet,* with echoes of the casket theme from *The Merchant of Venice* and a touch, in reverse, of the temptation scene from *Othello.* If a passage with such patterns behind it is found wanting in dramatic tension, it is surely more the actors' or reader's fault than Shakespeare's. In it Malcolm reveals on a smaller scale some of the most engaging traits of Hamlet: something of the same modesty, wisdom, circumspection, and poetic insight, the same tendency to dramatize himself, to pass himself off for less than he is, to lie low and play psychological games on others, but without a trace of Hamlet's antic disposition. He speaks in this scene mainly about evil, but in doing so his vocabulary manages to be full of such words as angels, grace, child, snow, lamb, milk. If we know Shakespeare, we know what this means. The man's imagination is contradicting his intellect. His metaphors are giving away the deeper truth. He speaks of himself as "a weak poor innocent lamb," yet proceeds a few lines later to assert that he is so full of

All the particulars of vice so grafted,
That, when they shall be open'd, black Macbeth
Will seem as pure as snow,* and the poor state
Esteem him as a lamb, being compar'd
With my confineless harms.

The projection on Macbeth of the attributes of snow and of the lamb need not deceive us as to whose they really are.

Nay, had I power, I should
Pour the sweet milk of concord into hell.

* Notice the echo of the casket theme from *The Merchant of Venice* in that "open'd," and of *Othello* in that "black" and "snow."

This is a sort of inverted or celestial irony. Malcolm thinks he is stigmatizing himself as the undying enemy of peace, but over his head the words are a prophecy that, when he comes to the throne, his love of peace will assuage the infernal state to which Scotland has been reduced under Macbeth. At the sight of Macduff's genuine grief Malcolm is convinced of his integrity and abjures the "taints and blames" he has just laid on himself as bait. In his retraction, however, he does not claim for himself "the king-becoming graces" he previously listed as his deficiencies, but we more than suspect that he possesses something of every one of them. The mere fact that he is able to give us the most nearly perfect picture in Shakespeare of the ideal king is in itself significant. He seems to have inherited the gentleness of his father along with a greater valor. The outlook for Scotland under him is bright.

X

At the end of the interview between Malcolm and Macduff comes the passage describing the heavenly gifts and graces of the English king (Edward the Confessor), particularly his power to cure "the evil" by royal touch. Historical scholarship tells us that here Shakespeare turns aside from his play to pay a compliment to King James. Doubtless he does pay such a compliment. But that he turns aside to do it is not so certain. Here, to begin with, is the most effective of contrasts between the English king and the Scottish tyrant. More than that. Here is explicitly announced the contra-theme to the main subject of the play. That subject is human traffic with infernal spirits. But King Edward—though "how he solicits heaven, Himself best knows"—has the capacity to become the agent of celestial powers, can use spiritual force to heal rather than to destroy, is an instrument not of darkness but of light. Nothing could be less of a digression than this passage. Without it, and without various little touches throughout the play that support what it says, the play would be a different thing. It is one thing to believe in infernal spirits alone, quite another to believe in both infernal and celestial ones.

Our age speaks of its own spiritual unrest, thinks it permissible to believe in spiritual influences and tendencies, but holds it rank superstition to believe in spirits. It wants the adjective without the noun. The absurdity of this position was long ago demonstrated once for all by Socrates in the *Apology:*

Did ever man, Meletus, believe in the existence of human things, and not human beings? ... Did ever any man believe in horsemanship, and not in horses? or in flute-playing, and not in flute-players? No, my friend; I will answer to you and to the court, as you refuse to answer for yourself. There is no man who ever did. But now please to answer the next question: *Can a man believe in spiritual and divine agencies, and not in spirits or demigods?*

And Meletus, driven to the wall, admits, "He can not."

Where there is a gravitational pull, there must be a mass of matter pulling. Where there is illumination, there must be something emitting light. Where there is attribute, there must be substance. Over thousands of years the habits of the human imagination in this matter have never deviated. Socrates and Shakespeare are obedient to them. Those habits, we may be certain, have not been altered by the materialisms and rationalisms of a few generations of the nineteenth and twentieth centuries. During those generations it became fashionable to believe that things psychical are a sort of product or secretion of the brain. Faced suddenly with psychic reality itself, as it has been in two world wars, this unheroic philosophy now cries out in consternation with Macbeth:

> The time has been,
> That, when the brains were out, the man would die,
> And there an end; but now they rise again
> With twenty mortal murders on their crowns
> And push us from our stools. This is more strange
> Than such a murder is.

It is indeed, and from end to end the play is saturated with this strangeness. We put it down with the ineradicable conviction that the instruments of darkness of which it tells are real. It has exposed the sensitive imagination to an experience which otherwise only personal indulgence in cruelty might impart.

There are some human consciousnesses, says John Cowper Powys,

who are tempted to give themselves up to a pleasure in cruelty; but if they knew the unspeakable ghastliness of the reality they are thus creating for themselves, they would stop dead, *there* where they stand, with a shiver of paralyzed self-loathing. That such cruelty is suicidal from a human stand-point, they know well. They know the ordinary human hell they are preparing for themselves. What they don't seem to know is the far worse cosmic Terror they are bringing down upon them. Insanity, that's what it is; not merely human insanity, but unutterable, unspeakable, *nonhuman insanity*. Sometimes in dreams of the night people who have been deliberately cruel get a glimpse of what they have done, and *what companions they have now got.*

The psychology of cruelty is a strange thing. The cruel person says to himself: "I have got beyond human law and human feeling. All is now permitted me, if I can but harden my heart." Little does he know! Better had he never been born *than have gone where he has gone* and attached to himself the ghastliness of the abyss that now clings to him. The "Hell" of the mediaeval imagination is a poetical joke compared with what he is on the way to experience—crying indeed "upon the mountains to cover him and the floods to overwhelm him"! Horror is a very peculiar and a very appalling thing; and those who have peeped through the cosmic chink into the Horror-Dance of the abyss would sooner henceforth hold their hands in a candle-flame and burn them to the bone, than give themselves up to deliberate cruelty.

This is precisely the Horror encountered at death by Kurtz, the European who reverted to African savagery, in Conrad's *Heart of Darkness*. It is the Horror of which Henry James gives more than a glimpse in *The Turn of the Screw*.

XI

But now at the end comes the strangest and most paradoxical fact about this play. And the loveliest. If *Macbeth* is Shakespeare's Descent into Hell, it is also his spring myth. This picture of blackness is framed in light, placed, we might almost say, against a background of verdure.

Shakespeare announces this theme, however faintly, in the first pages of the play. The bleeding Sergeant brings word that peace has been made with the rebels but that fresh war at the same moment has broken out with Norway. So storms, he says, sometimes come from the east where the sun rises, or discomfort from spring which promises comfort. Since word is immediately brought that Macbeth has averted the new threat with a second victory, we dismiss the Sergeant's metaphor from mind, not noticing how much better it fits the play as a whole than the minor incidents to which he applies it. For what is the tyranny of Macbeth between the reigns of Duncan and Malcolm but winter come back after the promise of spring only to be overcome in turn by spring itself? For, however delayed, spring always wins. So Malcolm and Macduff subdue the tyrant and Scotland looks forward to a dispensation of peace. Thus does a figure from its first page impart to the play its underlying pattern.

All this, however well it fits, might seem like making too much out of a metaphor thrown out so casually, if we did not know Shakespeare's habit of announcing important themes in the opening lines of his plays, and if, in this case, he had not so strikingly confirmed at the end what he hints at in the beginning. I refer to the coming of Birnam Wood to Dunsinane. When each of Malcolm's soldiers hews down a branch and bears it before him, it is only in a manner of speaking that the forest moves. But it does move in another and lovelier sense. The legend Shakespeare makes use of is a myth of the coming of spring. "The legend of the moving forest originated in the German religious custom of May-festivals, or summer welcomings, and . . . King Grunenwald is originally a winter giant whose dominion ceases when the May feast begins and the greenwood draws near."

War is winter. Peace is spring. Were ever symbols more inevitable than these, especially in the religion and poetry of northern peoples? Winter is a giant. Spring, in comparison, is a maiden. How powerless she seems in his presence! But because the sun is on her side and moves in every root and bud she undermines the sway of the tyrant. She has great allies. And so does peace in this play. The Old Man, for instance, who talks with Ross outside the castle and bids him farewell in those Desdemona-like words:

> God's benison go with you; and with those
> That would make good of bad, and friends of foes;

the Doctor who says at the sight of Lady Macbeth,

> More needs she the divine than the physician.
> God, God forgive us all!

the Waiting-Gentlewoman who bids him, "Good-night, good doctor"; little Macduff; the pious King Edward. These, and others, play no conspicuous part in the story. Yet perhaps Shakespeare is implying that it is only by the collaboration of thousands like them, whose contributions singly may seem as insignificant as single grassblades do to spring, that war, like winter, can be overcome.

Chapter XXIX

King Lear

I

King Lear, in a dozen ways, is the culmination of Shakespeare. It may be regarded from almost as many angles as life itself.

The theme of all Shakespeare's Tragedies is that of Zoroaster and Empedocles, of Aeschylus and Dante, of Milton and Blake, the conflict of the universal powers of light and darkness, of love and hate. *Hamlet*, except for its ghost, and *Othello*, except for transcendental overtones, express that struggle in predominantly human terms. *Macbeth*, on the other hand, gives the sense of metaphysical agencies at work behind the action, of being located as much in an infernal world as on this planet. *King Lear*, by a union of human intimacy and elemental vastness, exceeds the other three in the universal impression it produces. To say that in this respect it synthesizes *Othello* and *Macbeth* is to stamp it, by that fact, incomparable. That is one reason why it is hard to think of it as having been written before *Macbeth*.

II

From a biological angle, the theme of *King Lear* is the same one that dominates Greek drama, the relation of the generations, the same one that has been central in Shakespeare's Histories and Tragedies up to this time (and by no means absent from his Comedies), the authority of the past over the present as symbolized by the Father. This theme is so plain in the Histories, especially in the intensive study of Henry IV and his son, as to call for no comment. *Romeo and Juliet* and *Hamlet* would obviously be nothing without this mainspring. The idea is not as conspicuous, but under analysis turns out to be hardly less important, in *Julius Caesar* and *Othello*. Only from *Macbeth* does it seem absent. But when we recall the unforgettable moment when Lady Macbeth remembers her father,

> Had he not resembled
> My father as he slept, I had done 't,

we realize that the forces of the past are at work beneath the surface of that play too. In *King Lear*, however, the theme is both on the surface and under the surface from the first scene to the last.

Romeo, Henry V, Brutus, and Hamlet show, each in his own way, what comes from bowing the knee to force or authority as embodied in the Father. Juliet, Desdemona, and Cordelia show what comes from a refusal to obey the Father in the same sense. In worldly terms the result in all these cases, except that of Henry V, is disaster. But Henry, Brutus, Hamlet, and Romeo in so far as he resumes the ancient feud of his family, are involved in spiritual disaster likewise; while Juliet, Desdemona, Cordelia, and Romeo in so far as he is true to Juliet, know only spiritual triumph. In all Shakespeare's works there is nothing that goes deeper than this distinction, I believe, in its bearing on the salvation of humanity from force, nothing that proves more convincingly the necessity of regarding his works as a whole. Here, in play after play, it is intimated that the redemption of man from violence must come from woman—not from women alone, but from the generic woman who, whether expressed or hidden, is an integral part of both the sexes. If the Juliet within Romeo, the Desdemona and Cordelia within Hamlet, had had their way, how different the stories of those two plays would have been!

But *King Lear*, it should be pointed out, goes beyond *Othello* in its treatment of this theme. It is not that Cordelia surpasses Desdemona in beauty of character. That would be impossible. Indeed, Cordelia has to acquire through suffering what seems to be Desdemona's by birthright. Cordelia, with her abruptness and bluntness, her strain of disdain, is closer to most of us than the innocent and angelic Desdemona. If to err is human, to forgive divine, they are both divine, but Cordelia is more human. It is a triumphant mark of Shakespeare's art that the two supreme heroines of his tragic period should be so similar yet so different. It is not here, then, that *King Lear* probes deeper or soars higher than *Othello*. The difference resides rather in the relation of the generations at the end of the two plays. *Othello* in this respect stands midway between *Hamlet* and *King Lear*. *Hamlet*, as a kind of culmination of "father" plays that lead up to it, ends with the conversion of the son to the code of the father, the acceptance and practice of blood revenge. *Othello* shows youth freeing itself from the domination of the older generation—the father in this case, Brabantio, dying of grief and passing out of the play. But Lear does not pass out of the play. He is central in it to the end. In his case what we see, in complete contrast with what happens in *Hamlet*, is the conversion of the father into the likeness of the child. Here, if ever, the child is father of the man, and Lear ends with authority and force* put off, with love and tenderness put on. He longs for nothing in the world but to spend the rest of his days with the daughter who has brought him peace.

No character in *Hamlet* itself illuminates the Prince of Denmark more than Cordelia does. They act like polar opposites. Hamlet indulged in such extravagant protestations of love for his father that they come under suspicion. But for their manifest honesty they might remind us of Goneril-and-Regan's pretended adoration of their father, which, unconsciously, they resemble. Cordelia loves her father deeply and sincerely, but underplays her confession of affection—partly from a congenital truthfulness and hatred of display that bends backward at the hypocrisy of her sisters, but even more, perhaps, through a well-grounded fear, possibly unconscious, that if her father's plan goes through she will be given to the worldly Burgundy whom she could only have despised rather than to the unworldly France whom she loves. Not until we have Cordelia before us and above us as a North Star can we see how diametrically wrong Hamlet was, how antipathetic to his father his true self was underneath, how exactly he was steering backward.† The past and future of humanity are in these two figures. With rare exceptions man has been a slave to the past, but has refused to understand and love it. He ought to love and understand it but refuse to be its slave.

> She that herself will sliver and disbranch
> From her material sap, perforce must wither
> And come to deadly use.

Goneril, to whom that truth was spoken, dared defy it, and cried out, "No more; the text is foolish." Cordelia, though she defied it at first, lived to reassert it at last on a higher level. Her conduct involved the paradox of both discontinuity and continuity with the older generation. The present

---

* His boast at the end that he killed the "slave" that was hanging his daughter we hold against him no more than we hold Desdemona's "Nobody. I myself," or Cordelia's "No cause, no cause," against them.

† Shakespeare all but makes Hamlet say as much of himself. Words spoken in contempt generally fit the speaker better than they do the object of his scorn. "You yourself, sir, should be old as I am," says Hamlet to Polonius, "if, like a crab, you could go backward." Hamlet *was* the older of the two at the moment in the sense that when we speak with contempt we are regressing (II, ii, 201–10).

must break with the past, her story seems to say, in order to become conscious of itself and of its freedom; whereupon it must mend the breach it has made lest it cut itself off from the only energy whereby it can live. We must repudiate the past, for it has sinned against us; we must forgive and love it, for it has given us life. This is irrational, but it is true. Thus *King Lear* reconciles the polar principles of radicalism and conservatism and in doing so largely dissipates the riddle of *Hamlet*. The two plays are like the two sides of the same tapestry. But *King Lear* is the "right" side. As you cannot comprehend *Henry V* until you have read *Hamlet*, so you cannot comprehend *Hamlet* until you have read *King Lear*.

III

But the theme of *King Lear* may be stated in psychological as well as in biological terms. So put, it is the destructive, the ultimately suicidal character of unregulated passion, its power to carry human nature back to chaos. The political disorder of the fifteenth century, which he depicted in *Henry VI*, may have first called Shakespeare's attention to this truth. At any rate, from then on he never ceased to search for more and more vivid and violent metaphors through which to express it. It is "The expense of spirit in a waste of shame" of the 129th sonnet, the "bait On purpose laid to make the taker mad." It is the Universal Wolf of Ulysses, which, having devoured everything else, at last eats up itself. It is the occult force that led Duncan's horses to eat each other. Pride, lust, fear, anger: passion consumes itself, runs itself dry, burns itself out. Character after character in Shakespeare avows it, usually out of bitter experience. "Lechery eats itself," cries Thersites. "I have supp'd full with horrors," cries Macbeth,

> Direness, familiar to my slaughterous thoughts,
> Cannot once start me.

"Anger's my meat," cries Volumnia,

> I sup upon myself,
> And so shall starve with feeding.

But it remains for Albany in *King Lear* to give the thought its most ominous form as a prophecy of the doom of mankind itself:

> It will come,
> Humanity must perforce prey on itself,
> Like monsters of the deep.

The predestined end of unmastered human passion is the suicide of the species. That is the gospel according to *King Lear*. The play is in no small measure an actual representation of that process. The murder-suicide of

Regan-Goneril is an example. But it is more than a picture of chaos and impending doom. What is the remedy for chaos? it asks. What can avert the doom? The characters who have mastered their passions give us a glimpse of the answer to those questions. And Shakespeare, through them, gives us more than a glimpse. But that is the culmination of the play and should come last.

IV

He who masters his passions is king over them. Here the psychological theme of the play has its political implications. This metaphor of the emotions as a mob bound to dethrone its ruler if he loses control over them goes nobody knows how far back toward the beginnings of human thought. This comparison of the kingdom within to the kingdom without, of the microcosm to the macrocosm, is one of the immemorial and universal figures of speech. Plato founded his Republic on it. Jesus erected his Kingdom of Heaven on an extension and sublimation of it. Shakespeare evinced the keenest interest in it from the beginning.

In Henry VI the young poet found a king who, whatever his failures, had the almost unique success of retaining his individuality as a man in spite of his title, the beginning at least of a synthesis of the two kingdoms. The deposed Henry is in a situation not wholly unlike that of the deposed Lear, and the conversation in *III Henry VI* between him and Two Keepers on this very theme of man and king, with its talk of a spiritual crown that kings seldom attain, seems like a far-off gleam of the poet's supreme tragedy, as in another way does Henry's soliloquy on the Simple Life. In *King John* Shakespeare devoted a whole play to a demonstration that a man may be kinglier than a king. Henry IV's soliloquy on Sleep is a variation on the same theme, with its envy of the wet sea-boy to whom sleep comes on the giddy mast in the storm while it is denied to the king in his bed. The relation of king and subject is the explicit topic of debate between Henry V and the soldiers among whom he wanders disguised as one of them, the night before Agincourt. "I think the king is but a man, as I am," says Henry to Bates, ". . . his ceremonies laid by, in his nakedness he appears but a man." He would never have dared tell that truth but for the double protection of disguise and night. And the ensuing soliloquy on Ceremony follows out the same thought. Indeed, this entire group of plays is founded on the double personality of Henry: Henry as Hal, the man and pal of Falstaff, and Henry as Prince Henry, heir to Henry IV and later King Henry V. *Hamlet*, as its full title, *Hamlet, Prince of Denmark*, shows, rests on the same distinction between man and prince. Only in this perspective can we catch the significance of Hamlet's reply to Horatio when the latter says of his father:

I saw him once; he was a goodly king.

He was a man,

Hamlet retorts. He knows which title is more honorable.

And not a man, for being simply man,
Hath any honour, but honour for those honours
That are without him, as place, riches, and favour,
Prizes of accident as oft as merit.

In these words of Achilles in *Troilus and Cressida* we have the more generalized form of the theme, the contrast between the role a man plays before the world and the man himself. It is one of the most persistent ideas in Shakespeare. It is the subject of Isabella's great tirade on the abuse of power in *Measure for Measure* and of the King's long disquisition in *All's Well* on the indistinguishableness of various bloods. It is behind Hamlet's "insolence of office." It is in the "captive good attending captain ill" of the 66th sonnet and in innumerable other passages. But none of them quite reach the pitch of the mad Lear's revulsion against the very thing that he has been:

LEAR: Thou hast seen a farmer's dog bark at a beggar?
GLOUCESTER: Ay, sir.
LEAR: And the creature run from the cur? There thou mightst behold
             the great image of authority: a dog's obeyed in office.

With the standing exception of Henry VI (and Malcolm, whom we do not see on the throne), all Shakespeare's kings in both history and tragedy up to this point are weaklings, worldlings, or villains, sometimes two of the three or all three at once. "What is a king?" I once asked a little girl out of pure curiosity to see what she would say. Looking up at me with shining eyes, she replied without a moment's hesitation: "A king is a beautiful man." She was in her fairy-tale stage. Shakespeare would have understood her—for *King Lear* is the story of how a king in the worldly sense became a king in the fairy-tale sense, of how a bad king became a beautiful man. *Henry V* is an account of how a man became a king. *King Lear* is an account of how a king became a man. Until you have read *King Lear*, you have never read *Henry V*.

Nor is Shakespeare content with weaving this theme into his plot and rendering it explicit in almost every scene of the play. He makes it, both literally and symbolically, visible to the eye. We see Lear in the first act with crown and robe and all the other marks of authority and accoutrements of office, exercising, as in the banishment of Kent, an extreme form of absolute power. We see him in the fourth act, after his buffeting by night and tempest, crowned and robed with common flowers and wayside weeds, his authority exchanged for an emerging humility, his egotism for the sympathy and wisdom of an incoherent mind, his court for loneliness or the society of beggars and the blind. What inversions of everything!

> The trick of that voice I do well remember,

says the blinded Gloucester, hearing the tragedy in lieu of seeing it,

> Is't not the king?
>
> Ay, every inch a king!

replies Lear. We agree. It is now, not at the beginning, that he is every inch a king, for he has taken the first steps toward self-conquest: he has questioned his own infallibility; he has recognized the sufferings of others. From this it is but a step to mercy.

> When I do stare, see how the subject quakes,

the Old King, flaring up, cries to the phantasmal vassals of his insanity. But the New King quickly extinguishes him in the next line:

> I pardon that man's life. What was thy cause?

words which, I think, are generally mistaken. On the stage, as I remember, the implication always is that Lear first pardons one of the imaginary culprits who stand before him, and then, turning to a second, asks him *his* cause. But surely a single culprit is involved. The whole point is the fact that Lear offers pardon first and only afterward asks what the offense is that he has pardoned. When one is possessed of a spirit of universal forgiveness, of what moment is it to know the nature of the crime? It is like the Duke's

> I pardon thee thy life before thou ask it,

to Shylock, or the Duchess's

> "Pardon" should be the first word of thy speech,

in *Richard II*. Mercy, Shakespeare is saying, is the mark of the man who is every inch a king. It might have been from *King Lear* that Abraham Lincoln, one of the few rulers who ever practiced it, learned that truth.

It ought to be plain by now why the play is called *King Lear*. Macbeth was a king, Hamlet was a prince, Othello was a general, yet the plays in which they figure are simply *Macbeth*, *Hamlet*,* and *Othello*. But it is *KING Lear*. Unless we are merely labeling it, we should never refer to it,

---

* *Hamlet, Prince of Denmark* is of course the full title, and the subtitle should be coupled with the title oftener than it is to emphasize both Hamlet's princely qualities and his disdain of royalty. Cf. *Prince* Myshkin in Dostoevsky's *The Idiot*.

as so many do, as *Lear*. Shakespeare knew what he was about when he named his greatest play.

V

But important as are its biological, psychological, and political themes, none of them goes to its heart. Its innermost secret is religious. A clue to that secret, I believe, may be found, as is usual in Shakespeare, where one would be least likely to expect it, in the very scene that most readers and directors would be readiest to sacrifice: the blinding of Gloucester. The gratuitous horror of this incident has been condemned by critics over and over. It is cut out, or mitigated, in all stage performances.

But we are considering *King Lear*, not *Titus Andronicus*. Why did Shakespeare at the crest of his power see fit to include in an unequaled masterpiece this unendurable scene? The usual answer is that the Elizabethan was a ruder age than ours, men had steadier nerves and stronger stomachs then—the implication being that we are more refined. In that case, either Shakespeare was pandering to the lowest element in his audience without regard to the demands of the play, or else we have more delicacy and sensibility than the creator of Rosalind and Ariel. A hard dilemma.

Plainly we must seek some other explanation.

In science it is the exceptions to the rule that offer the most rewarding clues. It is the same in art. We may depend upon it that the tender and sensitive Shakespeare had some reason for the inclusion of this fearful incident as compelling as the one that led Dostoevsky, almost on his knees, to beg the censor not to cut out the not less insupportable stories of cruelties to children with which Ivan tortured Alyosha in *The Brothers Karamazov*.

The scene in question is centered on the eyes and eyesight of Gloucester. . . .

And here may I interrupt myself to ask that what, from this point on, may seem like a needless stress on irrelevant details may be forgiven until the end it is leading up to is perceived. A patient attention to what appear to be some of the most trivial things in the text will prove worth while if I am not mistaken in thinking that what they will reveal and what would be invisible without them is nothing less than the moment of most visionary loveliness in all Shakespeare, and, so far as my knowledge permits me to speak, of unsurpassed profundity of insight into the secret of life-and-death in the entire literature of the world. . . .

The scene in question, I was saying, is centered on the eyes and eyesight of Gloucester. But consider *King Lear* as a whole: does not practically everything in it turn on this subject of *seeing*? Darkness and light; blindness and vision—visions and blindnesses, indeed, of every kind. They are the warp and woof of the drama. The play is centered around a single image, dominated by a single metaphor. It is hidden until it is seen, and then it stands out in bold letters on nearly every page.

"Seek out the traitor Gloucester," Cornwall orders, when he hears of the letter the Earl has received promising revenge to the King.

"Hang him instantly," echoes Regan.

"Pluck out his eyes," cries Goneril.

Some have thought that these two speeches have become interchanged in the text, the crueler fitting better the more cowardly of the daughters. But they are not out of character as they stand, and Shakespeare undoubtedly wants us to link these words of Goneril with the first words she speaks in the play, when her father asks her, as "our eldest-born," to declare her feeling for him:

> Sir, I love you more than words can wield the matter,
> Dearer than eye-sight, space, and liberty.

Thus the image is introduced that is to run like a leitmotif throughout the rest of the play. Before the end of the same scene Cordelia has failed the King, he has disinherited and cursed her, and his faithful friend has tried in vain to intervene. "Out of my sight!" cries Lear, banishing him. And Kent replies:

> See better, Lear; and let me still remain
> The true blank of thine eye.

From this moment on, the story of King Lear is the story of the slow acquirement of that better vision. In the last scene of the play, when the loyal Kent, his disguise at last thrown off, stands in the presence of the dying King, a misty figure to a dimming eyesight, "Who are you?" Lear murmurs,

> Mine eyes are not o' the best: I'll tell you straight . . .
> This is a dull sight. Are you not Kent?

> > The same,
> Your servant Kent. Where is your servant Caius?

Kent replies. And Lear answers:

> He's a good fellow, I can tell you that.

The King's physical eyesight has faded. But he has learned to "see better." He can now see a man. And, what is more, he can recognize him under any name.

To enumerate the allusions to eyes and vision between these two scenes at the beginning and the end would be to review a large part of the play.

We hear of the "heavenly" eyes of Cordelia, of the "fierce" eyes of Goneril, of the deceitful eyes of Regan that to her deceived father seem to "comfort and not burn." When the King receives his first rebuff from Goneril, he exclaims:

> This is not Lear.
> . . . Where are his eyes?

Later, when his grief gets the better of him, and he cries to his "old fond eyes,"

> Beweep this cause again, I'll pluck ye out,

it is plainly an ironic preparation of the spectator's feelings for the blinding scene to come. And when in that scene, but before the deed, Gloucester tells Regan that he has taken the King to Dover,

> Because I would not see thy cruel nails
> Pluck out his poor old eyes,

it is as if he were reminding her, lest she forget, of her sister's "pluck out his eyes," and so inviting his own doom.

When the father would curse his eldest daughter, he calls upon the nimble lightnings to dart their blinding flames "into her scornful eyes," words that inevitably remind us of the "dearer than eye-sight" of her first speech. Later, on the heath, it is as if he had called down his imprecation on his own head. The winds in "eyeless rage" catch and toss his white hair in their fury.

And so one could go on collecting references to eyes and eyesight. But it is not so much their number, large as it is, as their significance, that is important. What that is, the relation between plot and subplot makes clear.

The parallelism between the faithful and unfaithful daughters of Lear and the faithful and unfaithful sons of Gloucester is so striking that it has been criticized as artificial and too obvious. It overloads the play with matter, we are told. This is a superficial view. There is a far more intimate tie between the two stories than this and it turns again on the question of vision.

Gloucester is a goodhearted but sensual man. His jocose attitude toward his adulteries is given the emphasis of the opening lines of the play. Because of his kindness to the King he suffers the frightful fate of having his eyes gouged out and being thrust forth to "smell his way" to Dover, as Regan phrases it.

It is immediately after this that, completely crushed, he utters the famous words:

> As flies to wanton boys, are we to the gods,
> They kill us for their sport,

a sentence which, lifted out of its context, has often been made the basis of a pessimistic interpretation of the play. In this mood, Gloucester thinks only of suicide and seeks a guide to the cliff over which he has made up his mind to leap to death. The scene is again the heath, with Edgar, as Poor Tom, in the background. Gloucester enters, led by an Old Man who has befriended him. It is one of his own tenants, who, by plain intention on the part of the poet, is of almost exactly King Lear's age, "fourscore." The blind man begs his guide to leave him, lest he injure himself with those in authority for helping their enemy. "You cannot see your way," the Old Man protests.

> I have no way, and therefore want no eyes;
> I stumbled when I saw,

Gloucester replies. It is the first hint of the birth within him of *in*sight. And he prays to his dear and wronged son Edgar, whose proximity he of course does not suspect:

> Might I but live to see thee in my touch,
> I'd say I had eyes again!

The prayer is instantly answered. Edgar comes forward. Gloucester, forgetting his own suffering in pity of Poor Tom's, sends the Old Man off to find covering for the beggar's nakedness. Here is a second symptom of rebirth. And, for a third, he gives Tom his purse, crying out to the powers above:

> . . . heavens, deal so still!
> Let the superfluous and lust-dieted man,
> That slaves your ordinance, that will not see
> Because he does not feel, feel your power quickly;
> So distribution should undo excess,
> And each man have enough.

Here is a vision that may well compensate for the loss of more than a pair of eyes. But two miracles must confirm it before Gloucester is brought to an acceptance of his fate: an act of combined kindness and psychological wisdom on his son's part that exorcises the demon of self-destruction, and a "sight" of the mad Lear, whose case is so much worse than his own. (To these two scenes we shall return later.) How utter is the change in him is seen by putting the lines about the gods killing men for sport, as boys do flies, beside

> You ever-gentle gods, take my breath from me;
> Let not my worser spirit tempt me again
> To die before you please!

Affliction has brought insight and submission. And yet Shakespeare has contrived the pitiable tale not primarily for its own sake but to throw into high relief the far sublimer story of Lear. For Lear, unlike Gloucester, is a figure of tragic dimensions.

VI

Lear, at the beginning of the play, possesses physical eyesight, so far as we know, as perfect as Gloucester's. But morally he is even blinder. He is a victim, to the point of incipient madness, of his arrogance, his anger, his vanity, and his pride. A choleric temperament, a position of absolute authority, and old age have combined to make him what he is. The night and the storm into which he is thrust out on the heath are Shakespeare's symbols for the truth that blindness and passion go hand in hand. The darkness that descends on Lear's mind in its impotent fury is the counterpart of the blackness in which the tempest rages. But, like the flashes of lightning that momentarily illuminate the landscape for the lost traveler, there is a spiritual lightning that illuminates the lost soul.

> No, I will be the pattern of all patience; I will say nothing.

Nothing! Cordelia's very word at the beginning when Lear sought to test her affection. However far behind, the father has at least caught sight of the daughter. "Nothing will come of nothing," he had warned her in that opening scene. But something "enskyed" and starry was to come of that "nothing," if no more than Lear's capacity to say "I will say nothing." The lightning has struck in his soul, and it is at the very moment when he cries "my wits begin to turn" that he thinks for the first time of someone else's suffering before his own.

> Come on, my boy. How dost, my boy? Art cold?

he cries to Poor Tom. More and more from that moment, the tempest in Lear's mind makes him insensible to the tempest without. Increasingly, he sees that madness lies in dwelling on his own wrongs, salvation in thinking of the sufferings of others:

> Poor naked wretches, wheresoe'er you are,
> That bide the pelting of this pitiless storm,
> How shall your houseless heads and unfed sides,
> Your loop'd and window'd raggedness, defend you

From seasons such as these? O, I have ta'en
Too little care of this! Take physic, pomp;
Expose thyself to feel what wretches feel,
That thou mayst shake the superflux to them,
And show the heavens more just.

Exactly Gloucester's conclusion! Agony leads the two men to one mind. But compare the passages, and it will be seen how much more concrete, moving, and tragic Lear's is. And besides, he had been king.

All through these three tremendous scenes, on the heath, before the hovel, and in the farmhouse, the night of madness grows blacker and blacker, the flashes of spiritual insight more and more vivid. It is imagination at grips with chaos. Vision with blindness. Light with eternal night. Here is a microcosm of the macrocosm. Here is War. Here, too, then, there should be a clue to what, if anything, can subdue that ancient and most inveterate enemy of man. Embryonic patience or ancestral passion: which will win? Even up to the terrific arraignment of the two recreant daughters in the chambers of Lear's imagination in which these scenes culminate, we do not know. Hatred and rage are in the ascendant when the phantasmal Regan dashes from the phantasmal courtroom and Lear cries:

Stop her there!
Arms, arms, sword, fire!

Here is revealed how entangled with the imagery of war are both the personal emotion of revenge and the hidden temper of those supposed instruments of social justice that are too often only judicial vengeance in disguise. And yet but a moment and the wind-struck vane has whirled through a hundred and eighty degrees and a diametrically opposite treatment of the same daughter is prescribed: "Then let them anatomize Regan; see what breeds about her heart. *Is there any cause in nature that makes these hard hearts?*" Here is another universe. Hell has given place to Heaven. The tolerance, one might almost say the scientific detachment, of that "anatomize," and the humility of

The little dogs and all,
Tray, Blanch, and Sweetheart, see, they bark at me,

tell us which side is winning. If there was War, here is Peace. And the gods seem to confirm it when the blessing of sleep finally descends on the exhausted old man. In his History Plays, Shakespeare had explored at length the feudal conception of the royal prerogative. In a few scenes in this play, of which this is one, he reveals the genuine divine right of kings—and of men. The angels that come to the aid of this stricken monarch are unrelated to those in whom Richard II had such confidence in virtue of his mere title, but who failed him so ignominiously at the crisis of his career.

But Shakespeare does not so much say it as make us see it. When we next behold the King, immediately after the attempted suicide of Gloucester, he enters fantastically robed and crowned with flowers. The symbolism of that, even without the echo of Ophelia, is unmistakable. The simple costless jewels of the fields and meadows have replaced the courtly pomp of gold and purple. Here is not merely Nature's king, but Heaven's. Before speaking further of that, however, we must return for a moment to Gloucester.

Surely a main reason why Shakespeare contrived the meeting of the two old men just when he did was to emphasize the fact that Lear, whatever his sufferings, unlike Gloucester, never for one instant dallied with the idea of self-destruction as a way out. Life: though nature, man, and apparently the gods conspired to make it an endless agony of crucifixion, even at fourscore and upward it never even occurred to Lear to question whether it was better than death. No more can we while we are under his spell.

> O, our lives' sweetness!
> That we the pain of death would hourly die
> Rather than die at once!

And then this play is called pessimistic! How inferior anyone who uses that word to describe it proves himself to its own glorious old hero! It may seem like a grotesque juxtaposition and the two may have little else in common, but King Lear and Falstaff embrace in their unbounded and unquenchable love of life for its own sake.

VII

But to get the full effect of this meeting of the two victims of their own and others' passions the remarkable scene that precedes it must be further analyzed. It is a superb example of Shakespeare's power to do whatever he likes with his auditors or readers. Of its kind he never performed a more remarkable feat of legerdemain than in the opening part of the sixth scene of Act IV of *King Lear*. In it he proves the primacy of the imagination by deceiving the whole world. Nearly everyone has seen or heard of Shakespeare's Cliff near Dover. Those who have never read *King Lear* suppose it is the scene of some part of the play. Those who have read it generally suppose so too. And even the few who know better find it hard to let reason get the better of the conviction that the action at this point takes place at the top, and afterward at the bottom, of an actual cliff. It doesn't, of course, except in the sense that Edgar's imagination is part of the play and the cliff does exist in Edgar's imagination. Yet, having proved this to our intellectual satisfaction, we proceed at once to slip back into our original illusion. Whether Edgar had once seen the physical cliff and was describing it from memory, or whether he had only heard of it and was creating it out of his own fancy at the moment, as he was quite capable of doing, we have no way of knowing. But what we do know is that if he relied on memory, his memory played him false.

But we can follow the miracle only in Shakespeare's footsteps.

Gloucester enters, accompanied by Edgar dressed as a peasant.

GLOU.: When shall I come to the top of that same hill?
EDG.: You do climb up it now; look, how we labour.
GLOU.: Methinks the ground is even.
EDG.:   Horrible steep.
        Hark, do you hear the sea?
GLOU.:   No, truly.

Gloucester, of course, is right. The ground is even and there is no sea to hear. But Edgar must convince him that he is deceived:

> Why, then, your other senses grow imperfect
> By your eyes' anguish,

—a complete inversion of the psychology of blindness.* Gloucester, however, is in no mood or position to dissent:

> So may it be, indeed.

But instantly he gives proof that it may *not* be so indeed by showing—as he does again later in the scene when he recognizes Lear's voice—that his ear is keenly alert:

> Methinks thy voice is alter'd, and thou speak'st
> In better phrase and matter than thou didst.

Edgar is caught! The natural emotion of being with his father, together perhaps with his change of dress, has led him to forget to maintain, vocally, the role he is playing, and his father's quick ear has detected the change.

> You're much deceiv'd. In nothing am I changed
> But in my garments.

This time, however, his father will not be talked down. He persists:

> Methinks you're better spoken.

* Cf. *A Midsummer-Night's Dream*, III, ii, 177:
    "Dark night, that from the eye his function takes,
    The ear more quick of apprehension makes."

So Edgar deftly changes the subject, or we might better say the scene:

> Come on, sir; here's the place: stand still.
> How fearful
> And dizzy 'tis, to cast one's eyes so low!

And thereupon begins the famous description of what Edgar sees as he gazes down into—his memory, or his imagination, or both. "He who does not imagine in stronger and better lineaments and in stronger and better light than his perishing and mortal eye can see," declares William Blake, "does not imagine at all." Edgar, and Shakespeare, pass Blake's test triumphantly, and have made this place that exists only in the imagination more real than the actual chalk cliffs of Albion. "It is not down in any map; true places never are," as Melville says in *Moby-Dick*.

Shakespeare is careful to show the attentive reader that Edgar is not describing what is before his physical eyes, by making him get his proportions somewhat out of kilter. But his most interesting error is at the end:

> The murmuring surge,
> That on the unnumber'd idle pebbles chafes,
> Cannot be heard so high.

Edgar has let slip out of mind his "Hark! do you hear the sea?" of a few moments back. The conclusion of his tale has forgotten the beginning of it—Shakespeare's sly way of proving that the two men are not standing where Edgar says they are. It is the son's memory that is "imperfect," not the father's senses.

Then follows Gloucester's attempted suicide. Possibly a supreme actor might carry off this difficult incident. But it may be doubted. The few times I have seen it in the theater it has come nearer to producing smiles than tears—I almost said, has fallen utterly flat. Yet it is completely convincing to the reader. How right that is, when one stops to think, in a scene whose theme is the supremacy of the imagination over the senses! It is Shakespeare's old habit of carrying his play leagues beyond and above the theater, making it practice what it preaches, as it were, act out its own doctrine, incarnate its own image within everyone who genuinely comes to grips with it. The cliff scene in *King Lear* is a sort of imaginative examination to test our spiritual fitness to finish the play. "It is not the height," says Nietzsche, "it is the declivity, that is terrible." And Thomas Hardy declares:

> If a way to the better there be, it exacts a full look at the worst.

Only he who can gaze into the abyss of this tragedy undizzied will ever realize that unknown to himself he has fallen and is now gazing up. Only from deep pits are the stars visible by daylight. As *The Merchant of Venice* is itself a casket, and *Hamlet* a mousetrap, so *King Lear* is a cliff.

Just the experience we have described, of course, is Gloucester's. Edgar grants a few seconds for his father's fall, and then, with his usual dramatic sense, instantly assumes a new role, that of the man-at-the-foot-of-the-cliff. The bewildered old man does not know whether he has fallen or not, until his companion assures him that he has. To clinch the fact, Edgar describes the fiend from whom his father parted on the crown of the cliff at the moment when he leaped. Again Shakespeare throws in inconsistencies and disproportions to distinguish sense from imagination. But the important point is that Edgar's instinct has proved sound: Gloucester has been cured by the shock of his supposed fall plus the assurance that he has escaped from a fiend—as indeed he has, if not in quite the literal sense he supposes. It is a wise child that knows his own father. Edgar knows his, and reckons correctly on Gloucester's superstitious-religious nature.

> GLOU.: Henceforth I'll bear
> Affliction till it do cry out itself
> "Enough, enough," and die.

Imagination has exorcised the suicidal temptation. Gloucester is done with the idea of voluntary death. The father is converted by the child. And Edgar adds, as if in benediction:

> Bear free and patient thoughts.

But it is not a benediction in the sense of an end. Gloucester's cure must be ratified. And to Edgar's quickly added, "But who comes here?" Lear—as if he were Patience herself in a morality play, entering on the cue of Edgar's "patient thoughts"—comes in "fantastically dressed with wild flowers."

VIII

What a meeting! The blind man and the madman. How insignificant the physical affliction in the presence of mental darkness! But it is not just darkness. The lightning flashes through the blackness of that head now crowned with flowers more vividly than did that other lightning through the night on the heath. "I am the king himself."

Here, if ever in Shakespeare, the poles of the universe rush together—as if stars suddenly began to gleam in the sulphurous pit, or the fury of an infernal ocean to toss up a foam of light. In a ferment of words more heterogeneous and, in spots, more noisome than the brew of the Witches in *Macbeth,* with images of violence and sensuality predominating, the forces of bestiality and forgiveness contend again, making their penultimate bid for possession of the old man's soul. As insane language so often does, it impresses us at first as just a mass of fragments, thoughts that tear past us like tatters of clouds after a storm. But on the whole, the coherency, like patches of blue sky, increases. It is madness, but a madness that in its rapidity leaves reason behind panting for breath and logic like a lame beggar far in the rear—ror into these volcanic outbursts of matter and impertinency mixed Shakespeare has managed, by a kind of poetic hydraulic pressure, to pack pretty much all he had had to say on force and sensuality and worldly power in such masterpieces as *Troilus and Cressida* and *Measure for Measure*.

Along with the shorter ones, there are four long, or fairly long, outbursts. In the first of them, Lear's memory goes back to the royal occupation, war. Then, mistaking Gloucester for "Goneril, with a white beard," his thoughts, in a second speech, pass to that flattery that cuts off kings from truth. How his youth was sinned against! When I was still but a boy, he says in effect, they began making me think I was wise. "To say 'ay' and 'no' to everything I said! 'Ay' and 'no' too was no good divinity"—no sound theology, as we should say. Not until that night on the heath does he discover that there are powers that will not bow to a king. "When the thunder would not peace at my bidding, there I found 'em, there I smelt 'em out"—those sycophants and false teachers, he means. "Go to, they are not men o' their words: they told me I was every thing; 'tis a lie."

How fitting that Shakespeare chose the moment when the King discovers the truth which the whole world is bent on hiding from kings to have Gloucester finally identify him: "Is't not the king?" "Ay, every inch a king!" And at last we know it is true, as Lear launches into his third speech, this time on sensuality, or, to put it more precisely, on adultery tinged with forgiveness. Some have thought this out of place on Lear's lips, have held it less his than the poet's. Shakespeare, it is said, was the victim of a sort of "sex nausea" at the time he wrote this play. He may or may not have been such a victim; but whoever thinks the speech out of keeping with King Lear has missed Shakespeare's conviction, reiterated from *Venus and Adonis* and *The Rape of Lucrece* onward, of the radical link between violence and lust. The horror of this outpouring, augmented as it is by the age of the man, is a measure not more of the part that sex, expressed or suppressed, has played in his life than of the part that war and power have.

> To't, luxury, pell-mell! for I lack soldiers.

How that line, to pick just one, sums up the interest of dictators in the birth rate! How little such things change down the centuries!

It is at the end of this eruption, and before coming to his fourth and last long speech, that Lear first seems to notice the presence of Gloucester, and here the theme of blindness and vision that hitherto has been implicit in the scene becomes explicit. "Dost thou know me?" asks Gloucester. "I remember thine eyes well enough," Lear replies, and with a flash of insane inspiration he identifies him as blind Cupid, and thrusts a "challenge" under his nose to read.

"Were all the letters suns, I could not see," says Gloucester.

"O, ho, are you there with me?" cries Lear, recognizing their common plight. "No eyes in your head, nor no money in your purse? Your eyes are in a heavy case, your purse in a light; yet you see how this world goes."

"I see it feelingly," replies Gloucester. He has indeed had to substitute touch for vision, but he has also learned through suffering that he whose senses, however perfect, are not backed by human sympathy perceives nothing.

"What! art mad?" Lear retorts. "A man may see how this world goes with no eyes. Look with thine ears." And then follows a terrific indictment of the rich and powerful ("which is the justice, which is the thief?"*) that sums up under the same metaphor of blindness all Shakespeare has had to say about Commodity-servers from *King John* on:

> Plate sin with gold,
> And the strong lance of justice hurtless breaks;
> Arm it in rags, a pigmy's straw does pierce it.
> None does offend, none, I say, none; I'll able 'em:
> Take that of me, my friend, who have the power
> To seal the accuser's lips. Get thee glass eyes,
> And, like a scurvy politician, seem
> To see the things thou dost not.

Then, with a sudden veer from contempt to pity, he cries to his blind companion:

> If thou wilt weep my fortunes, take my eyes.
> I know thee well enough; thy name is Gloucester:
> Thou must be patient.

Perhaps it is that word "patient," or it may have been Lear's declaration, "I will preach to thee: mark," which arouses to their expiring effort the demons that would drag him down to hell. At any rate, the sermon never

---

* Note, in retrospect, how this phrase justifies our interpretation of "Which is the merchant here and which the Jew?" in *The Merchant of Venice*.

gets beyond one sentence. A hat, real or imaginary, catches Lear's eye.* It reminds him, possibly, of his crown. His thoughts turn back to war, and he gives vent in terrible accents, but for the last time, to his longing for revenge:

> It were a delicate stratagem, to shoe
> A troop of horse with felt. I'll put 't in proof;
> And when I have stol'n upon these sons-in-law,
> Then, kill, kill, kill, kill, kill, kill!

the reiterated word being the cry, it is said, uttered by the English army at the onset. Yet the furies of war and murder do not possess themselves of the old man's soul, and when, a moment later, he sinks exhausted crying, "Let me have surgeons; I am cut to the brains," it is as if the laceration had been made less in the attempt of those demons to tear their way into his soul than in tearing their way out from it forever. When we next see the King, with Cordelia restored, his "insanity" is of the celestial, not the infernal, brand.

IX

But before coming to that, we must say a word about Cordelia. The extraordinary vividness of her portrayal, considering the brevity of her role, has often been commented on. The beauty of her nature—its sincerity and its combined strength and tenderness—goes far toward explaining the clarity of impression. But it is the fact that never for an instant do we forget her that compensates for the infrequency of her physical presence. Shakespeare sees to this in several ways. The antithesis with her sisters, to begin with, brings her to mind whenever they are on the stage. His sense of guilt with regard to her keeps her perpetually in Lear's memory—and so in ours. And the Fool's love for her, both on its own account and because he is forever insinuating thoughts of her into the King's mind, works the same way. Kent, too, makes his contribution. The best verbal embodiment I can think of for what Shakespeare's magic gradually turns Cordelia into in our imaginations is that starry phrase of Emily Dickinson's: Bright Absentee. *Bright Absentee:* that is exactly what Cordelia is during most of the play, and the phrase is doubly appropriate when we remember that the Cordelia-like New England poetess employed it to express a not less spiritual love than Cordelia's of a younger woman for an older man.

Now the fact and the success of this method of characterizing Cordelia are generally felt, I believe, but what is not recognized is that Shakespeare

---

* If, as is generally agreed, "block" is to be taken in that sense. "Felt" is a further punning link in Lear's association.

used it not just because it fitted the plot and was effective, but for a minute-ly specific reason. The last scene of this fourth act, the most tenderly pathetic in the play, begins to apprise us of what that reason is.

The place is a tent in the French camp. Lear is brought in asleep, and we hear and see administered the two of all the medicines in the world that in addition to sleep itself can bring back his sanity, if any can: music and Cordelia's kiss. The King gives signs of returning consciousness. "He wakes," says Cordelia to the Doctor, "speak to him." But like most of Shakespeare's physicians, this one has psychological insight as well as physiological skill, as his use of music as a healer has already hinted. "Madam, do you; 'tis fittest," he replies to Cordelia. Whereupon, with a wisdom equal to his, she addresses her father by his former title, seeking thereby to preserve his mental continuity:

> How does my royal lord? How fares your majesty?

But Lear believes he has awakened in hell and is gazing across a great gulf toward one in heaven:

> LEAR: You do me wrong to take me out o' the grave:
> Thou art a soul in bliss; but I am bound
> Upon a wheel of fire, that mine own tears
> Do scald like molten lead.
> COR.:   Sir, do you know me?
> LEAR: You are a spirit, I know. When did you die?

Lear is "still, still, far wide!" as Cordelia expresses it under her breath. Yet in another sense, as it befits Cordelia alone not to know, Lear was never before so near the mark. Cordelia, *we* know, *is* a spirit, and, in that shining line, Shakespeare harvests the promise of four full acts which have been subtly contrived to convince us of the same truth. That which without being apprehensible to the senses is nevertheless undeniably present is a spirit—and that Cordelia has been through most of the play. Now she becomes *visibly* that to Lear, and we, as readers or spectators, must be able to enter into the old man's vision, or the effect is lost. Shakespeare has abundantly seen to it that we shall be able. Here is that unknown some-thing that is indeed "dearer than eyesight"—something that is related to eyesight as eyesight is to blindness.

It is a pity to skip even one line of this transcendent scene. But we must. What a descent from king and warrior to this very foolish fond old man, fourscore and upward, who senses that he is not in his perfect mind! But what an ascent—what a perfect mind in comparison! He begins to realize vaguely that he is still on earth:

LEAR: Do not laugh at me;
    For, as I am a man, I think this lady
    To be my child Cordelia.
COR.:   And so I am, I am.
LEAR: Be your tears wet? Yes, faith. I pray, weep not.
    If you have poison for me, I will drink it.
    I know you do not love me; for your sisters
    Have, as I do remember, done me wrong:
    You have some cause, they have not.

"No cause, no cause," replies Cordelia: a divine lie that will shine forever beside the one Desdemona uttered with her last breath. "Am I in France?" Lear asks at last, coming back to earth. "In your own kingdom, sir," Kent replies, meaning England, of course; but we know that Shakespeare means also that Lear is now in a kingdom not of this earth. And in a moment more the scene closes—and the act. It would seem as if poetry could go no further, and yet it is scarcely an exaggeration to say that this scene is nothing in comparison with what Shakespeare still has in store for us in the scene to which this one specifically leads up.

X

The event which determines everything else in the last act is the battle between the British and the French. But what a battle! Except for the quick passage of the French forces over the stage, with an alarum and a retreat, it all takes place behind the scenes and exactly one line of the text is devoted to the account of it:

    King Lear hath lost, he and his daughter ta'en.

The brevity of it is a measure of how insignificant the mere clash of arms becomes in comparison with the moral convulsion that is its cause, and the strife between and within the human beings who are its agents. Shakespeare is here tracking Force into its inmost lair. To have stressed the merely military would have thrown his whole drama out of focus. Cordelia, for all her heroic strength, is no Joan of Arc, and it would have blotted our image of her to have spotted it with blood. Instead, we remember the final lines of *King John*, and, forgetting entirely that France is invading England, think only of the battle between love and treason. Even Albany, in effect, fights on the other side. His hand is compelled to defend his land against the invader, but his heart is with the King:

            Where I could not be honest
    I never yet was valiant.

Ubi honestas, ibi patria.

Lear and Cordelia are led in captive. But for him, she would be ready to "out-frown false Fortune's frown," and, as it is, she is willing to confront her captors. But all that he begs is to spend the rest of his life with her in prison. That will be paradise enough, and the words in which he tastes that joy in imagination are one of the crests of all poetry. Shakespeare in the course of his life had many times paid his ironic respects to worldly greatness and temporal power, but it may be doubted whether he ever did it more crushingly than in the last lines of this daydream of a broken old king who had himself so recently been one of "the great." Lear's words are elicited by Cordelia's glorious challenge to Fortune, which exhibits her at the opposite pole from Hamlet with his weak attempt to rationalize Fate into the "divinity that shapes our ends." Cordelia will be fooled by no such verbal self-deception. "For if the trumpet give an uncertain sound, who shall prepare himself to the battle?" Cordelia's ringing sentences are the very stuff into which the pugnacity of the race ought to be sublimated:

COR.:   We are not the first
      Who with best meaning have incurr'd the worst.
      For thee, oppressed king, am I cast down;
      Myself could else out-frown false Fortune's frown.
      Shall we not see these daughters and these sisters?
LEAR: No, no, no, no! Come, let's away to prison;
      We two alone will sing like birds i' the cage.
      When thou dost ask me blessing, I'll kneel down,
      And ask of thee forgiveness. So we'll live,
      And pray, and sing, and tell old tales, and laugh
      At gilded butterflies, and hear poor rogues
      Talk of court news; and we'll talk with them too,
      Who loses and who wins; who's in, who's out;
      And take upon 's the mystery of things,
      As if we were God's spies: *and we'll wear out,*
      In a wall'd prison, packs and sects of great ones
      That ebb and flow by the moon.

Even Shakespeare seldom concentrated thought as he did in those last lines. "That ebb and flow by the moon": what indeed is the rise and fall of the mighty but just that, the meaningless coming in and going out of a tide, never registering any gain, forever canceling itself out to all eternity? And who are these mighty? "Packs and sects of great ones." Into those half-dozen words the poet condenses his condemnation of three of the forces he most detests: (1) the mob, which is nothing but the human counterpart of the pack; (2) that spirit which, in opposition to the one that makes the whole world kin, puts its own sect or party above humanity; and (3) "greatness," or worldly place and power. Under each or any of these dispensations the harmony man dreams of is denied. The mob is its destroyer. The sect or party is its defier. Power is its counterfeiter. And the extremes meet, for power rests on the conquest and subservience of the mob. In the face of such might, what can the imprisoned spirits of tenderness and beauty do? "We'll wear out. . . ." And it does indeed sometimes seem as if all they can do is to wear it out with patience, even as the weak ancestors of man outwore, by outlasting, the dynasties of now extinct "great ones," the mastodons and saber-toothed tigers that dominated the earth in an earlier geologic age.

But Shakespeare, however profound his reverence for patience, does not leave it at that. His phrase, in this scene, for the opposite of packs and sects and great ones is "the common bosom," and Edmund does not intend—any more than Claudius did in Hamlet's case—that pity for the old King shall be able

> To pluck the common bosom on his side,

or that the general love for Cordelia shall have a like effect.

> Her very silence and her patience
> Speak to the people, and they pity her.

It might still be Edmund speaking of Cordelia. Actually the words are uttered of Rosalind by her envious uncle. As they show, a turn of Fortune's wheel could easily have converted the play of which she is the heroine into tragedy, and Rosalind herself into a Cordelia. She would have met the test, too! Meanwhile, Edmund is as relentless as the usurping Duke in *As You Like It*. His retort to Lear's mental picture of his final days with Cordelia is an abrupt

> Take them away,

and a moment later we are given a typical glimpse of one of Lear's "great ones" in action, as Edmund promises advancement to a captain if he will carry out his bloody purpose.

EDM.:   Know thou this, that men
        Are as the time is; to be tender-minded
        Does not become a sword. Thy great employment
        Will not bear question; either say thou'lt do 't,
        Or thrive by other means.
CAPT.:   I'll do 't, my lord . . .
        I cannot draw a cart, nor eat dried oats;
        If it be man's work, I'll do 't.

XI

The dying Edmund, mortally wounded by Edgar in their duel, changes his mind too late. Edgar's account of their father's death of mingled grief and joy obviously touches him. It is as if the incipient prompting to goodness that may for just a moment be detected in Iago in the presence of Desdemona had survived into another life and come to bud in Edmund. When the deaths of Goneril and Regan are announced, deeply moved again, he exclaims:

> I was contracted to them both. All three
> Now marry in an instant,

and when the bodies of the two sisters—one poisoned by the other, the other self-slain—are brought in, the balance is finally tipped:

> I pant for life. Some good I mean to do,
> Despite of mine own nature.

He attempts to rescind his fatal order.* But in vain, as we see a moment later when Lear enters with the dead Cordelia in his arms. "Dead as earth," he pronounces her. And yet the next second he is willing to believe that she may still be revived. He calls for a looking glass to see if her breath will mist it, and Kent, gazing at the pathetic picture, cries: "Is this the promis'd end?" "Or image of that horror?" echoes Edgar, while Albany begs the heavens to "fall, and cease!" All three utterances converge to prove that this is indeed Shakespeare's version of the Last Judgment.

Failing a mirror, Lear holds a feather to Cordelia's lips:

> This feather stirs; she lives! If it be so,
> It is a chance which does redeem all sorrows
> That ever I have felt

(words that must on no account be forgotten). Kent, and then Edgar, bend above the old man, but Lear, intent on his work of resuscitation, waves them away. They have jostled him at the critical moment, he thinks:

> A plague upon you, murderers, traitors all!
> I might have sav'd her; now she's gone for ever!

The test of breath, of touch, has failed. But there still remains the test of hearing:

> Cordelia, Cordelia! stay a little. Ha!
> What is't thou say'st? Her voice was ever soft,

* Bradley and Stoll both think the delay of Edmund is a sacrifice of reality to stage effect. I should say, on the contrary, that it is motivated with the very nicest gradations.

Gentle, and low; an excellent thing in woman.
I kill'd the slave that was a-hanging thee.

And an officer standing by confirms him:

'Tis true, my lords, he did.

The officer's word causes Lear to look up, and he gazes with groping vision at Kent. "See better, Lear," Kent had bade his master, we recall, when he rejected Cordelia. Lear has followed that injunction: he recognizes his friend and servant. (But of that we have already spoken.) "Your eldest daughters," Kent goes on,

have fordone themselves,
And desperately are dead.

And Lear, as though he had known it for a thousand years, replies with an indifference as sublime as if a granite cliff were told that an insect had dashed itself to death against its base:

Ay, so I think.

"He knows not what he says," Albany observes, and while Edmund's death is announced, Shakespeare, as if perceiving that the scene should inspire anyone who participates in it in the theater, leaves to the actor the immense freedom of devising business for Lear that shall bridge the dozen lines that the others speak. Albany, by right of succession, is now entitled to the throne. Seeking to make what amends he can, he steps aside:

For us, we will resign,
During the life of this old majesty,
To him our absolute power.

Lear is again to be king! His reign, however, as Albany does not know, is to be a matter of seconds. But what is time except for what it contains? and into those seconds is to be crowded such a wonder as never occurred in the longest reign ever chronicled of the most venerable of earth's kings.

What Lear has been doing while Albany is speaking is left, as I said, to the imagination, but that it is something profoundly moving is indicated by the sudden, "O, see, see!" with which Albany interrupts the train of his thought. And thereupon Lear begins what is possibly the most poetically pathetic speech existing in the English, if not in any, language:

And my poor fool is hang'd!

are his first words. . . . Hundreds of other words have been written about those six. Do they refer to the Fool, or to Cordelia?

Why did Shakespeare create one of the most beautiful and appealing of his characters—perhaps his masterpiece in the amalgamation of the tragic and the comic—only to drop him completely out a little past the middle of the play? To those who think Lear remembers his faithful jester at the end, those six words are the answer: he dropped him out precisely in order to stress this parting allusion to him. But why was the Fool hanged? And why, at this supreme moment, should Lear have a thought for anything but what is in his arms? No—another school of interpreters, a vast majority, tells us— "poor fool" is a colloquial term of endearment, and it is Cordelia to whom it is applied. Yet I challenge anyone in his heart of heart to deny that, so taken, *at such a moment* the phrase jars. Furthermore, Shakespeare is not in the habit of sending us to our glossaries at such emotional pinnacles: he has too sure a sense of what is permanent in language.

The solution of the enigma is simple. Remember the Third Murderer in *Macbeth*. Surely the whole point of the phrase is that Lear is referring to both Cordelia and the Fool. His wandering mind has confused them, if you will. But what a divine confusion! Has *wedded* them would be the better word. Think how the Fool loved his master! Think how he adored Cordelia and pined away after she went to France! Surely this is the main reason for Shakespeare's banishing the Fool from his play—that he might reappear united to Cordelia on his dear master's lips:

> Where dead men meet, on lips of living men.

In what other Heaven would the Fool have preferred to meet those other two? "Let me not to the marriage of true minds admit impediments."

> All three
> Now marry in an instant.

Goneril, Regan, Edmund. Cordelia, Lear, the Fool. (And the supererogatory Nahum Tate thought this drama lacked a love story, and proceeded to concoct one between Edgar and Cordelia!)

But the union of Cordelia and the Fool is but the first act of King Lear's reign. The restored King goes on speaking, holding his child's body closer as it grows colder. The tests of touch and hearing have failed.

> No, no, no life!
> Why should a dog, a horse, a rat, have life,
> And thou no breath at all? Thou'lt come no more,
> Never, never, never, never, never!

—a last line that fathoms the nadir of annihilation as utterly as that earlier

> kill, kill, kill, kill, kill, kill,

had touched the nadir of revenge. . . . But the uprush of emotion has been too much for the old man:

> Pray you, undo this button. Thank you, sir.

Lear has lifted his head while the service was performed. Now he looks down again at what is in his arms. And on the instant, like a bolt of divine lightning—that "lightning before death" of which Romeo told—the Truth descends:

> Do you see this? Look on her, look, her lips,
> Look there, look there!

Cordelia lives! The Third Test—of vision—has not failed, and those earlier words echo through our minds:

> She lives! If it be so,
> It is a chance which does redeem all sorrows
> That ever I have felt.

And Lear, clasping his restored child to his heart, falls "dead" of joy.* For all its sound and fury, this story at least is not a tale told by an idiot, signifying nothing. And here the rest is not silence.

XII

On the contrary, it will be said, Lear's delusion only makes the blackness blacker, another night fallen on mid-night. For *we* know that Cordelia *is* dead.

We do? How do we? And if we do, we know more than Shakespeare. For like a shower of golden arrows flying from every angle and every distance to a single target, every line of the play—almost—has been cunningly devised to answer our skepticism, to demonstrate that Lear is right and we are wrong. Why but to make the old King's dying assertion incontrovertible does Shakespeare so permeate his play with the theme of vision?

Only consider for a moment the grounds the poet has given—pre-eminently in this play, but also in all he had written from the beginning—for having faith in the testimony of Lear's imagination.

First—though least important and not indispensable to the point—Lear is an old old man, and Shakespeare has over and over indicated his adherence to the world-old view that age, which is a synonym for experience, coupled with a good life, brings insight and truth. Adam, in *As You Like It*

---

* Note how the death of Gloucester, whose heart "burst smilingly," prepares for Lear's.

It was Bradley, I think, who first pointed out that Lear dies of joy, not grief. A rare insight. But to leave it at that is to leave the harvest of that insight ungarnered.

(a part that Shakespeare himself may have played), Priam in *Troilus and Cressida*, Belarius in *Cymbeline*, or the Old Tenant who aids Gloucester in this very play are good examples. Lear has had long experience; and if he was tardy in attaining the good life, he has at least packed enough virtue into its last days to compensate for its previous failure. Here we have at least a foundation for a faith in Lear's power to see the truth. The wisdom of experience. The wisdom of old age.

But there is something more cogent than that.

Second, Shakespeare believes that suffering and affliction, to those at least who will give ear, bring power to see things as they are. To prove that in detail would be to pass his Tragedies in review. With what clairvoyance Othello, for example, sees the truth at the moment when he begs to be washed in steep-down gulfs of liquid fire. With what prophetic power Queen Margaret foresees the doom of the House of York. "Nothing almost sees miracles but misery," says Kent, at night, in the stocks, confident of sunrise. By which rule, laid down in this very play, Lear at the moment of supreme misery might be expected to see the supreme miracle. He does. To the vision and wisdom of old age are added the vision and wisdom of misery.

But Lear, if he is an old and a miserable, is also a dying, man; and if there is any ancient belief that Shakespeare credits, it is that "truth sits upon the lips of dying men." Over and over he has said it: "Holy men at their death have good inspirations";

> The tongues of dying men
> Enforce attention like deep harmony;

and over and over he has illustrated it in the death scenes, whether in bed or on the battlefield, of his plays:

> The setting sun, and music at the close,
> As the last taste of sweets, is sweetest last.

There is a human counterpart of the legend of the dying swan, or that legend, rather, is a symbol of this human truth. Even worldly men and women, like Warwick or Henry IV, if they regret or repent, may see their lives at last in something like true perspective, and evil ones, like Cardinal Beaufort, Lady Macbeth, or Edmund in this play, may confess, or may face the truth in nightmare or terror. The vision of death is a *third* form of inspired seeing.

And a fourth is the vision of insanity. Primitives, instead of degrading them as we do, worship the insane, holding that madness is in touch with the gods.

> Some madness is divinest sense,

says Emily Dickinson. *Some* madness. The fact that there is plenty of insanity of the infernal brand has not blinded poets to the same truth that primitives accept too indiscriminately. As with crime, so with mental abnormality, it is certain species of it only that are of tragic interest: the madness of Orestes, of Cassandra, of Don Quixote, of Kirillov and Ivan Karamazov. Lear, sane, is exiled from the truth. His egotism is intolerable. He is devoid of sympathy. It is Lear of so-called sound mind who disinherits Cordelia, banishes Kent, and curses Goneril. But as his mind begins to break, truth begins to break in on it. Indeed, Shakespeare chooses Lear's shattered brain as the vehicle of not a few of his own profoundest convictions, mixed, it is true, with wild ravings, as lightning is with wind and night. After the restoration to him of Cordelia, he is never again incoherent, and he never utters a word that does not enforce attention either by its truth or its pathos. But his mind is not in normal condition, and, just before his dying speech, Shakespeare is careful, for our guidance, to have Albany remark,

> He knows not what he says.

His last flash of insight is the perception of a supernormal mind.

Or better, it may be, of a *childlike* mind. For Lear, after the return of sanity, is in his second childhood, not in the ordinary sense of being afflicted with stupidity and dulness, but in the rarer sense of being gifted with a second innocence and ingenuousness, as if he had indeed been born again.* And so at the end it is more strictly the wisdom of simplicity than the wisdom of insanity with which he is crowned. The artlessness—not to say monosyllabic bareness, considering the tragic intensity effected—of his last speeches, especially the last of all, has often been the subject of comment. Shakespeare has already familiarized us with the insight of simplicity in scores of humorous and humble characters from Launce to Desdemona, always differentiating it sharply from commonness or uncouthness. In the present play, Edgar and the Fool are strikingly simple but penetratingly wise.

And so on that last line and a half of Lear's role are concentrated, like sunbeams by a burning glass, the inspired visions of old age, of misery, of death, of insanity and simplicity, to put beyond the possibility of challenge the truth of what Lear at this extremest moment *sees*.

> Death but our rapt attention
> To immortality.

* Emerson, in his last days, was "broken" in this beautiful sense.

It might have been this last scene of *King Lear*, with the father intent on nothing but what he saw on his daughter's lips, that elicited those astounding seven words of Emily Dickinson's.

> Prove true, imagination, O, prove true!

prayed Viola. So prayed Shakespeare, and, by writing *King Lear*, helped answer his own prayer. This is Keats's "truth of Imagination." Like Cordelia's, its voice is ever soft, gentle, and low, and the din of the world easily makes it inaudible. But in the end, Shakespeare seems to say, it is the only voice worth listening to. How many other wise men have said the same thing! "Power to appreciate faint, fainter, and infinitely faintest voices and visions," says Emerson, "is what distinguishes man from man." And Thoreau, improving even upon Emerson, exclaims: "I will attend the faintest sound, and then declare to man what God hath meant." This is the "genuine" way of knowing which Democritus differentiates from the "obscure" way. "Whenever the obscure way has reached the minimum sensible of hearing, smell, taste, and touch," Democritus asserts, "and when the investigation must be carried farther into that which is still finer, then arises the genuine way of knowing, which has a finer organ of thought." *King Lear* might have been written to make that distinction clear.

Such a piling-up of persuasions as we have been reviewing might seem sufficient. But it is not for Shakespeare. For him, there is still the obverse side of the coin. The objective must supplement the subjective. Not content with showing that Lear is capable at death of spiritual vision, Shakespeare must also show that there is spirit *there* to be seen.

But here we have forestalled the demonstration—for precisely this is what we have already abundantly seen. Why, all through the play, has Shakespeare exercised the last resources of his art to make us conscious of Cordelia's presence even when she is invisible, except in preparation for the end?

> You are a spirit, I know.

So we too say, and if we did not at that moment add to Lear's assertion his question, "When did you die?" it is only because the restoration scene is but a rehearsal of the death scene. In *it* all the poetical forces that verify Lear's first vision of Cordelia as a spirit come back with compound interest to verify his last one. Cordelia lived in the Fool's imagination, and in her father's before death; the Fool is united with Cordelia in his master's imagination at death; Cordelia still lives in Lear's imagination after death. And she lives in ours. In all these ways, Shakespeare confers upon her existence in the Imagination itself, which, as William Blake saw, is only our human word for Eternity. "Love without Imagination is eternal death." From *Julius Caesar* on, Shakespeare's faith in the existence of spiritual entities beyond the range of ordinary consciousness, and hence objective to it, increases in steady crescendo. Of his belief in the reality of infernal spirits, he has long left us in no doubt. In the storm scene of *Othello*, and in the "divine" Desdemona, we can sense the coming of the last scene of *King Lear*. But in *King Lear* more unequivocally even than in *Othello*—however embryonically from the merely human point of view—he asserts the reality of a celestial spirit. The debased current use of the word "imagination" must not be permitted to confuse us. The imagination is not a faculty for the creation of illusion; it is the faculty by which alone man apprehends reality. The "illusion" turns out to be the truth. "Let faith oust fact," as Starbuck says in *Moby-Dick*. It is only our absurd "scientific" prejudice that reality must be physical and rational that blinds us to the truth.

And right here lies the reason for the numerous references to the lower animals in *King Lear*. They are so used as to suggest that the evil characters of the play have slipped back from the human kingdom to the kingdom of beasts and brutes. Goneril, for instance, shows whither Henry V's injunction to imitate the action of the tiger ultimately leads. She has become a tiger. Hyenas, wolves, serpents—men under slavery to passion pass back into them by atavism; yet it is an insult to these subrational creatures to compare human abortions like Regan and Cornwall to them, and Shakespeare seems to be asking himself, as Bradley so admirably expresses it,

whether that which he loathes in man may not be due to some strange wrenching of this frame of things, through which the lower animal souls have found a lodgment in human forms, and there found—to the horror and confusion of the thinking mind—brains to forge, tongues to speak, and hands to act, enormities which no mere brute can conceive or execute.

Er nennt's Vernunft und braucht's allein,
Nur tierischer als jedes Tier zu sein,

says Goethe of man. For this monstrous state of affairs words stronger than brutal or bestial, infernal words, are demanded. Albany feels this when he calls his own wife a devil:

ALB.:   See thyself, devil!
          Proper deformity seems not in the fiend
          So horrid as in woman.
GON.:   O vain fool!
ALB.: Thou changed and self-cover'd thing, for shame!
          Be-monster not thy feature. Were 't my fitness
          To let these hands obey my blood,

They are apt enough to dislocate and tear
Thy flesh and bones. Howe'er thou art a fiend,
A woman's shape doth shield thee.

If this is not the doctrine of "possession," what is it? To Albany, Goneril is not a woman in the shape of a fiend, but a fiend in the shape of a woman. The distinction may seem slight or merely verbal: actually it involves two opposite views of the universe.

And so the play takes on what may be called an evolutionary or hier-archical character—but more in a transmigratory than in a Darwinian sense —with the dramatic persons on an ascending and descending scale, from the evil sisters and their accomplices at the bottom up through Albany and Edgar and Kent to the Fool, the transformed Lear, and Cordelia at the top. "O! the difference of man and man!" The effect is indeed Cosmic, as if the real battle were being fought over men's heads by devils and angels, and as if man's freedom (yet how could he crave more?) consisted, as in *Macbeth*, not in any power to affect the issue by his "own" strength, but rather in the right to stand, as he wills, in the light or in the shadow, to be possessed, as he chooses, by spirits dark or bright.

XIII

Spirits! The word sends us back to the Ghost in *Hamlet*. What a contrast! The son kneeling to the spirit of his father; the father kneeling to the spirit of his child. The warrior demanding vengeance in stentorian tones that every man and woman in the theater can hear and understand; the daughter breathing reconciliation in a voice so low that no one in the theater can hear—the only evidence to auditor or reader of its existence being its reflection in the voice and face and gestures of him who bends over her, when, though he cannot hear, he sees the movement of Life on her lips.

In this scene is finally registered the immense advance that Shakespeare's own vision had taken since *Hamlet*. From *Romeo and Juliet*, or earlier, to *Hamlet*, and perhaps beyond, Shakespeare held, so far as we can tell, that the human ideal, as Hamlet said, lay in a proper commingling of blood and judgment. But he grew wiser as he grew older. Blood is life itself. It is heat, intensity, passion, driving force: it is our inheritance from an indefinitely long animal and human past with all its vast capacity—for good, yes, but especially for rapacity and destruction. And that enormous energy is to be ruled by judgment! Judgment: what a colorless abstraction beside red blood!—as if a charging stallion were to be turned aside not by a bit but by politely calling his attention to the danger of his speed and fury. It just will not do. Hamlet himself discovered too late the terrible inadequacy of "reason" in this sense. And so did Shakespeare—but not too late. The infinite can be controlled only by the infinite—by something of its own order. In *Othello*, *Macbeth*, and *King Lear* invisible and superhuman spiritual agencies have taken the place of judgment as the hoped-for curb of blood. Love, tenderness, patience, forgiveness are our too too human names for the manifestations within human life of something which comes as incontrovertibly from what is beyond and above it as the appetites do from what is beyond and below. Because these rare words are tarnished with hypocrisy and soiled by daily misuse, they lose their power—until a Shakespeare comes along to bring them to life in a Desdemona or a Cordelia.

But it would be wrong to the point of grotesqueness to suggest that he implies that reason has no place. It has, he seems to be saying, but it is a secondary one. Reason is what we have to fall back on when imagination fails—as we have to fall back on touch when eyesight fails. Or, in another figure, reason is the bush that saves us from plunging down the declivity, not the wings that enable us to soar in safety above it. Such wings only some brighter spirit, like Dante's Beatrice, can bestow. Cordelia is one—of the first magnitude. *King Lear* is Hell, Earth, and Heaven in one. It is Shakespeare's reconciliation of blood and spirit, his union of the Red Rose and the White.

XIV

From *Henry VI* onward, Shakespeare never ceased to be concerned with the problem of chaos, or, as we would be more likely to say today, of disintegration. Sometimes it may be no more than a hint of chaos in an outburst of individual passion or social disorder. Often it is chaos under its extreme aspects of insanity or war. Always the easy and obvious remedy for chaos is force. But the best force can do is to impose order, not to elicit harmony, and Shakespeare spurns such a superficial and temporizing solution. "How with this rage," he perpetually asks,

> How with this rage shall beauty hold a plea,
> Whose action is no stronger than a flower?

In play after play he pits some seemingly fragile representative of beauty against the forces of inertia and destruction: a dream, the spirit of innocence or play, love, art—whether as poetry, drama, or music especially. Force and Imagination: they are the ultimate foes. Force or Imagination: that is the ultimate choice. But always up to *King Lear* the conflict seemed to fall short of finality. It remained for Shakespeare's supreme play to oppose physical force with imagination in its quintessential form of metaphysical Vision. Not only does the poet incarnate that struggle in the action of the drama; he has the Duke of Albany state it in so many words.

Anyone who reads those words, if he notices them at all, thinks he understands them. But it may be questioned whether he can understand them unless he reads them in the light of those other words, the last utterance of King Lear, to which, as I have tried to show, the entire tragedy in a sense leads up.

In this, his version of The Last Judgment, Shakespeare has demonstrated that hatred and revenge are a plucking-out of the human imagination as fatal to man's power to find his way in the universe as Cornwall's plucking out of Gloucester's eyes was to the guidance of his body on earth. The exhibition, in fearful detail, of this self-devouring process is what makes *King Lear* to many readers the most hopeless of Shakespeare's plays. But *King Lear* also exhibits and demonstrates something else. It shows that there is a mode of seeing as much higher than physical eyesight as physical eyesight is than touch, an insight that bestows power to see "things invisible to mortal sight" as certainly as Lear saw that Cordelia lives after her death.

What is the relation between these two aspects of Shakespeare's Last Judgment?

He states it with the utmost exactitude in the words of Albany to which I have referred. The last three of the five lines that make up this passage I have already quoted. The first two, as those familiar with the text may have noted, I omitted at that time. I suppressed them intentionally. Albany says:

> If that the heavens do not their visible spirits
> Send quickly down to tame these vile offences,
> It will come,
> Humanity must perforce prey on itself,
> Like monsters of the deep.

Such is the predestined end of humanity, if the heavens do not send down their spirits and if those to whom they are sent down do not achieve the power to see them. If the heavens do not. . . . But the heavens did—and King Lear did not fail them.

> You are a spirit, I know. When did you die? . . .
> Do you see this? Look on her, look, her lips,
> Look there, look there!

And so, in *King Lear* at least, humanity did not devour itself, and King Lear and his child were lifted up into the realm of the gods.

King Lear takes us captive. That is what it ought to do and what we ought to let it do, for only as we give ourselves up to it will it give itself up to us. "Enthusiastic admiration," says Blake, "is the first principle of knowledge, and its last." And it is right too that we should wish to share our wonder. "O! see, see!" cries Albany over the dying Lear. "Look there, look there!" cries the dying Lear over the dead Cordelia. This play draws those same exclamations about itself from everyone who feels its power. But that does not mean that anyone has the right to insist that his way of taking it is the only possible one. I hope that I have myself given no impression of speaking "the truth" about *King Lear* in this sense. All I have wanted to do is to point out the figures I see moving in this fiery furnace of Shakespeare's imagination, in the hope, naturally, that others may see them too. But if others do not see them, for them they are not there. Far be it from me in that case to assert that I am right and they are wrong. If, as the old King bends over his child and sees that she still lives, he is deluded and those who know that she is dead are right, then indeed is *King Lear*, as many believe, the darkest document in the supreme poetry of the world. And perhaps it is. There come moods in which anyone is inclined to take it in that sense. But they are not our best moods. And the chief reason, next to the compulsion of my own imagination, why I believe I have at least done no violence to Shakespeare's text is that I have so often witnessed the effect on youth of this reading of the final scene of his tragic masterpiece. I have already quoted the words of one such young person on first coming under its spell. They are worth repeating:

"*King Lear* is a miracle. There is nothing in the whole world that is not in this play. It says everything, and if this is the last and final judgment on this world we live in, then it is a miraculous world. This is a miracle play."

Chapter XXX

Timon of Athens

I

Timon of Athens is one of the doubtful plays in the sense that its Shakespearean authorship has often been questioned. It was apparently put in the First Folio to take the place of *Troilus and Cressida* when that play was moved from the position originally assigned to it among the Tragedies. This fact lends a certain plausibility to the view that someone besides Shakespeare may have had a hand in its composition, a view which, in turn, is given some support by the disparity in merit between its best and its worst passages.

Yet it is beyond comprehension how anyone could doubt that Timon himself, and hence the central conception and impact of the play, is a product of Shakespeare's imagination. The date of the work is not known. But it seems to be related to *King Lear* somewhat as *Troilus and Cressida* is to *Hamlet*. If *Troilus* may be called the intellectual twin of *Hamlet*, *Timon* might be called the emotional twin of *King Lear* (or better perhaps its dark satellite). The generalization of course immensely oversimplifies the truth, to say nothing of the fact that there is plenty of emotion in *Troilus* and plenty of thought in *Timon*. It might be closer to the truth to say that the two plays appear to be safety valves through which Shakespeare blew off excess thought and emotion, in the case of *Troilus* partly for the edification of a special audience, in that of *Timon* mainly perhaps for his own relief. In the latter play he seems to let himself go and to express through the mouth of Timon exactly what he thought and how he felt about humanity at some moment of mingled anger and disillusionment —disillusionment, however, not with life but with mankind, particularly with senators and their associates among the nobility. "All covered dishes!" a Second Lord exclaims at the banquet of lukewarm water Timon has prepared for his former friends. The symbolism is plain, though the Second Lord is unconscious of what he has said. When a man lets himself go, as Shakespeare apparently did in the character of Timon, we learn much about him.

However far his imagination may carry him beyond it, a poet must begin with his own experience, and it seems reasonable to believe that a dramatic poet conceives characters that are on the whole alien to his own personality by noting within himself evanescent moods or attitudes and asking himself what sort of person he would be if such transitory effects were to become frequent or permanent. *Timon of Athens* sounds like an extreme embodiment of that scorn of humanity of which flashes are observable in Shakespeare's works almost from the beginning, that contempt which in *Hamlet* and the "dark" Comedies and some of the *Sonnets* becomes conspicuous—the "contempt" Beatrice saved herself from by bidding it "farewell"—that fierce indignation which ever and anon shows there was a Jonathan Swift buried in the gentle Shakespeare, ready to erupt. In *Timon of Athens* he did erupt. Timon himself shows in what direction Shakespeare might have been carried if he had surrendered to bitter thoughts and emotions instead of controlling them, if he had thrown up the dramatic profession in despair. By contrast with his greatest masterpieces this play reveals how great was the restraint behind them, how superior imagination is to moral teaching or the schematism of conscious thought.

> What is your substance, whereof are you made,
> That millions of strange shadows on you tend?

We do not ask that of *Timon of Athens* as we do of *King Lear*.

Yet how much of Shakespeare this play echoes, or recapitulates! It is as much a satire on Commodity as *King John*: "Policy sits above conscience." It is at one with *The Merchant of Venice* on money and avarice, on the contrast between gold without and gold within. In a different key it says what *As You Like It* and *Cymbeline* say on the superiority of nature and simplicity to courts and flattery. In its portrayal of idealism turned sour and tinged with madness it is akin to *Hamlet*. Like *Hamlet*, too, it is a revenge play, but there it is still closer to *Coriolanus* with its picture of the embittered patriot turning against his country. Apemantus would be enough to tie it to *Troilus* by his combined resemblance to and sharp differentiation from Thersites, even if many passages in it did not remind us of the earlier play in thought and spirit. But as we began by saying, it is closest of all to *King Lear*, so close that much of it might have been made of rejected fragments of that play. Its central theme of ingratitude, its curses, its condemnation of flattery, its stress on the faithful servant, its references to the lower animals, its idea that misery leads to illumination, that loss is gain, and its final note of forgiveness and reconciliation are just a few of the things that link it to its mightier counterpart.

The style of *Timon of Athens* is frequently highly aphoristic, and the play is packed with brief telling phrases that are either of Shakespearean mintage or extraordinarily successful counterfeits of it: "minute-jacks," "time's flies," "feast-won, fast-lost," "high-vic'd city," "the common lag of people," "icy precepts of respect," the "bright defiler" (gold), "traffic's thy god," "you must eat men," "livelier than life," "now's a time," and dozens of others. The resemblance to what is certainly Shakespeare's often becomes minutely verbal, an extreme example being the remark to the jester of one of the servants:

> Thou art not altogether a fool,

which is almost verbatim Kent's

> This is not altogether fool, my lord.

But the most convincing, if the most imponderable, evidence in this matter of authorship is musical. Compare, for instance, the rhythm of "that's villanous, *and shows a most pitiful ambition in the fool that uses it*," from Hamlet's advice to the players with the last clause of this speech of the Painter's: "To promise is most courtly and fashionable; performance is a kind of will or testament *which argues a great sickness in his judgement that makes it*." Or match Timandra's words to the fallen Timon:

> Is this the Athenian minion, whom the world
> Voic'd so regardfully?

with Lodovico's on the falling Othello:

> Is this the noble Moor, whom our full senate
> Call all in all sufficient?

Such resemblances will mean little to those not given to listening for echoes. But to those who are, it is the same voice. And few things identify like a voice.

Finally, the underplot in which Alcibiades is central has just the illuminating relationship to the main story that is characteristic of Shakespeare. It expresses in extraordinarily direct language ideas which Shakespeare elsewhere insinuates more clandestinely.

II

The fifth scene of Act III is a perfect little play within a play that repeats the main situation in *Measure for Measure*, tinctured with a strong likeness to the occasion when Henry V tries out the three traitors, and with remoter echoes of the court scene in *The Merchant of Venice*. Alcibiades, the warrior of the piece, intercedes with the Athenian senate in behalf of a friend of his,

> who, in hot blood,
> Hath stepp'd into the law,

extenuating the offense because the man did not "soil the fact with cowardice." We are given few details, but gather that it was an affair of honor, that the friend acted in self-defense and killed his adversary. The senators are unmoved by Alcibiades' plea. You sound as if you were trying to make an ugly deed look fair, to bring manslaughter into good repute, the First Senator objects:

> You cannot make gross sins look clear;
> To revenge is no valour, but to bear.

The senator's plain implication is that Alcibiades' friend should have swallowed the affront. . . . Why, then, if there is such virtue in forbearance, Alcibiades wants to know, should we ever expose ourselves in battle? Why not endure all threats, and let the enemy quietly cut our throats while we are sleeping? A question as disturbing to a judge as to a soldier.

> To kill, I grant, is sin's extremest gust,

Alcibiades admits, but this man has "slain in fight many of your enemies." Therefore, he should be spared. A curious syllogism. And the senators are equally illogical. The Second Senator, in a highly intemperate speech, accuses Alcibiades' friend not of the crime in question but of a general sin of intemperance, while the First Senator, who a moment before was praising forbearance and denouncing vengeance, announces laconically: "He dies." At least, then, let him sell his forfeited life on the battlefield, pleads Alcibiades:

> If by this crime he owes the law his life,
> Why, let the war receive 't in valiant gore;
> For law is strict, and war is nothing more.

But the First Senator is obdurate, and, as if bent on confirming Alcibiades' opinion that war does not exceed law in rigor, he reiterates:

> We are for law. He dies . . .
> He forfeits his own blood that spills another.

The senator-judge does not pause to consider how well or how ill these two assertions hang together, but the fury to which he gives way when Alcibiades persists in his suit is a manifest confession that his heart gets the connection if his head does not. "We banish thee forever," he cries, duplicating the psychology of Lear's banishment of Kent. And to stifle his conscience and further assuage his pride, he sets forward the execution date of the man he has just condemned to death. Alcibiades, when the senators have departed, relieves his feelings in turn by calling them, in effect, exactly what they are—a set of hypocritical old profiteers:

> I am worse than mad: I have kept back their foes,
> While they have told their money and let out
> Their coin upon large interest,

and anticipating the situation in *Coriolanus*, Athens' strongest man, like Rome's, swears vengeance on his native city. The entire scene is a tissue of contradictions expressly contrived, one would suppose, to set us thinking of the relations of crime, law, war, and justice.

III

And the same thematic thread runs through Timon's part in the drama. Timon is not banished from Athens by law; but, overcome by the ingratitude of the false friends who flattered and fawned upon him in his prosperity only to desert him utterly at the first whisper of adversity, he banishes himself. We behold him outside the walls of the "detestable town" he has left, calling down confusion on it and begging the wolves that are its inhabitants to indulge in every outrage and atrocity.

> Bound servants, steal!

he cries,

> Large-handed robbers your grave masters are,
> And pill by law.

There, in so many words, is that moral identification of common theft with grosser but more respectable forms of robbery which, I am convinced, is the key to *Henry V*.

In the next scene in which Timon figures we find him standing on the seashore indulging in a tirade that sounds like a contemptuous refutation of Ulysses' famous utterance on "degree." According to Timon, it is not reverence for order, as Ulysses at first held, but a vile combination of envy and obeisance that accounts for the stratification of mankind:

> Who dares, who dares,
> In purity of manhood stand upright
> And say, "This man's a flatterer"? If one be,
> So are they all; for every grise of fortune
> Is smooth'd by that below. The learned pate
> Ducks to the golden fool; all is oblique;
> There's nothing level in our cursed natures
> But direct villany. Therefore, be abhorr'd
> All feasts, societies, and throngs of men!
> His semblable, yea, himself, Timon disdains.
> Destruction fang mankind!

Whereupon he begins digging in the earth for roots, and finds—gold.

The discovery of the precious metal is of critical importance, for, if it is his mere reversal of worldly estate that has precipitated Timon's misanthropy, with the restoration of riches he may be expected to revert to his former frame of mind. But Timon is no fool of time. Like Swift's, his abhorrence of his kind has deeper and more idealistic roots. He stands the test, and will use the treasure earth has yielded him, not to reinstate himself in Athens but to prove the universal corruptibility of man. The rest of the play is, in large part, given to this trial by gold of various groups and individuals who visit Timon in his banishment. The symmetry employed here, as in earlier parts of the play, which carries us back to *The Comedy of Errors*, adds to its parabolic at the same time that it detracts from its dramatic effect.

First, Alcibiades and his two mistresses appear. The meeting of the two men whose fortunes have fallen so low is not unlike the encounter of Gloucester and Lear, Timon, like Lear, being the tragic figure.

> Follow thy drum,

he cries, spurning Alcibiades and his martial profession,

> With man's blood paint the ground, gules, gules.
> Religious canons, civil laws are cruel;
> Then what should war be?

It sounds like the very echo of Alcibiades' own

> For law is strict, and war is nothing more,

except that Timon adds religion to his friend's equation. Alcibiades, who feels a strange affinity and genuine pity for Timon, undergoes the trial by gold successfully by offering his companion in banishment a share of his own small store of remaining money before he discovers that Timon himself has treasure to give. The two women, however, fail the test by accepting simultaneously showers of gold and insults.

> Believe 't, that we'll do anything for gold,

they abjectly admit. To which Timon retorts:

> There's more gold;
> Do you damn others, and let this damn you,
> And ditches grave you all!

Apemantus is Timon's next visitor, and we have the contrast between the professional cynic who revels in hurling dirt and spreading vexation and the man whose heart is really torn by the baseness of mankind. Though Apemantus accepts no gold, he does what is worse by threatening to tell all the world that Timon has it, to the end that his solitude may be destroyed.

Then, enter three thieves. But when Timon calls them by that name, they protest: "Soldiers, not thieves." "Both," replies Timon, implying that the words are synonyms, but adds:

> Yet thanks I must you con
> That you are thieves profess'd, that you work not
> In holier shapes; for there is boundless theft
> In limited professions,

and Pandulph, Beaufort, Canterbury come to mind out of a superfluity of Shakespearean examples.

> Love not yourselves; away!

Timon exclaims, dismissing them in another golden fusillade:

> Rob one another. There's more gold. Cut throats;
> All that you meet are thieves. To Athens go,
> Break open shops; nothing can you steal,
> But thieves do lose it. Steal no less for this
> I give you; and gold confound you howsoe'er!
> Amen.

And right here comes one of the most Shakespearean touches in the play. Deep down, Timon is no doctrinaire but a lover of the truth, and through his mad generalizations about mankind that love and truth somehow manage to shine, touching these vagabonds—two of them at least—who are less criminals at heart than army derelicts in desperate want.

THIRD THIEF: He has almost charmed me from my profession, by persuading me to it.

FIRST THIEF: 'Tis in the malice of mankind that he thus advises us; not to
   have us thrive in our mystery.
SECOND THIEF: I'll believe him as an enemy, and give over my trade.
FIRST THIEF: Let us first see peace in Athens: there is no time so miserable
   but a man may be true.

Sincerity has done its work. This little scene is an illuminating contrast to
the one where the senators vented their spleen under the name of justice.
And it is a preparation for something else.

But Shakespeare will not leave the doctrine that all men are thieves with
any such minor correction as the hypothetical redemption of one or more
of these men. Pat on the Third Thief's "there is no time so miserable but a
man may be true," the truest man in the play, one of the truest in all Shakespeare, enters: Flavius, Timon's faithful servant, the incarnation of everything a thief is not. Timon, at first, affects not to know him, whereat
Flavius breaks down in tears, and in those tears his old master's misanthropy
is instantly dissolved:

TIM.: What, dost thou weep? Come nearer. Then I love thee,
   Because thou art a woman, and disclaim'st
   Flinty mankind, whose eyes do never give
   But thorough lust and laughter. Pity's sleeping:
   Strange times, that weep with laughing, not with weeping!
FLA.: I beg of you to know me, good my lord,
   To accept my grief, and whilst this poor wealth lasts
   To entertain me as your steward still.
TIM.: Had I a steward
   So true, so just, and now so comfortable?
   It almost turns my dangerous nature mild.
   Let me behold thy face. Surely, this man
   Was born of woman.
   Forgive my general and exceptless rashness,
   You perpetual-sober gods! I do proclaim
   One honest man—mistake me not—but one;
   No more, I pray,—and he's a steward.

Here, in contrast with the many other gifts and honors that figure in the
play, is the conferring of a title of genuine nobility, and one more star of
the first magnitude is added to Shakespeare's constellation of simple noble-
men.

"To generalize is to be an idiot," says William Blake, "to particularize
is the alone distinction of merit." Timon, in prayer, begs the gods to forgive
him for his failure to recognize that truth in his indiscriminate condemnation of mankind:

> Forgive my *general* and *exceptless* rashness,
> You perpetual-sober gods!

How far Timon was at that moment of contrition from the mood of Hamlet when he palmed off that very rashness on himself as a divinity! But Timon can maintain his elevation no more than Isabella could hers in *Measure for Measure*, and he spurns Flavius' request to stay and comfort him:

> If thou hat'st curses,
> Stay not; fly, whilst thou art blest and free.
> Ne'er see thou man, and let me ne'er see thee.

Timon's next visitors are the sycophantic poet and painter who appeared in the opening scene of the play. They have heard that he again has gold and hold it their cue to ingratiate themselves with him once more. In the scorn that Timon heaps on these two slaves we feel Shakespeare's own contempt for men who prostitute art for gold, and possibly even a touch of remorse for those probably venial derelictions of his own in that direction which he laments in Sonnets 110 and 111.

And then, finally, by a high stroke of irony, two senators enter with open arms, the very two, we hope, that we met before:

> The senators with one consent of love
> Entreat thee back to Athens.

How account for this unpredictable reversal? Read "peril" in place of "love," and the miracle is explained. Alcibiades is threatening Athens with his army. Athens, gone soft, lacks military leaders. Timon—as we learn to our surprise unless we have paid close attention to the text—is a great captain. If he will come back, the senators announce, he can have absolute power.

Two Timons speak alternately from this point to the end of the scene: the hater of mankind, who toys with the senators' hopes in order to blast them more utterly, and the noble Timon, the man himself, who has reached the end of his course. If Alcibiades should sack Athens,

> And take our goodly aged men by the beards,
> Giving our holy virgins to the stain
> Of contumelious, beastly, mad-brain'd war,
> . . . I care not.

That is the mad Timon, if you will, but, as with the mad Lear, there is wisdom mingled with the frenzy, and his characterization of war is concise and comprehensive. And then the other Timon speaks:

> My long sickness
> Of health and living now begins to mend,
> And *nothing brings me all things.*

Nothing even in *King Lear* sums up Shakespeare's philosophy of "nothing" as succinctly as those five words of Timon's, enough in themselves to refute the common idea that he is just an embittered man venting his personal spleen. Echoing the earlier words of one of his own faithful servants,

> now all are fled
> Save only the gods,

they are the quintessence of those sublime words of Hecuba in *The Trojan Women* beyond which the poetry of Euripides seldom went:

> Lo, I have seen the open hand of God;
> And in it nothing, nothing, save the rod
> Of mine affliction, and the eternal hate,
> Beyond all lands, chosen and lifted great
> For Troy! Vain, vain were prayer and incense-swell
> And bulls' blood on the altars! . . . All is well.
> Had He not turned us in His hand, and thrust
> Our high things low and shook our hills as dust,
> We had not been this splendour, and our wrong
> An everlasting music for the song
> Of earth and heaven!

The misanthropic Timon has a final fling in his invitation to his Athenian friends to come and hang themselves on a tree which, if they do not hurry, they will find cut down. And then, in those oceanic lines beginning,

> Come not to me again; but say to Athens,
> Timon hath made his everlasting mansion
> Upon the beached verge of the salt flood,
> Who once a day with his embossed froth
> The turbulent surge shall cover,

Timon of Athens passes out of the action forever.

But not his spirit.

The play ends with Alcibiades freely relenting from his plan for revenge and bringing peace rather than war to Athens. Why?

Whether by choice or because the last scenes lacked revision, the main point of the play is left so merely intimated that the majority of readers miss it entirely. Yet nothing is really in doubt. An illiterate soldier brings an impression in wax of the epitaph Timon wrote for himself.* Alcibiades reads it, and then utters the moving words that conclude the play:

> These well express in thee thy latter spirits:
> Though thou abhorr'dst in us our human griefs,
> Scorn'dst our brain's flow and those our droplets which
> From niggard nature fall, yet rich conceit
> Taught thee to make vast Neptune weep for aye
> On thy low grave, on faults forgiven. Dead
> Is noble Timon, of whose memory
> Hereafter more. Bring me into your city,
> And I will use the olive with my sword,
> Make war breed peace, make peace stint war, make each
> Prescribe to other as each other's leech.
> Let our drums strike.

Timon is dead. But the spirit of the rarer Timon (how mistake it? the very accent is the same) has passed into Alcibiades and, in the teeth of the mad Timon's misanthropy, has brought peace to Athens. "He has almost charmed me from my profession," the Third Thief confessed to the living Timon. The dead Timon has the same effect, even more powerfully, on this professional warrior and revenger. Alcibiades' "occupation's gone."

Timon in the first part of the play was a deluded and foolish man, and in the last half a wild and frenzied one. But he was a lover of truth and sincerity. And the play seems to say that such a man, though buried in the wilderness, is a better begetter of peace than all the instrumentalities of law in the hands of men who love neither truth nor justice.

IV

Seduced by the early seeming successes of the democratic experiment, the nineteenth century held the easygoing belief that law is the opposite of war and therefore a remedy for it. As in *Measure for Measure*, Shakespeare is again pointing out in *Timon*—what the twentieth century is beginning to learn by bitter experience—that only in the rarest instances, when

---

* "*Here lies a wretched corse, of wretched soul bereft.*
  Seek not my name: a plague consume you wicked caitiffs left!
  Here lie I, Timon; who, alive, all living men did hate.
  Pass by and curse thy fill, but pass and stay not here thy gait."

The contradiction between "Seek not my name" and "Here lie I, Timon" has been relied on to show the double authorship or incomplete state of revision of the end of the play. It may be so. But this opinion, instead of being an example of critical keenness, is quite as likely an example of the ingenuousness of a scholarship so bent over the text as to be unable to see the play. The contradiction, even if not intentional, is at any rate in perfect keeping with the mad state of the dying Timon, one half of whom is a self-lacerating egotist, the other a noble and anonymous soul.

administered by some true lover of equity, is law ever even remotely synonymous with justice. "I went through law school," complained a disillusioned graduate of one of our leading institutions for legal education in the United States, "without ever once having heard the word 'justice'— except in one case where Justice was the plaintiff's name." What law is far more often synonymous with than justice is force, by which, as the will of the state or sovereign authority, it must be fully backed to be operative. It is a commonplace that a law without a penalty is a dead letter, and a penalty without police or militia to enforce it is a farce. "The necessity of war, which among human actions is most lawless," said Sir Walter Raleigh, "hath some kind of affinity and near resemblance with the necessity of law." "For both equally rest on force as their basis," says Thoreau, commenting on Raleigh's remark, "and war is only the resource of law, either on a smaller or larger scale,—its authority asserted. In war, in some sense, lies the very genius of law. It is law creative and active; it is the first principle of the law. . . . It is inconsistent to decry war and maintain law, for if there were no need of war there would be no need of law." There are laws, like reasonable traffic regulations, which are a genuine expression of the will of a vast majority of the community. There are others, like many tax laws, which are only a disguised process whereby a part of the community confiscates the liberty or property of the rest. (Whether it is a minority robbing the majority, or the majority robbing a minority, makes, in the morality of the act, not a particle of difference.) To call by the same name things so diametrically opposite in nature is like having a single term for black and white. One is indeed an opposite of war; the other is war in disguise.

> Religious canons, civil laws are cruel;
> Then what should war be?

Timon of Athens might have been written to help us keep these distinctions clear.

Chapter XXXI

Antony and Cleopatra

I

If one were asked to select the play of Shakespeare's that best represents all aspects of his genius and preserves the most harmonious balance among them, *Antony and Cleopatra* would be the inevitable choice. Here history, comedy, and tragedy are chemically combined; here the scope of the drama is world-wide; here sprawling and recalcitrant material is integrated with a constructive art that only many rereadings permit one to appreciate; here all the important characters of a huge cast are distinctly individualized, the central figures ranking among Shakespeare's masterpieces; here the humor is so inherent that we do not think of it and could not conceivably speak of it as comic relief; here poetry of the highest order remains continually in keeping with the immense variety of scene and subject; here, finally, a conclusion that borrows touches from the death scenes of *Romeo and Juliet, Hamlet, Othello,* and *King Lear* blends them into what is in some respects the most complex, sustained, and magnificent piece of musical orchestration to be found anywhere in Shakespeare.

And yet, as Bradley has pointed out, this play can never compete with the four most famous Tragedies for the affections of readers. The chief reason for this seems to be that Antony and Cleopatra, compared with Shakespeare's other heroes and heroines, even the Macbeths, are a pair soiled and stained by long submersion in the world. Yet the peculiar effect at which Shakespeare was aiming in this instance is dependent on that very fact. As far back as *Richard III* Shakespeare had intimated that love is the natural first choice of all mankind, but that, defeated in love, the "strong" nature will turn next to power.

> And therefore, since I cannot prove a lover . . .
> I am determined

not "to prove a villain," as Richard had too crudely phrased it, but to get power without end. So analyzed, the thirst for power is a sort of revenge on life for the loss of love. To put love above any form of merely mundane achievement accords with the normal instincts of youthful human nature. When even maturity rates it first, its supremacy is asserted as it were a fortiori. Love, it is true, has usually lost some of its pristine quality when it appears late or in natures already tarnished with carnality, but its miraculousness may on that account actually be enhanced. All of which will appear impertinent to those who think that this play has to do with lust and not at all with love.

II

If the distinction is not held too rigidly nor pressed too far, it is interesting to think of Shakespeare's chief works as either love dramas or power dramas, or a combination of the two. In his Histories, the poet handles the power problem primarily, the love interest being decidedly incidental. In the Comedies it is the other way around, overwhelmingly in the lighter ones, distinctly in the graver ones, except in *Troilus and Cressida*—hardly comedy at all—where without full integration something like a balance is maintained. In the Tragedies both interests are important, but *Othello* is decidedly a love drama and *Macbeth* as clearly a power drama, while in *Hamlet* and *King Lear* the two interests often alternate rather than blend. *Antony and Cleopatra* is the one play of the author's in which they are completely fused.

Where criticism has most often fallen short, in my judgment, in dealing with this play has been in its failure to stress sufficiently the role of Octavius Caesar. Octavius is the indispensable background against which Antony and Cleopatra must be seen and in contrast with which they take on their significance, for before the play is over Octavius has become practically a synonym for the Roman Empire. From this angle it might be said to be a study in the power of personality versus the impersonality of power. Antony and Cleopatra are two of the most vivid and most vital personalities Shakespeare ever drew. Octavius, save for a few moments when the man God intended him to be shines through, has no personality in any proper sense. He has sacrificed it to the place and position he holds and has identified himself with the power they afford him. It is as if he had extended himself so widely over his empire that there is nothing of himself left to reside within himself. It is precisely to emphasize that fact that the play is so spread out in space. Its geographical ramifications leave us with the feeling that this "universal landlord" in asserting his sway must have stretched himself very thin. The impression he produces on us, except in the rare moments mentioned, is one of coldness, of nullity, of death. And the impression is the stronger because of his many virtues. He is no villain like Richard III nor a man maddened by ambition like Macbeth. He is cold, like Iago, but instead of taking delight in the evil he does, he doesn't even know that it is evil. For aught he is aware of to the contrary he might be the noblest Roman of them all. He has intelligence, but not enough to have understood what Samuel Butler meant when he said "As we should not do evil that good may come, so we should not do good that evil may come." He might have smiled if he had heard the epigram, but would never have dreamed that it had any application to himself.

But trust Shakespeare not to let Octavius degenerate into a mere personification of power in the abstract. He keeps him human by a number of little touches. By convincing us of the sincerity of his love for his sister he multiplies many times the ignominy of his sacrifice of her to his career.

> No, my most wrong'd sister,

he tells her, speaking of Antony, on her return to Rome after her marriage,

> Cleopatra
> Hath nodded him to her. He hath given his empire
> Up to a whore.

He does not ask whether it is worse to give up one's empire to a whore or to give up one's sister to an empire. Yet it is in the same scene that he speaks those ringing stoic words:·

> Cheer your heart.
> Be you not troubled with the time, which drives
> O'er your content these strong necessities;
> But let determin'd things to destiny
> Hold unbewail'd their way.

But such lines are exceptional and serve only to intensify by contrast his general effect on us, which is just the opposite of what we remarked in connection with Cordelia in *King Lear*. Cordelia is felt even when she is not present. Octavius is not felt even when he is. The negativeness of the impression in the face of the power he represents is the paradox—and the point. Who can doubt that it was intentionally contrived? And so, when we find Bradley writing, "Shakespeare, I think, took little interest in the character of Octavius," we can agree if he meant that Octavius was not the sort of man to excite the sympathy or admiration of Shakespeare, but we have to dissent completely if he means that the poet took little interest in depicting him. How could he have failed to take the deepest interest? From Richard III and Cardinal Pandulph and Henry IV on, Shakespeare's plays contain portrait after portrait of King Lear's "great ones" who ebb and flow by the moon. But judged in terms of territorial dominion securely held, Octavius Caesar is the greatest of the great. He actually attained the summit up the slippery slopes toward which so many other Shakespearean thirsters after power struggled—only to fall. Octavius did not fall, and the play leaves him in possession of pretty much all the known world. But what of it—the poet compels us to ask—if in the process he has lost his own soul? "How Shakespeare hated people who have no joy!" I heard a young reader of the play remark in connection with Octavius. His verb was too strong, but his insight was right. "How intolerable people are sometimes," says Chekhov, "who are satisfied and successful in everything." It is this capacity in Octavius Caesar to be successful in everything that drives both Antony and Cleopatra to fury. Antony perceives truly that it is Caesar's fortune, not Caesar, the empire that backs him, not the man, that he is up against. The very greatness of the forces on which he relies is a measure of their agent's littleness:

> His coin, ships, legions,
> May be a coward's; whose ministers would prevail
> Under the service of a child as soon
> As i' the command of Caesar. I dare him therefore
> To lay his gay comparisons apart
> And answer me declin'd, sword against sword,
> Ourselves alone. I'll write it. Follow me.

Antony would challenge Caesar to a duel—and nothing would delight us more, as spectators, than to witness a personal encounter between the great warrior and the man who was once practically on his knees to him when he needed his help in conquering Pompey. But that time is past, and Enobarbus punctures Antony's foolish proposal in one of the wisest speeches in the play:

> Yes, like enough high-battl'd Caesar will
> Unstate his happiness and be stag'd to the show
> Against a sworder! I see men's judgements are
> A parcel of their fortunes, and things outward,
> Do draw the inward quality after them,
> To suffer all alike.

III

Nowhere in the drama, except at the very end, is the ridicule of worldly power more concentrated and effective than in the scene on Pompey's galley that concludes the second act. The situation is a counterpart of the one in *Julius Caesar* where we see the triumvirs seated around a table at a banquet of blood. Here they are again at a banquet, but this time, though it is there, they are unaware of the blood. Language fails in any attempt to characterize this incomparable scene. It is a fresh version of the skeleton at the feast. It is as perfect a fusion of burlesque and political wisdom as is to be found outside of Aristophanes, and yet, by a hair line, not burlesque. It is close to Shakespeare's last word on all the brands of intoxication. It is the spirit of tragedy masquerading as farce, the chariot of comedy driven by death. It is anything you please that is consummate.

In the preceding scene Pompey, relic of republican Rome, as someone has called him, talks loftily of Brutus and Cassius and of his purpose to be the avenger of his father; but by a slip in one of his tenses when he speaks of his navy

> with which I *meant*
> To scourge the ingratitude that despiteful Rome
> Cast on my noble father,

he gives away the fact that his purpose is already a thing of the past, and in the face of the "offers" of the triumvirate and the frank attitude of Antony, his defiance quickly melts into compliance. It ends by his inviting his new friends to a feast, and we are reminded of Enobarbus' reference to "thieves kissing." The scene shifts and we are on Pompey's galley.

"*Music,*" the stage direction reads. "*Enter two or three* SERVANTS *with a banquet.*" The music, in the circumstances, may be supposed to symbolize harmony, and as for "two or three servants," though only two speak, it surely should be three, for the whole point is that here is a little triumvirate in the world of servants to put in comparison with the Big Triumvirate that is about to enter. Comedy, from the beginning down to Bernard Shaw, has delighted in the servant who is superior to his master. It remained for Shakespeare to suggest that if the Roman Empire had to put itself in the hands of three men it might better have selected the servants who open the scene, one of whom in particular seems to be a man of high intelligence and moral perception. "To be called into a huge sphere, and not to be seen to move in 't," he says, "are the holes where eyes should be, which pitifully disaster the cheeks." The remark was made of Lepidus, but, in view of what is to follow, it seems of wider application.

A sennet sounds, and the three owners of the earth enter. They are all drunk. Or at least Lepidus and Antony are, and even the cautious Caesar, before the scene is over, finds that his tongue "splits what it speaks." They are drunk in character, of course. Lepidus is maudlin- and stupid-drunk. "I am not so well as I should be, but I'll ne'er out." And he does indeed have to be carried out a little later. Antony is witty- or silly-drunk—or, if you will, a mixture of the two. His account, for Lepidus, of the character of the crocodile achieves a wisdom-in-inanity that reminds one of the wisdom-in-insanity of Lear. To Caesar, as we should expect, the revelry is distasteful. He grows cold and circumspect. He would not be a spoil-sport, but he does not intend to be taken off guard. He speaks only four times, and three of those four speeches are in deprecation of the proceedings:

> It's monstrous labour, when I wash my brain,
> And it grows fouler. . . .
> . . . I had rather fast from all four days
> Than drink so much in one. . . .
> What would you more? . . .
> . . . . . . our graver business
> Frowns at this levity. . . .
> . . . . . . the wild disguise hath almost
> Antick'd us all.

It is a side-splitting or a sorry spectacle according to taste when Enobarbus makes all those still capable of standing join hands and dance a drunken song. The seeming harmony is in inverse ratio to the real. Here is comedy at its acme, politics become visible.

If this be drunkenness, what is sobriety?

For full measure, Shakespeare gives us a sample of that too. One man, Menas, a "pirate" friend of Pompey's, has deliberately kept himself "from the cup," and, in the midst of the frolic, whispers in Pompey's ear the suggestion that they cut the cable, and then the throats of the triumvirs. Whereupon the world will be Pompey's. This is a sober proposal. Pompey replies in effect: O good Menas! but you should have done it first and told me afterward,

> In me 'tis villany;
> In thee 't had been good service.

After which, Pompey's talk about his "honour" coming before his "profit" sounds hollow, and we see it was fear, not moral scruples, that withheld him.

What a situation! Here Shakespeare is plainly paying his compliments to the fatuousness of a humanity that can delegate all its power to three drunken men on a boat—let its destiny depend on the slender string of a galley's cable and the still slenderer string of one weak man's "honour."

> There's a strong fellow, Menas,

says Enobarbus, pointing to the man who is carrying out the dead-drunk Lepidus.

MEN.: Why?

ENO.: A' bears the third part of the world, man; see'st not?

MEN.: The third part, then, is drunk; would it were all,
That it might go on wheels!

Power tends to go on concentrating. Lepidus was included in the trium-virate in the first place only in order to make the arrangement look more respectable. Three is a less autocratic number than two or one. But ex-cept numerically Lepidus has been a cipher from the start. And Antony is a vanishing fraction.

"We are three of them," says Trinculo in *The Tempest;* "if the other two be brained like us, the state totters." It is the perfect comment on this scene and the political moral of the play, for the three triumvirs are drunk throughout most of the drama in another sense: Lepidus with flattery and fawning; Antony with infatuation; Caesar with thirst for power. And when, at the end of the banquet, Menas, the pirate and would-be cutter of the cable, calls for drums, flutes, and trumpets to "bid a loud farewell to these great fellows" we are again reminded that through all the revelry death has been present, has even drawn his sword, though for the moment he decided to lay it aside.

IV

The same satire on power that is so evident in the galley scene appears more subtly throughout most of the play. Only "satire" is the wrong word. Satire is a conscious intellectual weapon wielded by the author. Shake-speare is above that. What he does is to turn their metaphors against these pretenders to worldly might until their own words fairly wink and whisper in mockery of them.

Recognizing the difficulty of friendship with Antony, Octavius declares,

> Yet if I knew
> What hoop should hold us stanch, from edge to edge
> O' the world I would pursue it.

As if the two were to be held together as a keg of liquor is—as indeed they were for a moment on Pompey's galley! Whereupon Agrippa, put up to it doubtless by Caesar, suggests that Octavia might well serve as this hoop, though of course he does not state it quite so baldly. But what power have you, Agrippa, Antony asks, to bring your suggestion to fruition?

> The power of Caesar, and
> His power unto Octavia,

Caesar himself interjects, and at that the "brothers" clasp hands as he seals the bargain:

A sister I bequeath you (whom no brother
Did ever love so dearly). Let her live
To join our kingdoms (and our hearts),

while Lepidus, like a smirking justice-of-the-peace, puts an "amen" to the ridiculous ceremony. Octavius' legal figure ("bequeath") gives away the truth about this brother who thus disposes of his sister as if she were a feudal chattel, and justifies, as does the outcome, the liberty I have taken with the punctuation to distinguish the sincere from the insincere Caesar. That he himself has forebodings about that outcome is shown on his parting with his sister. "Most noble Antony," he says,

Let not the piece of virtue which is set
Betwixt us as the cement of our love,
To keep it builded, be the ram to batter
The fortress of it.

Octavia as cement is after all not much better than Octavia as battering ram. And the love of Antony and Caesar as a fortress is even more confusing. Octavius may exact the submission of kings and kingdoms, but his own imagination seems to be in a state of chronic rebellion. As an instrument of unconscious confession, however, it is perfect.

This same treachery of the metaphor extends to Octavius' friends. Thyreus, seeking to seduce Cleopatra from Antony to Caesar, declares,

it would warm his spirits
To hear from me you had left Antony
And put yourself under his shroud,
The universal landlord.

Landlord! That is the unkindest cut of all. And shroud! Thyreus of course means protection. But who can doubt what Shakespeare meant? There in perhaps the grimmest pun in the play he announces once for all that domination of the earth is death. The delusions to which it leads Octavius himself packs into the colossal irony of that mocking line:

The time of universal peace is near.

But all these devices, bold and subtle, for wrecking Caesar in our estimations are as nothing beside Cleopatra's savage contempt for his power, and fierce derision of it. " 'Tis paltry to be Caesar." The First Triumvir is "Fortune's knave" to her, "ass unpolicied," and his precious empire a dicer's paradise:

The luck of Caesar, which the gods give men
To excuse their after wrath.

This is no mere rationalization. Cleopatra is dying. The moment invests her words with something of the doom of those very gods.

V

And now, over against this Octavius who becomes more and more identified with Rome and rules by that impersonality of power for which the empire stands, Shakespeare puts Antony and Cleopatra—or perhaps we should say Cleopatra, and Antony in so far as he comes under her influence—who at their best, and even sometimes at less than their best, represent the power of personality to exact free obedience by what it is. The play has hardly opened when Antony, in the name of love and with a music that is unanswerable, hurls defiance once for all in the face of space and power:

> Let Rome in Tiber melt, and the wide arch
> Of the rang'd empire fall! Here is my space.
> Kingdoms are clay; our dungy earth alike
> Feeds beast as man; the nobleness of life
> Is to do thus. (*Embracing*)

The word "love" as it is commonly used in English is forced to cover a hundred shades of emotion from the highest spiritual and mystical feelings known to man down not only to sexual passion but to the basest perversions of it. It embraces literally both heaven and hell. The word means nothing until we know the context in which it is used. Yet its very confusion serves to convey the completeness with which man's loftiest and lowest experiences are entangled. "God and the devil are fighting there and the battlefield is the heart of man." That great sentence of Dostoevsky's—in the mouth of Dmitri Karamazov—was spoken of beauty. It might equally well have been said of "love." And *Antony and Cleopatra* might have been written to confirm and amplify it.

Let us grant that the mutual attraction of Antony and Cleopatra at the opening of the play is not love in any very lofty sense; allow even that it may be an illusion. At least it is not a delusion as lust for power is, and illusions, as Emerson bids us remember, often have a habit of pointing to or even turning out to be the truth.

> There's not a minute of our lives should stretch
> Without some pleasure now.

Is this the gospel of self-indulgence or that pursuit of happiness that philosophy has so often declared to be the purpose of life? Is it a mere urge to squander vitality or a longing to embrace and comprehend existence? In this pair it appears to be the strangest mixture of the two. No one can deny, at any rate, that both Antony and Cleopatra are filled with a passionate thirst for life. They are afraid to lose one instant of it. They want to try it out in all its multifarious variety.

> But that your royalty
> Holds idleness your subject, I should take you
> For idleness itself,

says Antony, appearing to deny this hunger for experience on Cleopatra's part. But there is no contradiction. In her the categories of Idleness and Activity are transcended. The worst the play records of this pair is a debasement and waste of life, not a perversion of it as is the pursuit of power. To test all the potentialities of human emotion is at any rate a nobler thing than to collect kingdoms. In comparison, Octavius impresses us as an adolescent who has never outgrown the stage of playing with toy soldiers.

But Antony too, it will be said, was a seeker after power. He also was a world-sharer. True, and it was perhaps to show how far the poison of success could infect him that Shakespeare inserted that otherwise superfluous scene that opens Act III in which Ventidius is careful to give Antony credit for military triumphs with which personally he had nothing to do. But compared with Octavius, Antony never put his whole heart into conquest and government, and the Soothsayer is right in divining that the geniuses of the two men are antipodal. The spirit that keeps Antony is a celestial one. Only in the presence of Octavius' power-demon does it wilt into fear. Had he been an unreserved worshiper of power this "greatest soldier of the world" whose "soldiership is twice the other twain" would have eliminated his final competitor instead of being eliminated by him. Who can doubt it? But Antony was interested in something beside ruling others, and the difference between him and Octavius comes down in the end to one more instance of Shakespeare's old contrast between man and king, in this case man and emperor.

At heart Antony was no more interested in governing than was Hamlet, of whom indeed he is another fragment, one of the biggest. One is willing to wager that the passage of self-analysis in which Antony likens himself to the dissolving clouds and colors in the sky comes close to what Shakespeare in some moods thought of himself. It ties Antony indissolubly to the cloud passages in *Hamlet* and *The Tempest*, and shows the Hamletian powers of introspection that lay within a man whose active life had left them half-repressed. He embodies many of the paradoxes of the Prince of Denmark: strength and weakness, courage and irresolution, masterful manhood and feminine sensibility. He was passionate, rash, and self-indulgent. But he had compensating virtues. He was a military genius who saw beyond war, a ruler who had no craving to dominate, a conqueror to whom kings had been servants who treated his own servants as kings. He was neither resentful nor revengeful. He could admit his faults without false modesty. Such a combination of traits is irresistible. Enobarbus dies of a broken heart because, after long loyalty, he has at last deserted his declining master.* Eros—who had agreed to take, whenever he should demand it, the life of this man who had given him his freedom—kills himself rather than keep his promise. Even Octavius is genuinely moved at the news of Antony's end, and when Agrippa declares,

> A rarer spirit never
> Did steer humanity,

we pardon the exaggeration and for a moment almost believe it.

And so when this Herculean Roman turns from the conquest of the world to the conquest of the most complex and in many respects the most astonishing woman Shakespeare ever created, this woman to whom Julius Caesar and Pompey succumbed but against whose seductiveness Octavius Caesar appears proof, we cannot accept it as a mere act of dereliction, nor even as a descent. Rather, we see here the whole purpose and scheme of the play for the first time. It is the conquest of the earth versus the conquest of Earth. For Cleopatra is Earth.

It is no mere caprice that leads Antony to call her Egypt. Whatever she may be as an individual human being, she is also Woman in her infinite variety. And Woman is the Earth, as various in her different moods as the landscape under changing effects of light and shadow, sun and rain. "We cannot call her winds and waters sighs and tears; they are greater storms and tempests than almanacs can report." Cleopatra has all the moral neutrality of nature. There she is, like the soil, equally ready to produce the most noxious weed or the rarest flower. Will this Serpent of old Nile drag Antony down and strangle him in sensuality or will he lift her up to the level of his own guardian angel, who, as the Soothsayer has divined, is "noble, courageous, high, unmatchable"? That is the question. And, generalized, it is the question of questions for humanity itself, compared with which the conquests and reconquests of the earth that have gone on throughout history, doing and undoing themselves like so much weather, are of no interest whatever, not worth remembering, nothing. Until Cleo-

---

* Shakespeare slips in an illuminating contrast here. When Enobarbus deserts *from* Antony, Antony accepts the act as if he were himself to blame and sends his friend's treasure after him to Caesar's camp. But when Alexas deserts *to* Caesar, and induces the Jewish Herod to shift his allegiance with him, Caesar hangs him for his pains.

patra sends the lying message to Antony that she is dead, it looks as if she were to be his Dark Lady and he her victim. And then something else happens.

VI

It is not by chance that Shakespeare puts the description of the meeting of Antony and Cleopatra at Cydnus right after the account of the selling of his sister by Octavius to Antony. Caesar issues his orders and Octavia obeys. Cleopatra does not have to issue orders. The winds fall in love with the very sails of the barge she sits in. The water is amorous of its oars and follows faster. Boys and maids, like Cupids and Nereides, fan and tend her. The city pours out its multitudes to behold her. But for the gap it would have left in nature, the air itself would have gone to gaze on her.

> I saw her once,

says Enobarbus,

> Hop forty paces through the public street;
> And having lost her breath, she spoke, and panted,
> That she did make defect perfection
> And, breathless, power breathe forth.

Here is power of another species than power military or political. Cleopatra's beauty may have been more the Dionysian beauty of vitality than the Apollonian beauty of form, but whatever it was it justifies Keats's dictum:

> 'tis the eternal law
> That first in beauty should be first in might.

And yet the magnetism that emanates from her at her first meeting with Antony at Cydnus is mere witchcraft and magic compared with the authentic "fire and air" that descends on her before her second immortal meeting with him at the end.

It is this magic and witchcraft that captivate Antony in the first place.

> I must from this enchanting queen break off.

The adjective shows that it is with the semi-mythological Cleopatra, the ancestral image of Woman she evokes within him, the gypsy, Egypt, the Serpent of old Nile, that he is in love. The fascination is mutual, and she in turn endows him with superhuman attributes. He is anything to her from the demi-Atlas of the Earth to Mars. The tradition that Antony was descended from Hercules, son of Zeus, abets this cosmic overvaluation of the human being, as does, for him, her assumption of the role of the goddess Isis. In so far as these things amount to a conscious affectation or attribution of divinity—and, even more, a willingness to make political use of them —they degrade the pair deeply in our estimations, proving them victims not only of infatuation with each other but of a self-infatuation far less excusable. But infatuation, analyzed, generally turns out to be more a failure to locate the origin of compelling forces from underneath or from overhead than mere vanity, folly, or egotism in the usual sense. "No man," says Robert Henri, "ever overappreciated a human being." And so when Cleopatra, about to part from Antony, exclaims,

> Eternity was in our lips and eyes,
> Bliss in our brows bent; none our parts so poor
> But was a race of heaven,

it strikes us less as affectation of divinity than as genuine perception of the divine element in love—insight into the heart of something which their wildest words about each other are abortive or rapturous attempts to express. In such poetry as Cleopatra attains in those three lines the illusion becomes almost indistinguishable from the truth.

Far more subtly than in the case of Cleopatra and earth, Shakespeare suggests correspondingly that Antony is like the sun. Not until near the end does this analogy shine forth so clearly that we know the author must have intended it. But looking back we can see that he has insinuated it from the beginning. Granted that if Antony is the sun he is an intermittent and often obscured luminary, uncertain of his course across the heavens and subject to frequent total eclipse or worse, as when he orders Caesar's emissary whipped and sends word that, if Caesar does not like it, he may "whip, or hang, or torture" an enfranchised bondman of Antony's in requital. But these things strike us as mere aberrations of that real Antony in whose presence alone Cleopatra germinates and blossoms and matures into her full self as does the earth under the sun. Antony's power to attract and hold men in his sphere is sun-like also, as is the bounty he dispenses as freely and widely in his degree as the sun does his warmth. It was Eros who referred to his face as

> that noble countenance
> Wherein the worship of the whole world lies.

Yet this is a sun that, reversing all known laws of heavenly bodies, when the planet he should illuminate and hold in her course flies off at a tangent at the Battle of Actium, follows ignominiously after her. What wonder that he cries, when he realizes what he has done:

> Hark! the land bids me tread no more upon't!
> It is asham'd to bear me. . . .

CLEO.:   O, my lord, my lord,
Forgive my fearful sails! I little thought
You would have follow'd.

ANT.:   Egypt, thou knew'st too well
My heart was to thy rudder tied by the strings,
And thou shouldst tow me after. O'er my spirit
Thy full supremacy thou knew'st, and that
Thy beck might from the bidding of the gods
Command me.

But the shame is not the whole story. Even here Shakespeare seems less interested in the outcome of the Battle of Actium than in the nature of that force that at the height of the action can obliterate utterly in the mind of this greatest soldier of the world all thought of military conquest and glory, all concern for what the world will think of his disgrace. Here is a mystery indeed. In the Battle of Actium, war and love—or at least war and something akin to love—grapple, and war wins. Yet does it win? To deepen the enigma the poet proceeds to show that it is precisely out of the dishonor and defeat that the spiritual triumph emerges which is always found at the heart of the highest tragedy. More and more as it nears its end, *Antony and Cleopatra* seems to recede from mere history into myth, or, if you will, to open out and mount above history into a cosmic sunset of imagination.

Sunset is the inevitable figure, and Antony himself gives us the cue for it in the superlative passage in which he compares himself with black vesper's pageants.

But even before this, Shakespeare has given our imaginations a hint of the element into which the action is to pass when it rises above earth. In a little scene that reminds one of nothing so much as the opening of *Hamlet*, a group of soldiers discuss rumors of strange happenings about the streets. Suddenly mysterious music is heard. Where is it? "Under the earth," says one.

'Tis the god Hercules, whom Antony lov'd,
Now leaves him,

says another. But still another one (of rarer sensibility than the others, we cannot but believe) locates the sound in the air. It is a premonition of the transubstantiation that is to overtake Antony in defeat. In defeat he puts off the strength and renown that are like those of his mythical ancestor, and with them, by implication, his spurious claim to divinity through descent from the gods, putting on, in exchange, the true divinity of his own guardian angel who, as the Soothsayer foresaw, is the enemy and the opposite of the demon of power. Antony's metaphor of the sunset is but a confirmation of this scene, adding, however, the element of fire to the element of air.

The marks of a sunset are beauty and insubstantiality—a splendor that makes whatever it touches more real than earth, a transiency that makes it seem less than a dream. It is all in the evanescence and dissolution of the shapes and colors in the sky that Antony sees the likeness to himself:

> Here I am Antony;
> Yet cannot hold this visible shape.

But we see more than that. Only when the sun nears or goes under the horizon do men catch a glimpse reflected on the clouds of what they dared not gaze on directly when it was overhead. The sun, when it goes down, has an alchemic power to transmute the material world into its own substance.* It is the same with a great man when he dies. The world in which he had lived is lit up with his afterglow; the common scene where he once walked seems changed into a vision. This is the miracle that Antony, dead, performs on Cleopatra. His devotion to her, even unto death, is what does it, bringing to the surface at last a Cleopatra that his love has long been shaping underneath. In this revolution of everything, Cleopatra the enchantress disappears forever—except in so far as she survives as the willing servant of the new Cleopatra that takes her place. So fully does this new Cleopatra realize the splendor of Antony at death that her memory of him transforms what little of life is left for her on earth into heaven. She enters heaven, as it were, in advance. And we enter it with her.

VII

Incredibly, many readers and critics find in the conclusion of *Antony and Cleopatra* only the old Cleopatra, thinking at bottom just of herself, bent above all things on saving herself from being shown in Caesar's triumph. That the old Cleopatra, bent on precisely this end and with every histrionic device still at her command, is still present cannot indeed be questioned. But that she is now the only or the predominant Cleopatra everything in the text converges to deny. What has happened is that a new Cleopatra is now using the old Cleopatra as her instrument. It is the new one who issues the orders. It is the old one who obeys.

When Cleopatra, frightened by Antony's reaction to his belief that she has betrayed him and caused the surrender of his fleet, sends word to him that she is dead, it is the culmination of Cleopatra the actress and deceiver, of the woman who will go to any extreme to attain her end. Little does she

* Compare the 33d sonnet for alchemy at sunrise.

realize at the moment—though soon afterward she has a premonition of what she has done—that by her lie she has thrust a sword into the man she loves and who loves her even unto death, as certainly as if she had done it with her own hand. But from the moment when the dying Antony is lifted into her monument and she finds no word of reproach on his lips for what she has done, scales seem to drop from her eyes, and never from then on does she waver in her undeviating resolution to join him in death. What looks like hesitation and toying with the thought of life is but deception utilized with the highest art to make certain that her determination to die is not thwarted. The fact is that the new Cleopatra, with all the histrionic devices of the old Cleopatra at her command, acts so consummately in these last hours of her life that she deceives not only Octavius Caesar but full half the readers of the play. She stages a mousetrap beside which Hamlet's seems melodramatic and crude, enacts its main role herself, and, unlike the Prince of Denmark, keeps her artistic integrity by never for a second revealing in advance what its purpose is or interrupting its action for superfluous comment. Blinded by victory and the thought of his triumph in which she is to figure, Octavius is clay in her hands, infatuated in a sense and to a de-gree that she and her lover never were. She twists him, as it were, around her little finger. If this still be acting, it is acting of another order. It is no longer "art" vaingloriously exhibited as personal triumph or the pride of personal power. It is art, rather, tragically impressed in the service of death. Those who think that Cleopatra is driven to suicide only when she is cer-tain that if she does not kill herself she will be shown in Caesar's triumph are taken in by her as badly as is Caesar himself.

The text corroborates this interpretation to the point of supererogation.

Antony in almost his last words begs Cleopatra to seek of Caesar her honor and her safety. "They do not go together," she replies with a ringing finality. Trust none about Caesar but Proculeius, Antony adds.

> My resolution and my hands I'll trust;
> None about Caesar.

Who cannot hear the tone in which that "none" is uttered, and who can fail to understand from that reference to her hands that her determination to do away with herself is already taken? Antony dies, and no one will ever debate, as in the case of Lady Macbeth, whether the swoon into which Cleopatra falls is genuine or not. It is as if in those few moments of uncon-sciousness she visits some other world and comes back divested forever of all mere earthly royalty. Now for the first time she is a woman—and not Woman.

> No more but e'en a woman,

are her first words as consciousness returns,

> and commanded
> By such poor passion as the maid that milks
> And does the meanest chares.

It is as if she must compensate for having been queen by being not merely a woman, but the humblest of women, a menial, a servant. And as the fourth act ends, she confirms to Iras and Charmian the promise she made to Antony before he expired:

> We'll bury him; and then, what's brave, what's noble,
> Let's do it after the high Roman fashion,
> And make death proud to take us....
> Ah women, women! come; we have no friend
> But resolution, and the briefest end.

Resolution: it is the same word she had used to Antony. This Egyptian has become a Roman, not an imperial Roman like Caesar, but a noble Roman like the angel of her own Emperor—

> Noble, courageous, high, unmatchable.

The change in Cleopatra is again confirmed in the first words we hear from her in the last act:

> My desolation does begin to make
> A better life.

Better!—a word, in that sense, not in the lexicon of the original Cleopatra. The rapidity of the change going on within her is registered in another word in the message she sends by Proculeius to Caesar:

> I *hourly* learn
> A doctrine of obedience.

Caesar, poor fool, thinks, as she intends he shall, that it is obedience to his will that she is hourly learning. But it is obedience to her own new self and to her own Emperor, Antony, to which she of course refers. The very words with which she hoodwinks Octavius most completely are made to express, on another level, the highest fidelity to her own soul. When Caesar first enters her presence, she kneels to him:

> CAES.: Arise, you shall not kneel.
> I pray you, rise; rise, Egypt.

He wishes to dupe her into thinking she can still remain a queen. But to be a queen in that sense is the last thing that she wishes.

CLEO.:   Sir, the gods
          Will have it thus; my master and my lord
          I must obey.

"You, Caesar, are now my lord and master; I have no choice but to kneel and obey," Caesar thinks she means. It sounds like obeisance to the point of prostration. But what Cleopatra is really saying is that she now listens only to divine commands. She must obey her master and her lord, her Emperor Antony, not the mere emperor of this world to whom she is kneeling in mockery.

The interlude with her treasurer Seleucus is to the undiscerning overwhelming proof that Cleopatra is still angling for life, if she can only get it on her own terms. But surely this is the old histrionic Cleopatra placing all her art at the disposal of the new Cleopatra who is bent only on death and immortal life. Whether this little play within the play was planned in advance in consultation with Seleucus and he too is acting, or whether it is a piece of inspired improvisation on her part alone, struck off at the instant of her treasurer's betrayal of her, makes little difference. The reason Cleopatra kept back some of her treasures is the same in either case: to throw the gullible Caesar off the track of her intention. How completely he is deluded by her hint that she is planning to sue with gifts for the mediation of Livia and Octavia! It is the old wily Cleopatra of course who knows how to devise this trap, and her undertone of exultation at her success in springing it is heard almost to the end. But the wily Cleopatra is now the mere servant of another Cleopatra who is intent only on her own freedom, to whom traps for others are nothing except as they help her to escape from the trap that has been set for her.

Caesar is so beguiled that he makes a fulsomely magnanimous speech in which he thinks he is finally ensnaring his victim but in which he is really only entangling himself. His comparisons and metaphors, as usual, fairly blurt out the very truth he is trying to conceal. "Caesar's no merchant," he protests, revealing that a merchant is precisely what he is at heart. "Feed, and sleep," he advises—as if Cleopatra were a beast being fattened for the slaughter and he were already licking his lips at the prospect. "My master, and my lord!" once more, is all she says. To him the words confirm her abject submission. To her—however aware she may be of the irony—they are no less than a prayer to Antony for strength. "Not so," says the overconfident Caesar, seeming to reject her obeisance, as he goes out. The two words, as he means them, are the mark that his self-stultification is complete. But, in a sense he could never divine, they are the very truth echoed from Cleopatra's heart.

> He words me, girls, he words me, that I should not
> Be noble to myself,

she cries the moment she is alone with her women. His pretended mercy has not fooled her.

> But hark thee, Charmian,

and she whispers in her maid's ear. What she tells her of course is that she has already ordered the instrument of death, the asp.

> I have spoke already, and it is provided,

and bids her "Go, put it to the haste." This tiny incident is calmly left out of account by those who think that Cleopatra has been seriously debating between life and death in the previous scene and that the interlude with her treasurer is just what it seems to be—a provision for avoiding death if a way of escape with safety to her person should present itself at the last moment. Caesar, as I said, is not the only one these scenes deceive.

Shakespeare sees to it that it is only *after* this sending for the asp, with its clear implication that the die is cast, that Dolabella—with one exception the last of many men to come under Cleopatra's spell—confides to her the fact that Caesar does indeed intend the worst. The effect of the information is merely to fortify further what needs no fortifying.

Left alone with Iras, Cleopatra draws a final picture of the fate she has escaped. Charmian returns from her errand.

> Now, Charmian,

she cries without a second's hesitation,

> Show me, my women, like a queen; go fetch
> My best attires; I am again for Cydnus
> To meet Mark Antony. . . . Bring our crown and all.

Here, it will be said, Cleopatra gives the lie to everything I have just been saying. Here, once for all, she proclaims herself actress, first, last, and forever. As if she were about to appear upon the stage, she calls for her costume, her robe and crown. Once more she will assume the role of queen—in her "best attires." She will play-act the very act of death. The woman is an incorrigible exhibitionist.

On the contrary, it is the extreme opposite of all this, I believe, that Shakespeare intends. We become new not so much by rejecting the old as by imparting to the old a new meaning. So here. What we have is not the old Cleopatra reverting to the theatrical and all its meretriciousness, but a new Cleopatra, rather, aspiring to make the symbol indistinguishable from the thing, to rise into that region where art is lifted into life and life into art, the goal, alike, of art and life.

As the clown brings the asp, she cries:

> I have nothing
> Of woman in me; now from head to foot
> I am marble-constant, now the fleeting moon
> No planet is of mine.

What follows confirms this inversion and reversal. (And we can be the more confident of this interpretation because, strangely, however much more swift, the change in Cleopatra parallels a change of like character in her creator, who, as in the cases of Falstaff and Hamlet, has endowed her with not a little of his own dramatic genius. Shakespeare, by his own confession, was at one time almost "subdued" by the theater, and his evolution traces his successful effort to elude its grasp. From *The Comedy of Errors* to *Antony and Cleopatra*, the story is one of the gradual subjection of the theatrical to the poetical. Cleopatra's development is a sort of parable of Shakespeare's. "Shakespeare led a life of allegory: his works are the comments on it.")

Four times, in her haste to be rid of him, Cleopatra says "farewell" to the loquacious clown who has brought the asp. When he is gone and Iras has returned, she begins her own farewell:

> Give me my robe, put on my crown; I have
> Immortal longings in me. Now no more
> The juice of Egypt's grape shall moist this lip. . . .

As she renounces the intoxicants of earth a celestial intoxication comes over her—she feels herself being transmuted from earth into fire and air. Whoever, as he listens to her, does not feel, in however diminished degree, a like effect within himself, misses, I believe, one of the supreme things in Shakespeare. The atmosphere of sunset—which Charmian's single phrase, "O eastern star!" turns into sunrise—the universal character of every image and symbol, and above all perhaps the sublimity of the verse, conspire with the action itself to produce this alchemic effect. Here, if ever, is the harmony that mitigates tragedy, the harmony, better say, that creates it.

VIII

Whoever questions or is insensible to all this should consider the contrast between the two meetings of Antony and Cleopatra at "Cydnus," the earthly meeting as described by Enobarbus, and the spiritual meeting to which the death scene is the vestibule. Around these two passages, as we can see fully only when we have finished the play and hold it off in perspective, the drama is described as an ellipse is about its two foci. The antithesis between them is complete: the "poetry" of the senses versus the poetry of the imagination. In the first we have Cleopatra as the earthly Venus, enveloped in incense, waited on by everything from the winds to the populace, conscious to the last degree, we cannot but feel, of the universal adulation. Antony is absent, and is brought in at the end almost as an afterthought. In the second he is in a sense more present than she is, and she unconscious of everything save him, her Emperor, whom she is about to meet—of him, and of the courage with which his love has endowed her. The only memories that cross her mind of a world that "is not worth leave-taking" are those of *its* emperor that by contrast serve to make her Emperor great. "Ass unpolicied"! It is her Last Judgment on all Caesars—hers and Shakespeare's—the revenge of poetry, which is the politics of heaven, on empire. For the rest, what unprecedented words on the lips of Cleopatra: "husband," "baby," "nurse"! Even that "kiss" which it is to be her heaven to have is of another order from the many thousand kisses that Antony once placed upon her lips, of which his dying one, he thought, was the "poor last." The first meeting at Cydnus, as Enobarbus gives it to us, is like an immense tapestry or historical picture, a word painting, just the overdecorated sort of thing that the world mistakes for supreme art. The second is more than the greatest art. It is an apocalypse.

IX

Yet, even after this, Shakespeare, incredibly, has something in reserve, the most miraculous single touch in the whole play, a touch that, like a flash of lightning at night, illuminates everything.

Caesar enters. He is first told the truth and then looks down upon it. The sight seems to lift him outside of himself. Quite as if he had overheard those earlier words of Cleopatra,

> I dream'd there was an Emperor Antony.
> O, such another sleep, that I might see
> But such another man,

and had come to declare that prayer answered, he exclaims:

> she looks like sleep,
> As she would catch another Antony
> In her strong toil of grace.

Another Antony indeed, her Emperor! Whatever has happened elsewhere, here on earth, in those perfect words, the lovers are reunited. And Octavius, of all men, spoke them!

Many, including Bradley (who says that to him they sound more like

Shakespeare than Octavius), have declared the lines out of character, entirely too imaginative for this boy politician whom Cleopatra herself derided so unmercifully. They are. And yet they are not. And when we see why they are not we have seen into the heart of the play.

Caesar, practically alone, has shown himself immune to the fascination of this woman, and only now is he in a position to realize how utterly, even at his own game, she has outplotted and outwitted him, led him, as it were, by the nose. Conqueror as he is, she has dragged him behind the chariot of her superior insight and power. But all that now is nothing to him, less than nothing, not even remembered, and, gazing down as if entranced, this man, who had been cold to her and to her beauty while she lived, utters the most beautiful words ever spoken of her. Dead, she proves more powerful than the most powerful of men alive. She makes him realize that there is something mightier than might, something stronger than death. She kindles the poet within him. She catches him in her strong toil of grace. She leads him in her triumph!

X

Nothing in his works perhaps illustrates better than the conclusion of *Antony and Cleopatra* what I have called the integrity of Shakespeare, by which I mean the psychic interdependence of those works and their consequent power to illuminate one another.

The imaginative germ of *Antony and Cleopatra* is found in Romeo's opening speech in the fifth act of *Romeo and Juliet*:

> I dreamt my lady came and found me dead—
> Strange dream, that gives a dead man leave to think!—
> And breath'd such life with kisses in my lips
> That I reviv'd and was an emperor.

So specific is this, down even to the conception of a spiritual emperor, that it not merely presages the situation at the end of *Antony and Cleopatra* but is a perfect comment on and interpretation of its transcendental meaning.

Cleopatra and Othello seem incongruous figures to connect. Yet Cleopatra in the end is in the same position as Othello: she has killed the one she loves, not with her own hand, to be sure, as he did, but not less actually. And in one respect her situation is far worse. He did his deed under a complete delusion, but in good faith. She did hers by a lie that was wantonly selfish. But if Cleopatra and Othello make strange companions, Antony and Desdemona make even stranger ones—the greatest soldier in the world and the simplest and most modest girl. Yet here the link is even closer—and we remember Othello's greeting, "O my fair warrior!" Desdemona dies with no reproach for the wrong he has done her, and when he discovers the truth he is shaken to the foundation by a profound spiritual change. Similarly, not one word, not one thought, of the part Cleopatra has played in his death crosses Antony's lips, or his mind, in his last moments. Instead he merely says:

> I am dying, Egypt, dying; only
> I here importune death awhile, until
> Of many thousand kisses the poor last
> I lay upon thy lips.

Here is the counterpart of Desdemona's last words:

> Commend me to my kind lord. O, farewell!

and here the only conceivable cause commensurable with the change effected in Cleopatra. If it seems a more incredible change than that which occurs in Othello, it is because Othello had from the first a nobility to which the earlier Cleopatra could make no claim. The motif of the transcendental reunion of the lovers, which is only faintly hinted at and kept wholly in the overtones in *Othello*, becomes the main theme, openly announced and developed like music, at the end of *Antony and Cleopatra*. It is as if what the violins vaguely suggested there were played here by the full orchestra. At last we know that we were not deceived in what we hardly dared believe we heard in the earlier play.

But it is *King Lear* that comes closest of all. King Lear, summing up a dozen figures that preceded him, shows that it is greater to be a man than to be a king, greater to be a king in the imaginative than in the worldly sense. Antony's story says the same. He refuses to sacrifice to the Roman Empire his heritage as a man. He shows that it is greater to be an Emperor in Romeo's and Cleopatra's sense than to be emperor of the earth. "A man needs but six feet of ground," an old proverb has it, and though he has owned the whole earth six feet is enough when he has become a corpse. Even having been a universal landlord will not help him. "The earth I have seen cannot bury me," said Thoreau in one of the most astonishing sentences that even his genius ever struck off. The conclusion of *Antony and Cleopatra* makes clear what he meant.

The analogy between King Lear and Cleopatra is even more striking than that between King Lear and Antony, if for no other reason than that a contrast between the sexes is here involved. Just as Lear had to lose his title and recognize that he was only

> a very foolish fond old man
> Fourscore and upward, not an hour more or less,

before he could regain his kingdom as spiritual King, so Cleopatra had to realize that she was

> No more but e'en a woman, and commanded
> By such poor passion as the maid that milks
> And does the meanest chares,

before she could become a spiritual Queen worthy to meet her Emperor. Through humility both Lear and Cleopatra discover their humanity. Anger and violence in him are tamed to patience. Pride and passion in her are lifted to love. So faithful even in detail is Shakespeare to his earlier pattern that Lear's crown and robe of weeds and common flowers is the very counterpart of Cleopatra's symbolic robe and crown which she puts on before her death. And yet—what could be more splendidly different from the piercingly swift and simple ending of *King Lear* than the prolonged sunset glory of *Antony and Cleopatra?* The difference corresponds precisely to the two characters. But the likeness goes deeper than the difference. The end of the earlier play gives us a single lightning-like glimpse into heaven; that of the other ushers us to its very threshold.

Further plays, *Troilus and Cressida* especially, afford more comparisons and contrasts. But we must restrict ourselves to a last one, a link with *Hamlet* which is of another sort. When the Prince of Denmark discovers the truth about the poisoned rapier and realizes that he is trapped, he turns it on the King with the cry,

> The point envenom'd too!
> Then, venom, to thy work.

Cleopatra, as she applies the asp to her breast, exclaims:

> Poor venomous fool,
> Be angry, and dispatch.

It is as if Shakespeare had chosen the dying Cleopatra to make his ultimate comment on the dedication to the most futile of human passions, revenge, of the most gifted character he ever created.

XI

Antony and Cleopatra may be taken not only by itself, but as the final part of Shakespeare's Roman trilogy—*Coriolanus, Julius Caesar, Antony and Cleopatra*—last not in order of composition but in historical sequence. Coriolanus, Brutus, Antony; Volumnia-Virgilia, Portia, Cleopatra: the men, and even more the women, give us a spiritual history of Rome from its austere earlier days, through the fall of the republic, to the triumph of the empire. What lights and shadows, what contrasts and illuminations this immense canvas affords, surpassing even those in each of the separate plays! Only in the light of the whole, for instance, is the full futility of the conspiracy of Cassius and Brutus evident. This is Shakespeare's historical masterpiece.

Considered as three related Tragedies or even as a tragic trilogy, there are notes of triumph and even of hope to redeem the suffering at the end of each play and at the end of the whole. But considered as a single history or as the story of the evolution of imperialism, there is little but disillusionment and a sense of the predestined tendency of freedom, when it has once been wrested from slavery, to return again to slavery as if in a perpetual circle.

Can anyone doubt for a moment whether Shakespeare considered the tragic-poetical or the historical-political the profounder way of regarding life? Certainly the last thing Shakespeare was offering us at the end of his trilogy was any doctrine of "all for love" in the cheap popular sense of that phrase as suggested by the title of Dryden's famous version of the story of Antony and Cleopatra. But he certainly is saying that there is something in life in comparison with which battles and empires are of no account. As statesman and soldier it was Antony's duty to fight to the bitter end at the Battle of Actium for his half of the empire. If he had, at the price of depriving the world of the story of Antony and Cleopatra—including Shakespeare's play—is it certain that the world would be better off? The destiny of the world is determined less by the battles that are lost and won than by the stories it loves and believes in. That is a hard saying for hardheaded men to accept, but it is true. Stories are told, grow old, and are remembered. Battles are fought, fade out, and are forgotten—unless they beget great stories. We put up massive monuments to military heroes because otherwise their very names will be erased. We do not need to put up monuments to great poets nor to those heroes they have made immortal.

Antony was at times a pitiably weak man. His conduct at Actium was ignominious and shameful. But instead of trying to deify that weakness, saying foolish things like Richard II and the later Hamlet about angels and divinities, and killing under their supposed sanction, in the end he forgot, like Desdemona and Cordelia, that he had been sinned against and went on loving the one who had injured him. Was that not better than winning the Battle of Actium or any other battle? He that ruleth himself is better than he that taketh a city. And the weaker the man is, Shakespeare seems to add, the greater the victory.

Chapter XXXII

Coriolanus

I

In proportion to its merit, *Coriolanus* is possibly Shakespeare's most neglected play. It is rarely staged, and one wonders how often it is read except
by scholars and students. Its relative unpopularity can undoubtedly be
attributed in part to the fact that its hero, who dominates its action no less
than the Prince of Denmark does that of *Hamlet*, is not a general favorite,
is, indeed, repellent to not a few readers. He is a paragon of valor and, in
the opinion of many, of egotism also, takes his name from Mars, is spoken
of as Mars's "son and heir," and in the words of one of his admirers "wants
nothing of a god but eternity and a heaven to throne in." His contempt for
the plebeians has given the drama the reputation of being the extreme
example of Shakespeare's own supposed antidemocratic convictions. If its
author had been historically minded, much of the play might be explained
as an attempt to present the spirit of an early austere Rome where war and
the struggle for power were the primary concerns. But anything of that
sort is at best incidental, and, strangely, this public drama is scarcely surpassed in family interest by anything the author wrote except *King Lear*.
It has touches of tenderness that are like windflowers found on the face of
a crag. Yet, by and large, the play lacks poetry in the narrower sense. Its
clarity is the clarity of full daylight, and only rarely does it give us that
sense of the unfathomable that most of the Tragedies impart. It is possibly
significant that the poet makes no use of several passages involving the
supernatural to be found in his source.

II

The links between *Coriolanus* and preceding plays are many and illuminating. We can glance at only a few of them.

In situation *Coriolanus* is closest of all to *Timon of Athens*. Like Timon, who exiles himself, Coriolanus is banished from his native city, and, like Alcibiades, takes up arms against it. In a sense not evident at first he is himself a kind of Timon-Alcibiades.

The theme of ingratitude ties the play not only with *Timon* but with *King Lear*, in which still another exile made war against his own kingdom. Here the revengeful man learns mercy as there the angry one acquired patience. But there is a closer bond than this. Consider Coriolanus and Cordelia. It is just coincidence of course that their names begin with the same syllable, which in Latin means heart, though Shakespeare, like the unconscious mind, shows the strongest interest in just such punning resemblances. But the moment we notice this one, if not before, we realize that Lear's youngest daughter and the conqueror of Corioli have much in common:

CORDELIA: I love your majesty
                According to my bond; nor more nor less.
CORIOLANUS: But your people,
                I love them as they weigh.

Not only the thought but the accent the same. More and more, from *Hamlet* on, Shakespeare delighted in creating incorrigible truth-tellers who discomfort and undo the hypocrites and knaves: Emilia (at the end), Kent, Cordelia herself, Timon, Paulina, even Thersites and Apemantus, for whom—who can doubt it?—Shakespeare had more respect than for Osric or Parolles. Coriolanus is a pre-eminent member of this group.

He would not flatter Neptune for his trident.

Menenius is right, and Aufidius damnably wrong when he justifies the assassination of his old enemy by charging that

He water'd his new plants with dews of flattery,
Seducing so my friends.

As truth-teller, at least, the poet undoubtedly admired his hero more than some of his more timid readers do.

Hamlet and *Coriolanus* are the two works of Shakespeare in which a mother is of paramount importance—the two *Richard* plays, *Romeo and Juliet*, *All's Well*, and *Cymbeline* coming distinctly behind them in this respect. Fathers in his dramas, as we have seen, are plentiful, mothers, fully drawn, rare. Into this and another more important tie with *Hamlet* we will look later.

Lady Macbeth and Volumnia inevitably challenge comparison: two unsexed women, one ambitious for her husband, the other for her son. So, too, for the contrast, do Octavius Caesar and Coriolanus, two conquerors who relied, respectively, on the power of position and the power of personal force. If there was anything that Coriolanus did *not* rely on, it was his reputation, his place, or his possessions. Octavius wanted the world as his loot; Coriolanus scorned the soldier who would steal a spoon.

> Our spoils he kick'd at,

says Cominius,

> And look'd upon things precious as they were
> The common muck of the world. He covets less
> Than misery itself would give, rewards
> His deeds with doing them, and is content
> To spend the time to end it.

This refusal to value life in terms of anything but life itself puts Coriolanus in the strangely alien company of Falstaff, Cleopatra, and their kin, and advises us at the outset that in this respect at least his creator thinks well of him.

III

Coriolanus has often been taken as a political treatise in dramatic form. Its subject, in that case, is the struggle between the ruling and the oppressed classes, and Coriolanus himself is a typical tory who prefers the privileges of his class to the good of his country, as tories have been prone to do from time out of mind. It sounds plausible, but it will not do. Tories there are in this play—and a class struggle—but Coriolanus is not one of them. His one speech on custom—

> Custom calls me to 't.
> What custom wills, in all things should we do't,
> The dust on antique time would lie unswept,
> And mountainous error be too highly heapt
> For truth to o'er-peer,

—is sufficient to disqualify him once for all. And as for loyalty to his class, he comes to hate the members of it who acquiesced in his banishment worse, if anything, than the plebeians and their tribunes who engineered it. A comparison with its source will show that Plutarch's *Life of Coriolanus* fills the prescription of a plebeian-patrician treatise far better than Shakespeare's tragedy. It may be a political play, but its scheme is not so simple as that.

An opposite view holds that Shakespeare here, as usual, is just portraying an interesting and tragic individual. The fact that the background happens to be political is unimportant. But surely the politics of the play is far more than background, anything but incidental. The point is that Shakespeare does not divorce his politics from his general science of human nature, as we so often do. The children of this world are still in our generation wiser than the children of light, and it has been the tragedy of the twentieth century that the latter left it to the former to discover before they did that politics is just a branch of psychology—and to put that discovery to diabolical use. Shakespeare apparently never had to make this discovery, or, if he did, he had made it by the time he wrote *Richard II*. He used it for the emancipation, not the enslavement, of his fellow men.

And so the "education" of Coriolanus by his mother becomes of consuming interest. Shakespeare was naturally unacquainted with twentieth-century psychiatry. Yet, whether by instinct or wisdom, what he sets down in this play with clinical precision is a case of not wholly normal mother-son relationship (the sort of thing that some critics have wrongly found in *Hamlet*). Until this is analyzed, it is futile to say anything about the politics of the play in the narrower sense.

IV

Volumnia is often spoken of as a woman of heroic mold calculated to give us an idea of the stern stuff of which the early Romans were made. "This Volumnia," declared Menenius to the tribunes,

> Is worth of consuls, senators, patricians,
> A city full; of tribunes, such as you,
> A sea and land full.

She may have been on the occasion referred to; but it should be remembered that Menenius was speaking just after she had performed the most uncharacteristic act of her life: falling on her knees and begging someone *not* to fight. Up to that point she had been little other than an Amazon, a woman—to call her that—who so rejoiced in battle and military glory that for her vicarious satisfaction she pushed her son into bloodshed almost before he had ceased to be a child. She fairly feasted on wounds and scars. A wolf is said to have suckled Romulus and Remus. Coriolanus did not need such nourishment. He had its human equivalent. "Anger's my meat," she proudly proclaims, and when her son, incensed, says of the people, "Let them hang," she characteristically adds, "Ay, and burn too." The admiration Volumnia has at times elicited is a comment on the suppressed desires of those who have belauded her.

She talks a great deal about honor, but at the political crisis she is perfectly willing to fall back on policy and employ craft and lies. Her argument is that all is fair in war and politics. And Shakespeare clinches the point by showing that, however physically courageous she may be, she lacks the corresponding moral fiber:

> Nay, mother,
> Where is your ancient courage?

her son chides her when fortune has turned against them and she dares not practice what she has preached—a strong heart in adversity. That Volumnia is not a typical woman of even these primitive times Shakespeare makes clear by putting in the domestic Valeria and the laconic Virgilia, who out-Cordelia's Cordelia in the eloquent brevity of her role.

A mother like Volumnia would be a liability to any boy. She was the most unfortunate of mothers for such a rare and sensitive child as Caius Marcius evidently was. Whoever fancies him a young ruffian spoiling from the first for a fight must revise his picture. His mother herself says that, when he was yet "tender-bodied," he was so comely that, when she took him abroad, he was the focus of all eyes. Congenitally he must have been closer to a young poet than a young warrior. True, he grows up to be a prodigy of physical strength. "What an arm he has!" says one of Aufidius' servants. "He turned me about with his finger and his thumb as one would set up a top." But his grace is just as much stressed as his strength. It must have been more that of Helios than of Hephaestus, whatever it became under his mother's tutelage. The fact seems to be that Volumnia, who was a widow, played father as well as mother to her son and made the most of the double docility that comes from a child's natural affection for his mother and reverence for his father. Indeed, she was far more father than mother to him. What wonder that, beginning in his infancy, she could shape him into anything she liked! Praise for any audacity on his part seems to have been her main instrument, and praise can be as fatal to youth as blame. Who has not seen a child awkward and embarrassed at being openly commended in the presence of others?—and the finer the child's instincts the more marked the self-consciousness. Caius Marcius must have been like that, and retains as a man something of the same feeling:

> My mother,
> Who has a charter to extol her blood,
> When she does praise me grieves me.

His hatred of boasting or of hearing his own bravery lauded is generally diagnosed as inverted pride. It may be partly that, but it is much more the native modesty of a man who on instinct feels that "whatever praises itself but in the deed, devours the deed in the praise." And so, when we hear how the crude Volumnia ground her own ax on this sensitive boy, we are reminded of Blake's design, *Aged Ignorance*, in which an old dotard with a huge pair of scissors is clipping off the psyche-like wings of a boy who is struggling to escape. "The vilest abortionist," says Bernard Shaw in the

same vein, "is he who attempts to mould a child's character." By that rule
Volumnia qualifies as vilest of the vile. She all but succeeds in turning into
a Hercules a child who evidently no more resembled Hercules by nature
than Hamlet did in his own estimation. Furthermore, Hamlet was a grown
man before his father set out to convert him to the doctrine of blood. And
his father was then only a ghost. What chance, comparatively, had the
infant Marcius against this portentous mother-father of flesh and blood?
The man Coriolanus seems expressly drawn to record the results of the
martial indoctrination of childhood.

V

That this is indeed just what he had in mind Shakespeare makes plain by
a reiterated metaphor.

Caius Marcius has a son, little Marcius. His role is brief, but it is long
enough to make it evident that his grandmother—Virgilia's mother-in-law—
has taken the child in hand and intends to repeat in him the "education" she
gave his father.

"How does your little son?" Valeria asks Virgilia in the inimitable scene
of the three women whose names all begin with a *V*, for which Shakespeare
found no hint in Plutarch. "I thank your ladyship; well, good madam,"
replies Virgilia, with what sounds like conscious restraint and with a side
glance, I fancy, at her mother-in-law. The boy's grandmother is both more
specific and more emphatic: "He had rather see the swords and hear a
drum than look upon his schoolmaster." "O' my word," exclaims Valeria,
"the father's son. I'll swear, 'tis a very pretty boy." And she goes on to
narrate an incident that shows that young Marcius, whatever he thinks of
his schoolmaster, is not yet wholly subdued to his grandmother's formula.
He can still chase butterflies in the meadow.

VAL.: O' my troth, I looked upon him o' Wednesday half an hour together:
has such a confirmed countenance. I saw him run after a gilded butterfly; and when he caught it, he let it go again; and after it again;
and over and over he comes, and up again; catched it again; or
whether his fall enraged him, or how 'twas, he did so set his teeth
and tear it. O, I warrant, how he mammocked it!*

VOL.: One on 's father's moods.

But a butterfly throughout myth and poetry is psyche, the soul, the
winged and immortal part of man, and this little incident is a parable of the
struggle going on inside the boy between his real self and the self his grand-

---

* "Mammocked it"—tore it. Chekhov uses the same metaphor in the same way in
The Steppe, where the little boy Yegorushka first just listens to the music of the grass-
hopper, and then, under the tutelage of the coachman, tortures it.

mother would impose upon him. Why does Shakespeare take the trouble to tell us in the same scene that Volumnia's son as a child was so comely that he "plucked all gaze his way," and that her grandson was so attractive that Valeria watches him "half an hour together"? Plainly to impress on our minds the common beauty and spiritual kinship of father and son. And why has he let the child play out a little play that reads like the biography of his father written in advance ("whether his fall enraged him, or how 'twas, he did so set his teeth and tear it")? Plainly, again, to show what havoc to their souls this old war horse of a mother-grandmother has caused, and is causing, to son and grandson alike.

"One on 's father's moods"? One on 's grandmother's moods, would be more accurate. His father's only in so far as Marcius is Volumnia's son. Not his father's in so far as Marcius is himself and his soul's son.

The butterfly metaphor occurs again in Act IV, when Cominius and Menenius are frightening the tribunes by describing the prowess of this former Roman who is now advancing on his native city at the head of a Volscian army. Says Cominius:

> He is their god. He leads them like a thing
> Made by some other deity than Nature,
> That shapes man better; and they follow him
> Against us brats with no less confidence
> Than boys pursuing summer butterflies,
> Or butchers killing flies.

Volumnia's doctrine has done its work with a thoroughness that she did not anticipate. Her son—"whether his fall enraged him, or how 'twas"—is now mammocking the butterflies in a fashion she does not relish, threatening to tear both the bodies and the souls of his former countrymen as ruthlessly as the "gods" of Gloucester in *King Lear* who, as wanton boys do flies, kill men for their sport. Cominius compares him to a god—presumably Mars. But Menenius puts it still more effectively in a later scene when he gives the same entomological metaphor an infernal turn. "There is differency between a grub and a butterfly," he explains to the tribunes, "yet your butterfly was a grub. This Marcius is grown from man to dragon: he has wings; he's more than a creeping thing." From man to dragon!* That is the metamorphosis that Volumnia all but effects in her son. And when, ironically, the hour comes when that son is an enemy of Rome and it is mercy rather than mercilessness that she longs to discover in him, it is through no fault in the way she has brought him up that she does not find

---

* Coriolanus likens himself to a lonely dragon when he goes into exile, and Aufidius declares that he fights "dragon-like" on the side of the Volscians—showing that the metaphor is not a casual but a carefully calculated one on Shakespeare's part.

a creature with "no more mercy in him than there is milk in a male tiger." She had loaded his childhood with precepts of valor. But in the critical hour it is not those precepts, it is that childhood—or some remnant of it—that tells him the truth—tells him that valor can mean something higher than the mere audacity in battle for which it has always stood in his mother's mind. The butterfly wins out over the dragon. (But this is anticipating.)

If there is anything in all this, Coriolanus is in the same situation as Hamlet, forced into a role intolerable to his soul. Only the miscasting began so much earlier that Marcius is wholly unconscious of the perversion his mother has effected.

The moment we grasp this violence that was done him as a child, a dozen traits of the man are explained. His arrogance, first and foremost—which is nothing but his tenderness turned inside out. His sense of honor—because he has not been honorable to himself. His at times almost quixotic insistence on the truth—because his military career is founded on a lie. Even his physical courage—which in its frenzied intensity is revenge for his failure in moral courage in not being himself. Hamlet overidealizing his father, Hamlet tearing loose from his companions to follow the Ghost, Hamlet sending Rosencrantz and Guildenstern to their doom, gives us in flashes what Coriolanus, except in flashes, is, one might almost say, professionally. But here we must discriminate nicely between the genuine courage, honor, and truth of a congenitally courageous, honorable, and truthful nature and the exaggeration of these virtues to balance the outrage they underwent from infancy—on and at his mother's knee.

VI

To enforce his point further, Shakespeare uses another reiterated metaphor that translates the figure of the butterfly, as it were, from terms of childhood into those of manhood. Play the soldier Coriolanus can, for, though he was made for better things, after all, personal combat calls for not a few of the manly virtues. But play the boaster and the beggar Coriolanus cannot, and when he is told that if he is to be consul he must exhibit his wounds to the people and humbly solicit their votes, his soul revolts and he cries:

> It is a part
> That I shall blush in acting.

As Shakespeare doubtless reverted to his own boyhood in Stratford for the figure of the butterfly, so now he goes to his own profession of actor-playwright for his metaphor of a man playing a theatrical role for which he is not fitted. Little does Coriolanus know that, cast for it by his mother before he had any choice, he has been doing practically that all his life.

Pushed on by Menenius, Coriolanus, in spite of his reluctance, dons the gown of humility and gets through the ordeal by sheer dint of mockery at himself—as if he were both bad actor and derisive audience—salving his conscience by an irony the citizens cannot understand. But some of them sense something wrong and, when they are out from under his magnetic presence, report to their tribunes that he mocked them—and are induced by their leaders to withdraw their approval. Coriolanus and the tribunes exchange verbal blows, and when he suggests the abolition of their office, they charge him with treason and are for hurling him down the Tarpeian rock. Any chance of his being made consul seems to have disappeared.

It is just here that Volumnia reveals herself in her true colors. This supposed paragon of Roman honor turns Machiavellian politician and, like a totalitarian in our day, begs her son to dissemble a little until the office is his. If it is honorable to seem what you aren't in war, she argues, why not in peace?* How bad her conscience is in thus subordinating truth to ambition is revealed by the devious style of speech into which she immediately lapses, so bad that critics whose grammatical is greater than their psychological perspicacity have pronounced the text corrupt at this point.

Coriolanus, as ever, listens to Volumnia with deepest respect. It is a grotesque spectacle (so only grotesque language can depict it): the greatest warrior of the world tied to his mother's apron-strings! But their hold is weakening:

> You have put me now to such a part which never
> I shall discharge to the life,

Marcius exclaims.

> Come, come, we'll prompt you,

says Cominius. Shakespeare doesn't intend that we shall miss his metaphor and he stresses it a third time when he has Volumnia add:

> My praises made thee first a soldier, so,
> To have my praise for this, perform a part
> Thou hast not done before.

* In the first scene of the second act, when news comes of the wondrous things Marcius has done against the Volscians, Virgilia, Volumnia, and Menenius exclaim in order:

> "The gods grant them true!"
> "True! pow, wow."
> "True! I'll be sworn they are true."

A man's idea of the truth is an index of the man. Here are these three in a nutshell.

"Well, I must do 't," her son replies. But the picture he proceeds to draw of himself bending like a beggar so humiliates him that he cries out in contradiction:

> I will not do 't,
> Lest I surcease to honour mine own truth
> And by my body's action teach my mind
> A most inherent baseness.

Yet, in spite of that, he complies like a good boy, and goes out to a chorus of admonitory "mildly's."

VII

But the tribunes are ready for him. Ignorant as they are, they know the trick that will draw him, and at just the right moment they hurl the word "traitor" in his face, counting on it to set him aflame.

It is the crisis of the play (or the first of its two crises). And it is a touchstone for readers. "How! traitor!" cries Coriolanus. "Nay, temperately; your promise," warns Menenius. But in vain:

> The fires i' the lowest hell fold-in the people!
> Call me their traitor! Thou injurious tribune!
> Within thine eyes sat twenty thousand deaths,
> In thy hands clutch'd as many millions, in
> Thy lying tongue both numbers, I would say
> "Thou liest" unto thee with a voice as free
> As I do pray the gods.

"To the rock, to the rock with him!" the citizens shriek. But undeterred, and brushing by Menenius'

> Is this the promise that you made your mother?

Marcius flings his mother and everything but sincerity to the winds and at last obeys his soul:

> Let them pronounce the steep Tarpeian death,
> Vagabond exile, flaying, pent to linger
> But with a grain a day, I would not buy
> Their mercy at the price of one fair word;
> Nor check my courage for what they can give,
> To have 't with saying "Good morrow."

Granted that the words lack tact and common sense. They are the words of a free man. A certain verbal violence is pardonable in breaking the bonds of a lifetime. Never from that moment is Coriolanus the slave of Volumnia.

I shall be told of course that in saying so I have forgotten his cry

O mother, mother!
What have you done?

when, at the end, he relents and spares Rome the revenge he has prepared. There, by his own confession, he is again under his mother's dominion.

To that there are two answers, either adequate without the other.

The situation will be remembered. Coriolanus, in the Volscian camp before Rome, has been interceded with in vain by Cominius and Menenius, though the fact that in both cases he cuts the interview short almost before it has begun and makes his own communication in writing suggests that he does not dare trust his own voice not to reveal the danger he is in of relenting; and when he says of Menenius to Aufidius,

This last old man,
Whom with a crack'd heart I have sent to Rome,
Lov'd me above the measure of a father,

the ambiguity as to whose heart it was that was cracked is plainly intentional on the poet's part, whatever it was on Coriolanus'. .

And now Virgilia, Volumnia, with little Marcius, and Valeria come to make a last plea. It is the common view that it is Volumnia who wins her son over from war to peace, from revenge to mercy. And Coriolanus seems to think so himself, as his cry "O, mother, mother! What have you done?" makes clear. But there is little to suggest that Shakespeare agrees with him. The author is not in the habit of giving the deciding voice to the utterer of the longest speech—and Volumnia speaks about a hundred lines in this scene, mostly in two long instalments. And what is more, the poet makes plain that in his heart Coriolanus has begun to give in before even one of these words is spoken.

What does he notice as the procession of intercessors approaches? "My wife comes foremost" are his first words. (They are prophecy as well as fact.) He gazes in her eyes—

those doves' eyes
Which can make gods forsworn

—and as if to steel himself against their influence, asks what they are worth. But his answer to his own question shows that as inducements to mercy their power is measureless:

I melt, and am not
Of stronger earth than others.

But if eyes that presage peace can make the gods forsworn, what will they do to one who is only human? Of his mother, significantly, he remarks only her gesture when she bows to him,

> As if Olympus to a molehill should
> In supplication nod,

not, as in the case of his wife and of his child, the effect also of her presence on him—for of little Marcius he says,

> my young boy
> Hath an aspect of intercession, which
> Great nature cries, "Deny not."

Again he feels a power mightier than himself making him relent, and again he tries to fortify himself:

> I'll never
> Be such a gosling to obey instinct, but stand
> As if a man were author of himself
> And knew no other kin.

"My lord and husband!" cries Virgilia, who is the first to greet him, and by the time she has spoken one line and a half more, the instinct he has just sworn never to obey overwhelms him utterly:

> Like a dull actor now,
> I have forgot my part, and I am out,
> Even to a full disgrace.

The old metaphor! But with what irony Shakespeare now uses it! So far from being a dull actor who forgets his part, it is all his life since childhood up to now that Coriolanus has been a dull actor—though, because he was scarcely to blame, *miscast* would be a better word—and now for the first time he finds the role for which he was made. He has caught the butterfly, but he does not mammock it. With words sufficient in themselves to foretell that the one who utters them will never be able to set vengeance above love, he takes Virgilia in his arms:

> O, a kiss
> Long as my exile, sweet as my revenge!
> Now, by the jealous queen of heaven, that kiss
> I carried from thee, dear; and my true lip
> Hath virgin'd it e'er since.

(Only Brutus to Portia the morning before the assassination of Caesar, and Othello to Desdemona on his arrival at Cyprus, can vie with that!) Volumnia is left ungreeted until the embrace of Virgilia is over. It may seem a trifle, but it confirms the fact that "my wife comes foremost." "First he kissed his mother," says Plutarch. Shakespeare altered that!

> Sink, my knee, i' the earth,

he says as he falls before her,

> Of thy deep duty more impression show
> Than that of common sons.

Duty has replaced love. But she bids him stand while she falls on her knees herself. Inevitably we think of King Lear kneeling to Cordelia. But what worlds away from that moment is this one! That father was all humility and self-forgetfulness. This mother takes care to point out how hard the flinty ground is on which she kneels and how improper the duty she is performing, involving as it does an inversion of the natural relation of parent and child.

> What is this?
> Your knees to me? to your corrected son?

that son cries,

> Then let the pebbles on the hungry beach
> Fillip the stars; then let the mutinous winds
> Strike the proud cedars 'gainst the fiery sun,
> Murd'ring impossibility, to make
> What cannot be, slight work.

The exaggerated rhetoric of that seems expressly fashioned to contrast with the noble simplicity and poetry of his greeting to his wife. It is easy enough to tell which is God's Coriolanus—Virgilia's or Volumnia's—and which, if either, will be the one who will forgive. Volumnia, however, forgetting she has come for the unaccustomed task of making her son forget war, is so delighted with his old tone that she exclaims:

> Thou art my warrior;
> I holp to frame thee.

But as Coriolanus turns from her to greet Valeria, the poet in him instantly revives:

> The noble sister of Publicola,
> The moon of Rome, chaste as the icicle
> That's curded by the frost from purest snow
> And hangs on Dian's temple. Dear Valeria!

Surely Shakespeare means something by these sudden shifts of style and imagery! And perhaps the most revealing one of all comes as the grandmother points to the grandson, little Marcius, and says:

> This is a poor epitome of yours
> Which by the interpretation of full time
> May show like all yourself.

"I hope this boy will grow up to be like his father, another great warrior," she says in effect, and the implication is that, so far, her education of him has not been wholly successful. If her treatment of her own son is any precedent, however, we know she will not leave the "interpretation" to time alone but will collaborate vigorously in molding the boy's future. But Coriolanus will not let it rest at that. Almost as if in rebuke of his mother, he prays that his son may be invested with three virtues: nobility of thought, invulnerability to shame, and steadfastness—

> Like a great sea-mark, standing every flaw,
> And saving those that eye thee!

—a prayer that is being answered at the very moment it is uttered as Coriolanus stands there "eyeing" his son and drinking in salvation. It is as if he thinks of him as a rock, or even, to translate the image into more modern terms, a lighthouse.

Volumnia, at this point, launches into an argument of over eighty lines which is interrupted in just one place by two lines of Virgilia's, a line and a half of the boy's, and two and a half of Coriolanus'—the last a cry from the bottom of his heart that shows that the few words of his wife and child have availed far more than his mother's reasons. It is the crisis (the play's second one):

> Not of a woman's tenderness to be,
> Requires nor child nor woman's face to see.
> I have sat too long. (*He rises*)

To what woman he refers, or at least to what one he does not refer, the word "tenderness" reveals, the last one in the language to fit Volumnia. And that it is of the effect of seeing a woman's face, not of hearing her voice, that he speaks shows again what force is converting him, for Virgilia, it will be remembered, he has named "my gracious silence."

Volumnia loves to talk, but even she, at last, seems to get an inkling of the fact that her prating like a man in the stocks (her own image) is getting her nowhere, and the persistence with which she begs some one of the other three (four counting Valeria) to say something becomes almost comic. She is stranded as it were on their silence. "Speak to me, son," she entreats, and, again, five lines later, "Why dost not speak?"

> Daughter, speak you;
> He cares not for your weeping.

(But her weeping is precisely what he does care for.)

> Speak thou, boy;
> Perhaps thy childishness will move him more
> Than can our reasons.

Of course it will, reviving, as it is bound to do, memories of his own child-hood. And, with high irony, Shakespeare chooses the very moment when Coriolanus is inarticulate with his wife's tears, his boy's innocence, and his own heart, to have Volumnia say:

> There is no man in the world
> More bound to 's mother.

With none of them coming to her rescue with so much as a word, she fairly flounders from one thing to another, complaining that her son has never shown her any courtesy, comparing herself to a clucking hen, and even threatening, if he spurns a just request, that the gods will plague him for neglecting the duty a son owes his mother! She descends almost to scolding, as if he were indeed still a child.

> He turns away,

she exclaims. Who can doubt that it is to hide his tears? But she, insensitive as ever, thinks he is turning his back on their petition, and bids them all kneel in one final appeal. Even the little Marcius falls on his knees and lifts his hands in entreaty to his father. If that father had been made of stone that must have touched him, and so far from being made of stone, Coriolanus is all tenderness at the center. Even Volumnia gets a hint of what is happening and perceives that if the child does not decide things in their favor nothing will:

> This boy, that cannot tell what he would have,
> But kneels and holds up hands for fellowship,
> Does reason our petition with more strength
> Than thou hast to deny 't.

Declaring that she is done with words and will speak no more till Rome is on fire, she bids them rise from their knees:

> Come, let us go:
> This fellow had a Volscian to his mother;
> His wife is in Corioli, and his child
> Like him by chance.

Why does Shakespeare seize just this moment to remind us of the likeness between father and child? Why but to show us what force has finally melted Coriolanus? A second more and he has capitulated.

O mother, mother!
What have you done?

Characteristically he thinks she has done it all, as if everything had happened just between her and him. And no one would wish to underestimate her contribution. But whatever that contribution was, it would have amounted to nothing if the wife and the boy had not been there to translate its logic into love and imaginative power. Volumnia admits that the child is like the father. What she does not perceive is that the father is still like the child. Another mother and another son are acting through their very inaction over the heads of the apparent actors; the effective forces are the dove-like eyes of Virgilia, her tears, her silence, the innocence of the boy and the innocent memories he stirs of another boy not yet utterly crushed by a false education and example. It is not the mother, then, who performs the miracle, nor the child. It is the-mother-and-the-child.

Shakespeare leaves so much to pantomime and stage business in this scene that a director with his eye only on its general effect (probably preconceived) can easily produce it so as to obliterate the significance of the many tiny details and hidden stage directions with which it is filled. But every one of them must be taken into account.

A characteristic touch in the next scene seems to confirm our interpretation of the one we have been discussing. The muddle-headed Menenius gives all the credit to Volumnia for her son's change of heart! It is almost enough in itself to prove that Shakespeare doesn't. It is a way he often uses for slipping in his own opinion—as in the case of John of Lancaster's comment on the rejection of Falstaff.

But assume, if you will, that all these things mean nothing, that it is Volumnia who tips the scales against revenge. Would that mean that her son has lost his hard-won freedom, is again under her old dominion? Decidedly not; for however little her character may be changed, her object in this scene is the very opposite of everything she formerly fought for. She may still be at heart the same Amazonian father-mother to whom he was once a slave. But at least it is not bloodshed for which she is now pleading. Whatever her spirit, her goal is now a genuinely maternal one. Whatever her motive, it is forgiveness, mercy, tenderness, love, she now seeks in her son. And these things are what a mother means. In that sense, Coriolanus never had a mother till this moment. Mother and child had previously pulled in opposite directions; now they are pulling in the same one. Motherhood is indeed a mighty influence in this crisis—but it is something mightier than the force of this individual mother Volumnia and not to be identified with her. Whether Volumnia herself was permanently softened by this unwonted experience and by the ultimate tragedy we shall never know. It seems unlikely.

<h2 style="text-align:center">VIII</h2>

To the metaphors of the butterfly and the actor—positive and negative symbols of the same idea—is added a third figure, a simile this time, that indirectly confirms them and carries us into the political heart of the play: Menenius' parable of the belly.

Menenius appears to be a genial and hearty old gentleman, kindly, humorous, and humane, with the ripe wisdom that comes of experience, a patrician yet a man whom a commoner can describe as "one that hath always loved the people." But whoever thinks so had better beware—for Menenius is one of Shakespeare's triumphs in leading readers by their noses to conclusions diametrically opposed to the evidence he places right under those noses. As life so often does.

The best that can be said of Menenius is that he loves Coriolanus—in his doting fashion—and that Coriolanus loves him. The younger man is both "son" and hero to him. The hero-worshiper subscribes fully to Volumnia's idea of her warrior "boy," vies with her in counting up his wounds, and when he gets a letter from him is as delighted as a child. Let Coriolanus be but mentioned, and Menenius' style rises into a kind of grandiloquent poetry. At the end, by touching his "son's" heart, just before his critical interview with the women, he contributes to the final act of mercy. For all this we can forgive him much. But he cannot be judged by his amiableness with his own kind. It is a man's relationship with his social inferiors that is a better test of his character. And the moment we bring Menenius to that test we see that his graciousness is largely veneer and that underneath is a hypocrite, a fool, and a snob. These are harsh terms, but they are justified by the text, though we may feel like mitigating them in view of the man's encroaching second childhood, which makes even his vanity a bit disarming. Menenius loves an audience above everything. He is even willing to talk endlessly with the plebeians and their tribunes for the sake of hearing himself talk. He considers himself a blunt fellow who always blurts out the truth ("What I think, I utter, and spend my malice in my breath"), a great "democrat" as we would say today. Because they are entertaining, his tart wit and command of picturesquely abusive language can easily blind us here. His long tirade, for instance, against the tribunes for wasting time in talk and calling names fits himself as well as it does them. It shows how lacking he is in what he has been so often praised for—a sense of humor. He has about as much of it as Polonius himself, a figure with whom he, though far less tedious, has other points in common. As does Ophelia's father, he prides himself most on the very qualities in which he is most deficient—humor, wisdom, psychological insight, and diplomacy. The result—as in the case of Malvolio—is both comic and pathetic. There must have been some reason for the care and detail with which Shakespeare drew this old man. What that reason was ought to be clear: Menenius is what Coriolanus is generally held to be and isn't—an inveterate tory and patrician.

Politically, Menenius reminds us in some respects of that well-meaning weakling York in *Richard II*, and of Richard himself in that the word "peace" or its equivalent is so often on his lips. The peace he believes in in a crisis is the kind of colorless compromise and "good" feeling that quickly leads to worse complications than before, accompanied usually by an outburst of irritation or temper from the pacifist himself.

But the key to Menenius is his stomach. This is forever at the center for him figuratively as well as literally, and continually perverts his perspective. He is a gourmand and diner-out, and one of the few good things that Brutus the tribune contributes to the play is his thrust at Menenius: "Come, come, you are well understood to be a perfecter giber for the table than a necessary bencher in the Capitol." How well deserved that was is proved near the end when Menenius declares that Cominius, who went to intercede with Coriolanus for mercy to Rome, chose the wrong psychological, or rather gastronomic, moment for his interview:

> He was not taken well; he had not din'd,

and the old man craftily plans to find out the propitious moment and himself seek the one on whose will Rome's destiny hangs—when his stomach is full. Digestive comfort, or repletion rather, might well have tipped the balance in Menenius' case, had the roles been reversed. But it would have made as little difference to Coriolanus as to Saint Francis himself. Money talks, we are in the habit of saying. The belly talks, Menenius might have said in the same sense. In fact he does say it:

> For, look you, I may make the belly smile
> As well as speak.

A smiling belly! it could pass as a succinct description of Menenius himself.

All this is contrived, of course, to make the fable of the belly both highly appropriate and fatally ironic on Menenius' lips. That fable, rightly understood, contains profound political and social wisdom. But the truth in the mouth of a man like Menenius is as dangerous as a sword in the hands of a child. As "to thine own self be true" sounds when Polonius says it, so sounds the parable of the belly coming from Menenius.

He tells it, it will be remembered, in the first scene of the play. Rome is suffering from a dearth and the drama opens with the entry of a *"Company of mutinous* CITIZENS, *with staves, clubs, and other weapons."* The crowd of plebeians is represented vocally by just two, one of them, the ringleader, like most ringleaders, doing most of the talking.* He is marvelously individualized: an egotistical, loud-mouthed, malicious, illogical troublemaker and knave who has not a few of the characteristics of Jack Cade—and yet not natively bad, but made bad by a hard life and amenable as a child to better influence. The grievances he complains of are real, but the relative state of his blood and judgment at the moment is revealed when he exclaims: "Let us revenge this with our pikes ere we become rakes; for the gods know I speak this in hunger for bread, not in thirst for revenge." The end of his sentence has forgotten its beginning.

The people are famished: this man's ready remedy is the killing of Caius Marcius, whom he dubs "chief enemy to the people." Holding the balance even, as he always does, among the common people as individuals, Shakespeare puts into contrast with the First Citizen a Second Citizen, whom the ringleader permits only a few words, but who is as deliberate, reasonable, and lacking in malice as his fellow is not. The poet relies on mass psychology in his auditors as fully as the ringleader does in his mutinous company, and it is a tribute to his art that the First Citizen hypnotizes not a few modern readers as completely as he does the Roman crowd in the play. Ask a group who have just read this scene (not seen it in the theater, for where is the stage director who can be trusted not to tamper with the text?) to describe the temper of the crowd, and practically all of them will give a description of the temper of its ringleader, and, from this, will pass to the conclusion that the rest of its members are just like him and that here we have Shakespeare's opinion of the common people—never so much as noticing the character of the Second Citizen, for instance. Now the proper inference to be drawn, of course, is not that all the common people are like the First Citizen but that they *are* just docile and weak enough to let him represent and fool them. How can the reader who has only now been fooled by the same man in the same way object to the veracity of the psychology?†

Menenius comes in. Caius Marcius, we were told, is the chief enemy of the people. Here is their chief friend.

---

* In this discussion I follow the many editions that give most of the lines to the First Citizen.

† George Brandes, discussing this play, shows how insensitive he is to Shakespeare's astonishing discrimination of individuals among the common people. "For the people," he says, "he felt nothing but scorn, and he was now, more than ever, incapable of seeing them as an aggregation of separate individualities; they were merged in the brutality which distinguished them in the mass. Humanity in general was to him not millions of individuals, but a few great entities amidst millions of non-entities."

> Why, masters, my good friends, mine honest neighbours,
> Will you undo yourselves?

the old gentleman begins. We can hear his grieved tone and almost see him knead his hands.

> We cannot, sir, we are undone already,

the ringleader retorts wittily and quite to the point. And then follows a scene which is the political key to the play, an amalgam of humor, under-intention, irony, and wisdom that puts it almost beside the galley scene in *Antony and Cleopatra*.

> I tell you, friends, most charitable care
> Have the patricians of you,

the Chief Friend of the People begins.

> > For your wants,
> Your suffering in this dearth, you may as well
> Strike at the heaven with your staves as lift them
> Against the Roman state, whose course will on
> The way it takes, cracking ten thousand curbs
> Of more strong link asunder than can ever
> Appear in your impediment. For the dearth,
> The gods, not the patricians, make it, and
> Your knees to them, not arms, must help. Alack,
> You are transported by calamity
> Thither where more attends you, and you slander
> The helms o' the state, who care for you like fathers,
> When you curse them as enemies.

It is a shame to subject this sympathetic pronouncement to scrutiny. But we must. It reduces to this:

1. The patricians care for you plebeians most charitably.
2. You must look to the gods to supply your wants in answer to prayer.
3. The chariot of the state will ride over you if you get in its way.
4. We patricians are "the helms o' the state" (and so, though the speaker does not point that out, presumably the drivers of the chariot).
5. We patricians—as I said before—care for you plebeians like fathers.

"Care for us!" cries the ringleader with contempt, and he counters this silly attempt of Menenius to put the blame on the gods with a bill of particulars that puts it squarely on the patricians. "If the wars eat us not up," he concludes, "they will; and there's all the love they bear us." Remembering Shakespeare's gallery of "fathers," including the Amazonian "father" in this play, we suspect he is correct.

It must be that "eat us not up" that ͵uts into Menenius' head the fable of the belly: the story of the revolt of the other members of the body against it because, while they were busy ministering to one another's needs, it remained inactive in the middle of the body, hoarding the food. He forgets that he has just told his auditors to look to the gods, not to the patricians, in their trouble, and he proceeds to set up a comparison that utterly contradicts that advice and tallies fatally with the plebeian analysis of the political situation in Rome. Menenius is better at telling a story than at understanding it.

MEN.:   I shall tell you
        A pretty tale. It may be you have heard it;
        But, since it serves my purpose, I will venture
        To stale 't a little more.
FIRST CIT.: Well, I'll hear it, sir: yet you must not think to fob off our dis-
        grace with a tale. But, an 't please you, deliver.
MEN.:   There was a time when all the body's members
        Rebell'd against the belly, thus accus'd it:
        That only like a gulf it did remain
        I' the midst o' the body, idle and unactive,
        Still cupboarding the viand, never bearing
        Like labour with the rest, where the other instruments
        Did see and hear, devise, instruct, walk, feel
        And, mutually participate, did minister
        Unto the appetite and affection common
        Of the whole body. The belly answer'd—
FIRST CIT.: Well, sir, what answer made the belly?

(He who but a moment ago was a ringleader is now an open-mouthed child listening to a story.)

MEN.:   Sir, I shall tell you. With a kind of smile,
        Which ne'er came from the lungs, but even thus—
        For, look you, I may make the belly smile
        As well as speak—it tauntingly replied
        To the discontented members, the mutinous parts
        That envied his receipt; even so most fitly
        As you malign our senators for that
        They are not such as you.

Menenius has made exactly Hamlet's mistake of beginning to expound and point out the application of his story before he is through telling it. And that "kind of smile" that did not come from deep down but was a taunt in disguise—what a perfect description of his own state of mind at the moment!

And just here comes the great surprise of the scene. The enthralled ring-leader, no longer ringleader but creative listener, again interrupts, and with an accent and an insight that seem incredible coming from a man who a moment ago was inciting a mob to murder, shows that a great fable, even if told by a stupid man, can still produce an authentic effect on an imaginative mind.

> Your belly's answer?

he breaks in,

> What!
> The kingly-crowned head, the vigilant eye,
> The counsellor heart, the arm our soldier,
> Our steed the leg, the tongue our trumpeter,
> With other muniments and petty helps
> In this our fabric, if that they—

But now it is Menenius' turn to interrupt, for he senses in some dumb way that his story is being taken out of his mouth.

> What then?
> 'Fore me, this fellow speaks!

What a giveaway! This fake democrat and Chief Friend of the People is going to have no low fellow *before him*, and in that phrase, as if in one flash, his fable explodes. "Helms o' the state" and "fathers" we now perceive, if we didn't before, are what he really considers the patricians. Any resemblance on their part to this altruistic belly is destined to cease the moment the mutiny is quelled.

And more than this. Which is the philosopher here and which the fool? Which of the two, plebeian or patrician, has caught the truly aristocratic interpretation of the fable? The comparison of the body politic to the body is one of the oldest in human thought. With what irony Shakespeare lets this Plato of the people* seize on the vital distinction between organs that like the head, the heart, and the eye, are in a way ends in themselves, and organs like the arm, the leg, and the stomach, that are means only—while his supposed aristocrat goes on to identify the ruling class with the inferior organ around which his own life revolves, quite oblivious of the

---

* This anonymous plebeian Plato has a famous forerunner in Shakespeare's pages, a man of high birth but of genuinely democratic instincts: Falstaff. Falstaff, with no interest whatever in the commonweal, in his apostrophe to wine seizes on the same distinction as the ringleader but imparts to his analogy, characteristically, a less aristocratic flavor than his Roman compeer. Wine, he declares, "illumineth the face, which, as a beacon, gives warning to all the rest of this little kingdom, man, to arm; and then the vital commoners and inland petty spirits muster me all to their captain, the heart, who, great and puffed up with this retinue, doth any deed of courage." The best political philosophers are plainly the unconscious ones.

fatality to his argument of this identification! Thus does unconscious common sense expose patrician sham. Menenius is as blind to the full meaning of his parable as Polonius was to the truth of his maxims. The First Citizen has punctured his casuistical moral in advance.

But Menenius in his interruption of the ringleader has been worse than inconsistent. The rude snobbery of his tone is instantly registered in the Citizen's change of temper and vocabulary. He reverts from his role of inspired child to that of indignant ringleader and thug. If these higher organs —he cries in reply to Menenius' "What then? what then?"—

> Should by the cormorant belly be restrain'd,
> Who is the sink o' the body,

and should complain at their treatment,

> What could the belly answer?

The man is as bellicose and abusive as before. Menenius has missed the opportunity of a lifetime. He all but stumbled on the miracle of converting a dangerous rebel into a child, philosopher, and friend. But he is totally unaware of it and blunders on into his transformation of "the belly's answer" into a moral and political boomerang:

> Your most grave belly was deliberate,
> Not rash like his accusers, and thus answer'd:
> "True is it, my incorporate friends," quoth he,
> "That I receive the general food at first,
> Which you do live upon; and fit it is,
> Because I am the store-house and the shop
> Of the whole body: but, if you do remember,
> I send it through the rivers of your blood,
> Even to the court, the heart, to the seat o' the brain;
> And, through the cranks and offices of man,
> The strongest nerves and small inferior veins
> From me receive that natural competency
> Whereby they live. And though that all at once,
> You, my good friends,"—this says the belly, mark me,—

Menenius evidently hesitates, a bit embarrassed, at this point. And well he might. For what is his argument? Nothing—in the circumstances—but the old sophistry that has been the resort of the powerful and the privileged in all ages: *If only we are prosperous, some of our prosperity is bound to trickle down to you. Let the stomach flourish and the smallest capillaries will be nourished.* To which the First Citizen—whose power to detect fallacies is not equal to his imagination—can only stammer in reply, "Ay, sir;

well, well," and Menenius, regaining courage, goes on, still speaking for the
belly:

> "Though all at once cannot
> See what I do deliver out to each,
> Yet I can make my audit up, that all
> From me do back receive the flour of all,
> And leave me but the bran."

And we picture this pious old epicure, Menenius himself, as a sample patrician, humbly breakfasting on bran—hastily, that he may get the sooner
to his honest morning's work as auditor—while these very mutinous citizens, for example, sit down to thick steaks. Even as physiology, Menenius'
narrative will not do: as political philosophy, in the situation, it is pitiful.
Imagine Coriolanus being guilty of any such sad stuff. "What say you
to 't?" demands the triumphant orator of his gaping audience.

"It was an answer," replies the First Citizen, aware that something is the
trouble but at a loss to discover what it is. "How apply you this?"

> MEN.: The senators of Rome are this good belly,
>   And you the mutinous members,

(including brain, heart, and eye, presumably)

>   for examine
>   Their counsels and their cares, digest things rightly
>   Touching the weal o' the common, you shall find
>   No public benefit which you receive
>   But it proceeds or comes from them to you
>   And no way from yourselves. What do you think,

he concludes, turning directly and derisively to the ringleader,

>   You, the great toe of this assembly?

It is a hit, but the tone of it shows in one line how utterly Menenius rejects his own parable in practice.

> FIRST CIT.: I the great toe! Why the great toe?
> MEN.:   For that, being one o' the lowest, basest, poorest,
>   Of this most wise rebellion, thou go'st foremost;
>   Thou rascal, that art worst in blood to run,
>   Lead'st first to win some vantage.
>   But make you ready your stiff bats and clubs;
>   Rome and her rats are at the point of battle,
>   The one side must have bale.

There is the sweetness and light of the born patrician! It is as if Caius Marcius, whose approaching footsteps have grown louder during this speech,

had sent before him the spirit of sincerity. Menenius at last says exactly what he thinks, and there is more honesty in the half-dozen lines of that Thersites-like outburst than in the fourscore of his preceding flatteries. "Rome and her rats!" "at battle!" What a comment on

> Why, masters, my good friends, mine honest neighbours,

with which the scene began. And what a commentary on the fable of the belly! Here is another ending that forgot not only its beginning but its middle.

IX

And this is the play, and this particularly the scene, that is relied on to demonstrate Shakespeare's prejudice in favor of the upper classes and his lack of sympathy for the common people and the democratic ideal! On what insane root, one wonders, have those critics eaten who argue so?

The unperverted implication of the fable of the belly is of course the idea of mutual participation, a hint of which Menenius, to his own logical confusion, lets slip out. It is the Pauline doctrine that we are all members one of another, one of the best expressions of the Christian, and of the democratic, ideal—which on this point are indistinguishable—that can be imagined. It is good political as well as good physiological science—and good religion. The whole play *Coriolanus* is a poetic demonstration of this truth, and its hero, with all his virtues, made, by his own confession, the capital mistake of trying to live

> As if a man were author of himself
> And knew no other kin,

the same mistake, strangely, that that archvillain Richard III made when he avowed as his creed at the beginning of his career,

> I am myself alone.

Coriolanus was a great individual. And no one loved individuals, "great" or "small," more than Shakespeare. But to be an individual, his plays increasingly show, it is not enough to be one's self in a limited sense; it is necessary also to live sympathetically in the lives of others.

> Heaven doth with us as we with torches do,
> Not light them for themselves; for if our virtues
> Did not go forth of us, 'twere all alike
> As if we had them not.

When Coriolanus embraces Virgilia and lets tenderness and mercy get the better of pride and consistency and revenge, when he sacrifices his head to his heart, his lifelong code to his gentler instincts, then for the first time he lets his various "parts" become members one of another and becomes himself something like the complete man he never was on the battlefield for all his valor. The dragon reverts to the butterfly. Virgilia's kiss is literally a dissolvent of war.

How easy it is to misread completely the man this brave and gentle woman loved so profoundly! Hasty, superficial, or prejudiced readers think this proud idealist wanted to be dictator of Rome. A wild notion, contradicted on almost every page of the play:

> Cor.:　　　　　　Know, good mother,
> I had rather be their servant in my way
> Than sway with them in theirs.

That is inverted pride, or egotism, if you will, but the dictatorial spirit it is not. No would-be tyrant was ever wise enough to speak even insincerely in that fashion, much less sincerely, and the stray line or two of Marcius' that without their context might be construed as an expression of class feeling fall from him in extreme anger.* Coriolanus' sin was not an ambition to dictate to the people, but the deeper one of presuming to dictate to the gods. It is true that he despised the common people, not, however, because they were the lowest class but because in his estimation they were common—cowards and fools, men who cared more for sports than for valor,

> Time-pleasers, flatterers, foes to nobleness.

And he had faith in the patricians, not as the ruling class as such, but because he held them to be friends to nobleness. Shakespeare supplies evidence that Coriolanus was blind to the facts in both cases; but his blindness is another article entirely from class prejudice. It may appear to work out to much the same thing in its practical political effects—though I do not think so—but at least it is totally different in the man's soul.

Whoever judges otherwise will find himself in the flattering intellectual company of Brutus and Sicinius, the tribunes, as pretty a pair of demagogues and rascals as will be encountered in all political literature. Their technique may be illustrated from the scene where the type of Coriolanus' punishment is in question. Says Sicinius:

> Assemble presently the people hither;
> And when they hear me say, "It shall be so
> I' the right and strength o' the commons," be it either

---

* The incident of the poor man in Corioli who had been his host but whose name he forgets shows both sides of Coriolanus. In Plutarch the man is an old friend of Marcius', formerly of great wealth. Shakespeare clearly left out that touch, for a reason.

For death, for fine, or banishment, then let them,
If I say fine, cry "Fine!" if death, cry "Death!"
Insisting on the old prerogative
And power i' the truth o' the cause.

It is all exactly in the manner of "pressure groups" in our own day who induce thousands of persons to send identical telegrams to representatives and senators. The negation of democracy in democracy's name.

It was these two, Brutus and Sicinius, who believed, or rather gave it out that they believed, that Coriolanus wanted to be dictator, "affecting one sole throne, without assistance"; and, in the picture they draw of the people being turned into camels and mules at his behest, they let escape the secret craving for power in their own hearts. Nearly all the characters in this play are sharply individualized. These two are scarcely more distinguished than Rosencrantz and Guildenstern. Two of a kind is all we can say of them. The eternal petty politician. Ibsen's *An Enemy of the People*—whose title might have been taken from this play—shows that they do not alter from century to century. After all the sly and cowardly attempts of the two tribunes to butter their bread on both sides, the most pacific reader finds it hard not to glow with delight to see them shivering at the expected subjugation of the city by their old enemy. Even the dove-eyed Virgilia tells them, in effect, exactly where they may go.

Though, as a crowd, the people in this play are quite under the thumbs of these creatures, Shakespeare is again careful to show that individuals among them, when speaking for themselves, have plenty of insight. In the scene where the people report to the tribunes how Marcius conducted himself when asking for their voices, one man declares that he mocked them; another that he flouted them downright.

No, 'tis his kind of speech; he did not mock us,

says a third, sizing up Coriolanus as perfectly as could be done in one line. You can't fool all the people all the time. Shakespeare too believed that. It is an obscure Volscian servingman who makes what is perhaps the most illuminating remark on war and peace the play contains. Peace makes men hate one another, one of his fellow-servants has just observed, meaning by the word, as most men do, not peace but the absence of war. "Reason": this humble political philosopher retorts, "because they then less need one another." The oblique allusion to the fable of the belly is unmistakable.

For those who are alert to them, Shakespeare's works abound in these little touches that reveal an almost Wordsworthian faith in the existence of nobility and wisdom in obscurity. Why does their author leave these things themselves in obscurity, as it were, so hidden, so unitalicized, so abandoned to us to discover? Is it not because life does just that? Shakespeare does not make the mistake of the nineteenth century. The nineteenth century mistook a dogma and a word, democracy, and a bit of political machinery, the ballot, for democracy itself. Only a few of its major prophets detected the error. Emerson was one of them—Emerson whom John Jay Chapman called the "younger brother of Shakespeare" and who cannot be quoted too often in an attempt to understand his predecessor. "I have just been conversing with one man," says Emerson in the last sentence of his neglected essay on Politics, "to whom no weight of adverse experience will make it for a moment appear impossible that thousands of human beings might exercise towards each other the grandest and simplest sentiments, as well as a knot of friends, or a pair of lovers." There we have a glimpse of that society of individuals wherein democracy, if it ever comes, will consist—the polar opposite in every respect of the crowd, and still more of the mob. "The mob," says Emerson, who was once howled down by one, "ought to be treated only with contempt. Phocion, even Jesus, cannot otherwise regard it in so far as it is mob. It is [the] mere beast of them who compose it; their soul is absent from it." Whether he did or not, Shakespeare might well have helped his "younger brother" to grasp just the distinction these two passages involve. The elder poet understood the difference between the many who loved Rosalind and Hamlet and the rabble that backed Laertes and Jack Cade.

But the best brief description of the spirit of the mob with which I am acquainted is that of Eugene V. Debs. To get it in perspective it is necessary first to recall Debs's words to the now forgotten judge who was about to sentence him to prison. "Your honor," he said, "years ago I recognized my kinship with all living beings, and I made up my mind that I was not one bit better than the meanest of the earth. I said then, and I say now, that while there is a lower class, I am in it; while there is a criminal element, I am of it; while there is a soul in prison, I am not free." That, admittedly, does not sound like Coriolanus. But now listen to Debs on the mob:

I never saw one that was against me; my experience has been entirely with mobs that were on my side. They were awful. When I got out of jail after my first big strike in Chicago, a crowd of thousands met me; they surged upon me, seized me, and, lifting me up, passed me from hand to hand over their heads. I was safe, of course, but I was afraid. I was afraid as of a beast, for those men that bore me aloft all looked alike, they all stared in the same direction, and their eyes were not the eyes of men, but of animals. They smelt like a beast, too. That odor of hate, the smell of animal ferocity! No, I never want to meet that again.

Coriolanus and Eugene Debs! the ancient Roman aristocrat and the despised and loved American labor leader. What a pair to discover in agreement! One knew only mobs that were against him, the other only those that were for him. Yet they pick out identical criteria of the Hydra-headed monster they both hate: its nauseating odor and its resemblance to a beast. The words of Debs may well give pause to the many readers and critics who have denounced Shakespeare as a snob and hater of the common people for his emphasis on these things. Not that I am comparing Coriolanus with Eugene Debs, or suggesting that because he abhorred men in the mass he was a pre-eminent lover of them as individuals, though the incident of the poor man at whose house he lay in Corioli suggests that he had unrealized powers in that direction.

X

Why did Coriolanus loathe the mob—not with the philosophic contempt of an Emerson nor with the defensive shrinking of a Debs, but with a positive and fierce abhorrence?

We hate—in that way—what we fear. And the more unconscious the fear the more intense the hatred. Coriolanus hated the mob because, without knowing it, he feared it. Why should he, of all men, fear it? Not physically at all, and not politically in any high degree. He feared it imaginatively and symbolically. To see this is to see into the very heart of the man.

Coriolanus is built on an antithesis, a figure and an anti-figure: mankind as a mass versus mankind as an organism. The ancient companion metaphors of the body politic and of man as a little kingdom identify the appetites and the slave class as the lowest strata, respectively, of the mind and of mankind. The slave becomes for this reason the inevitable symbol of the animal nature, and, conversely, the animal instincts are, psychologically, slaves. Hence emerges the symbolical equation *beast = mob = passion*. The mob *is* passion. The passions *are* a mob. It is so in mythology, it is so in dreams, it is so in poetry. The imaginative literature of all ages offers examples. In modern times the Russian classics, written under the czarist despotism, offer particularly striking ones.

When Anna Karenina, against her highest instincts, gives way to her lower ones with Vronsky, her dreams are haunted by a dirty unkempt peasant who clearly embodies for Tolstoy both her own lower nature and the class in Russia that Anna's class has injured. (We hate what we have hurt.) In *The Brothers Karamazov* the little peasant whom Ivan treads on and abandons in the snow before his interview with the devil, but whom he picks up and helps after his better instincts have conquered his worser ones, is a veritable barometer of Ivan's spiritual condition. And Chekhov's stories abound in the same symbolism.

Now *Coriolanus* is based on precisely these images. Marcius himself, molded from infancy by his mother, becomes a warrior against the fine grain of his nature. But offensive war is founded on the passions: on lust, on greed, on pride, and on revenge. In strict proportion to the violence his soul has undergone is the violence of Coriolanus' unconscious detestation of his lower nature. But being nothing of a psychologist, he projects his hatred of that lower nature into the mass of mankind, and sees it as a monster. The nauseous odor of it which he can never forget is the measure of his loathing for himself. The emotion it elicits goes far beyond the unpleasant reaction that the unpleasant smell itself might warrant.

That we may not miss his point, Shakespeare makes Coriolanus make it himself, though of course he does not realize what he is saying:

> For the mutable, rank-scented many, let them
> Regard me as I do not flatter, and
> *Therein behold themselves.*

A mob without gazing at a mob within. Each is looking in a glass. What wonder that they hate each other! And the final proof that this diagnosis is correct is the fact that it is the word "traitor" that explodes Coriolanus as a match does a keg of powder. It touches the sorest spot in his soul, for he has been a traitor, not to Rome, but to himself in obeying his mother and not *it*. Because she has praised him into being a warrior, he resents any praise of his heroism from others or any exhibition of it on his own part. Here the false pride of his mother's son gets entangled with the genuine modesty of his real self, to the bewilderment of readers and the wrangling of critics. But however we assess the mixture, we can all agree that Coriolanus lacks unconsciousness of his virtue. "And above all, my children, says William Law, the Quaker, in his *Serious Call*, "have a care of vain and proud thoughts of your own virtues. For as soon as ever people live different from the common way of the world, and despise its vanities, the devil represents to their minds the height of their own perfections; and is content they should excel in good works, provided that he can but make them proud of them. Therefore watch over your virtues with a jealous eye, and reject every vain thought, as you would reject the most wicked imagination; and think what a loss it would be to you to have the fruit of all your good works devoured by the vanity of your own minds." It might have been written of Coriolanus, so perfectly does it fit his case. He had virtues, but he could not forget the fact that he had them. Not, at least, until near the end. What warfare, literal and spiritual, might have been avoided, if the Puritans, before they closed the theaters, could have read or witnessed *Coriolanus* and understood it!

XI

Coriolanus embraced the truth at the moment when he kissed Virgilia, but he could no more hold the truth continuously in his mind than he could hold his wife perpetually in his arms. His moment of illumination saved Rome. But it would have been cowardly of him to seek personal safety after his "betrayal" of the Volscians. The glory of his giving in is that it is a supreme act of courage as well as of renunciation. He knows that it means his death.

And so he goes back to Corioli to fall under the daggers of Aufidius' hired assassins. The contrast between Aufidius and Coriolanus is complete. Even the Coriolanus who gave way in anger to bitterness of speech could never have been guilty of petty jealousy or treachery. The Roman ascended toward self-conquest. The Volscian descended to revenge and suborned murder. The end of Coriolanus is like that of that other hero, Hector, who fell overpowered by numbers, Aufidius and his assassins playing the same role as Achilles and his Myrmidons—further evidence possibly that the conclusion of *Troilus and Cressida* is Shakespeare's.

The last words of Coriolanus are known the world over, the metaphor in which he couches them having passed into the common speech of man. Aufidius, as the tribunes had done before, "draws" Coriolanus by twice calling him "traitor." But he has in reserve a still more insulting word that is to penetrate even deeper into the underconsciousness of his enemy. He leads up to it gradually. First he taunts him with betraying their common cause "for certain drops of salt"; then with breaking his oath like "a twist of rotten silk"; and finally with whining away victory at the sight of "his nurse's tears."

> Hear'st thou, Mars?

cries Coriolanus, stung, lifting his arms. To which Aufidius retorts,

> Name not the god, thou boy of tears!

Boy! The word infuriates Coriolanus to the point of suffocation. For a second all he can utter is an interjected, "Ha!" But, his breath recovered, his words descend on Aufidius' head like a thousand hammers:

> Measureless liar, thou hast made my heart
> Too great for what contains it. "Boy!" O slave! . . .
> Cut me to pieces, Volsces; men and lads,
> Stain all your edges on me. "Boy!" False hound!
> If you have writ your annals true, 'tis there
> That, like an eagle in a dove-cote, I
> Flutter'd your Volscians in Corioli;
> Alone I did it. "Boy!"

And in a moment more he has fallen.

Three times in those eight lines Coriolanus echoes Aufidius' derisive "Boy!" Why? Because he had all but spoiled his life by remaining the boy-traitor to his soul, the boy-slave of his mother (" 'Boy!' O slave!"). It was the past, not the present, that gave such truth as it contained to Aufidius' insult. The Roman's fierce outburst in reply has in it all the pride, all the arrogance, if you will, of the old Coriolanus. It is full of the spirit of that "boy" his mother most admired. But in its transcendent poetry and courage is there not more than a memory of that other boy his mother did her best to strangle—a boy who long ago loved to explore dove-cotes and still resembles his own child who chases butterflies in the meadow?

"An eagle in a dove-cote"! When we remember Virgilia of the dove-like eyes, and try to imagine her as she must have been after she had parted with her husband and when the news of his death reached her, suddenly one of the harshest of all Shakespeare's endings becomes one of his tenderest and most pathetic. Virgilia! Her reticence makes her role above almost any other in Shakespeare one to which the imagination of the reader must contribute a determining share. For me, she stands with Othello's wife and Lear's youngest daughter. She was called to no such extreme and dramatic sacrifice as they. But, if she had been, she would have been equal to it. I think of her as a sort of Cordelia-Desdemona.

XII

Nothing illuminates the end of *Coriolanus* like the end of *Hamlet*. Each has been a tragedy of revenge. In each the protagonist dies after a burst of anger. Hamlet translates his fury into death dealt to the King with an envenomed sword. Coriolanus presents his own body to the swords of others. The difference is abysmal. The old Coriolanus could have held off a dozen assassins, slaughtered them all perhaps, or at the very least sold his life dear. But he does not. And that he does not demonstrates that he is another man. His old self may echo in his last words. But his last act—or failure to act— is that of the new man created by Virgilia's kiss and the love of his child. It is the best commentary on those who laud Hamlet's final deed of rashness as the accomplishment of a great purpose and hold that a divinity shaped the end he had so rough-hewn.

Chapter XXXIII

Pericles

Pericles was not included in the Shakespearean canon until the second issue of the Third Folio (1664). Yet with a consent rare in such cases there is now wide acceptance of the view that while Shakespeare had little, and possibly nothing, to do with the first two acts, he either wrote most of the last three or contributed liberally to them. Practically all critics admit that he and he only could have composed the storm scene that opens Act III or the recognition scenes, particularly that between Pericles and Marina, of Act V. Nearly everything in these scenes suggests the presence of Shakespeare's genius.

> Thou God of this great vast, rebuke these surges,
> Which wash both heaven and hell.
>   The seaman's whistle
> Is as a whisper in the ears of death,
> Unheard.
>
> A terrible childbed hast thou had, my dear;
> No light, no fire.
>   . . . the belching whale
> And humming water must o'erwhelm thy corpse.
>
>   But are you flesh and blood?
> Have you a working pulse? and are no fairy?
>
> This is the rarest dream that e'er dull sleep
> Did mock sad fools withal. This cannot be.
> My daughter's buried.
>
> Now, blessing on thee! Rise; thou art my child.

Scattered elsewhere throughout the play, mainly in the last three acts, are lines and phrases that are either Shakespeare's or extraordinarily successful imitations of his style.

Pericles is an interweaving of stories but the main interest lies in the separation of Pericles from his daughter, Marina, and his wife, Thaisa, and their reunion at the end. Marina is so clearly and attractively drawn, and she makes such a fitting companion for Perdita and Miranda, that it is natural to assign her entire role to Shakespeare, though it would be easier to believe that he wrote the brothel scenes if they were more nearly contemporary with *Measure for Measure*.

But two excellent scenes, other good ones, and numerous felicities of expression and characterization elsewhere do not suffice to make a drama in the full sense and, as distinguished from what it is in parts, *Pericles* as a whole falls far below the level of the other dramatic romances. It is as if Shakespeare let his imagination, already instinct with the material of these coming creations, play over the surface of someone else's story leaving traces of his genius in place after place, but lingering only long enough to transmute the lead of the original into his own pure gold—not long enough over the whole to constellate it into anything resembling his greater masterpieces. The play remains an exciting series of adventures that violate the unities of time and place in most undramatic fashion. It is held together by narrative suspense and a certain interest in the three main characters, not by any dominating theme. So, while there are passages that approach or reach perfection, the piece as a whole lacks the universality that sends us back again and again to such a play as *The Tempest* or even to *Cymbeline* and *The Winter's Tale* in search of more and more hidden truth. After we have read *Pericles* a few times we feel that we have largely exhausted it, however ready we may be to return to its rarest passages. In this respect the drama is highly uncharacteristic of Shakespeare.

In dramatic, as distinct from theatrical interest on the one hand and poetical interest on the other, the work suffers from its loose structure and romantic plot. Take what is perhaps its greatest scene: the one in which Pericles and Marina are reunited. It is practically perfect as poetry and characterization. Why, then, does it fail to affect us as does the reunion scene between Lear and Cordelia of which it is in many respects an echo? Is it not because here we have no such interest in the two characters for their own sakes built up from the very opening of the play as we have in the other case? Then, too, the father here has never known the daughter, and meets her for the first time—except for a glimpse on shipboard just after she was born—in the last act of the play. However poignant the situation, the interplay of the two lives is much less complicated and significant than in the earlier work.

In spite of this the father-child theme is the heart of the whole. In this respect *Pericles* looks forward specifically to *The Winter's Tale* and *The Tempest*. Thaisa and Marina, the long-lost wife and daughter finally restored to Pericles, correspond to Hermione and Perdita ultimately recovered by Leontes, while in Cerimon we have what might be considered a preliminary sketch of Prospero. Incidentally, the wicked and jealous Dionyza gives us a foretaste of the Queen in *Cymbeline*. And there are other similarities. But the significance of these things lies not so much in the detailed correspondences as in the proof that the parent-child, particularly the father-daughter, relationship was assuming increased importance in Shakespeare's mind toward the end of his life.

Chapter XXXIV

Cymbeline

1

As is well known, Shakespeare's last plays, *Cymbeline, The Winter's Tale,* and *The Tempest* (along with the Shakespearean parts of *Pericles*) are generally grouped together and referred to as romances, dramatic romances, or tragicomedies. As the title *The Winter's Tale* implies, they are romances in the sense that they are narratives in dramatic form. Their plots are complicated, ingenious, improbable in places, but intriguing just as plots. "I am amaz'd with matter," cries Cymbeline, as revelation follows revelation toward the end of the story to which his name gives the title. It "is so like an old tale, that the verity of it is in strong suspicion," remarks a gentleman when the wonders pile up in *The Winter's Tale.* There are readers of these dramas who feel the same way about them. If the term "romantic" be taken in the sense of "like an old tale still," it fits them well enough. But if it is also held to imply that therefore their verity is in strong suspicion, it is open to challenge. For what is more likely to be true than an old tale?

Shakespeare always had a keen eye for theatrical fashion, but there is no evidence that he ever knuckled under to it. He took advantage of it rather to do in a new way what he wanted to do anyway. With the increase in courtly influence under James I, dramatic taste came to favor more and more a type of play associated with the names of Beaumont and Fletcher, in which interest in plot was the predominant factor. It has been held by some that Shakespeare conformed to this veering of the theatrical wind. But even if we assume that his powers diminished after the immense expense of spirit that produced the Tragedies, it is unthinkable that, short of a kind of senility, he could have so gone back on the practice of a lifetime as to begin writing plays with a main eye to the plot, spinning yarns, so to speak, for their own sake. He had always known the importance of the story, but he had always, even in his apprenticeship, kept the story in its place. Then, too, there at the end is that masterpiece, *The Tempest*, a poem which so transcends its story that, though practically all readers have a theory about it, probably no two will ever agree as to its meaning—a refutation in itself of the notion of imaginative decline. *Cymbeline* and *The Winter's Tale* do admittedly in places betray a somewhat easygoing attitude on the author's part toward his material. But what looks like carelessness is often casualness, a totally different thing. These plays may show a certain indifference to audience or reader. They certainly do not show mental enfeeblement or fatigue. Indeed, their overloaded plots and extraordinarily close-packed elliptical style—which at times can become very annoying—suggest a pressure of incident and a rush of metaphor, together with an impatience with rules and language, that approach an imaginative flood. These are not the signs of a man who has worked himself out. Granted that this group of plays does re-employ themes, situations, bits of plot, from their author's earlier works and often reveals the practiced playwright relying on well-tested theatrical devices and successes, still the impression they convey is anything but that of a tired man resting on his laurels. And least of all a man capitulating to fashion or truckling to his audience.

Cymbeline is Shakespeare's most recapitulatory play. It does for a large number of his works what *Twelfth Night* does for the earlier Comedies: echoes them while remaining completely *sui generis*. It exceeds even *Troilus and Cressida* in defying classification, being the strangest mixture of authentic history, legendary history, medieval romance, pastoral, comedy, tragedy, and half-a-dozen other things. Neat, orderly, common-sense, and historical minds ought properly to be driven frantic by it, as, for other reasons, should minds that insist that a play should always remain a play.* With poets, on the contrary, it is a favorite. Tennyson and Swinburne put it near the top. And so did Hazlitt.

It would be tedious to attempt to list all the reverberations in *Cymbeline*. The link of this play with *The Rape of Lucrece* we mentioned when discussing that poem. In ingenuity of plot it recalls *The Comedy of Errors*, but its ingenuity is of a higher order. In its contrast of court and country life, of artificiality and simplicity, it is another *As You Like It*, yet as differ-

---

* "Of all the completed plays of Shakespeare's unaided authorship, this seems to me the poorest. The nine lines of 'Hark, hark! the lark,' now inseparable from Schubert's perfect setting, and the first stanza of 'Fear no more the heat o' th' sun,' have more of Shakespeare's genius in them than all the tedious plot, characters, and sentiments in a lump." (Hazelton Spencer.)

ent—as Hazlitt indicated—as the mountainous retreats of Wales are from the Forest of Arden. Like *King Lear,* it is legendary British history and another story of a daughter, disobedient to a father, who preferred love to worldly place and power. The daughter marrying against the father's wishes links it also with *Othello,* and, as the name Iachimo ("little Iago") suggests, it includes, like its prototype, the plot of a villain against a faithful wife in the course of which the husband is driven close to insanity. Indeed, the play might be called a "little" *Othello* with a happy ending, a bridge in this respect between it and *The Winter's Tale* of approximately the same date. It is *Troilus and Cressida* reversed, the woman here being faithful as the man was there; the man here faithless, for a time, as the woman there was, so far as we know, forever. Not a few passages in the play echo *Macbeth:* the wicked queen, her ambition for her son, and her fearful death remind us of Lady Macbeth, her ambition for her husband, and *her* fearful death. But the mother-son relationship puts the play here nearer to *Coriolanus,* though Volumnia and Cymbeline's wife are worlds apart, and a greater contrast could scarcely be conceived than that between Cloten and Coriolanus. Cloten is closer to that other weakling son-of-his-mother, King John. Historically the action occurs during the emperorship of Augustus Caesar, and, in one sense, in spite of its abysmal difference, it may be considered a sequel to *Antony and Cleopatra* and a continuation of the Roman group. This is the most neglected aspect of the play and a possible clue to its meaning, justifying the chronological place usually given it in the last group of plays. It looks back to the other Roman plays and on to the "romances." And this fact offers a good handle by which to take hold of it.

II

To one reading *Cymbeline* just as a story, the location of certain of its scenes in Italy may seem as accidental and lacking in significance as the same thing in, say, *The Two Gentlemen of Verona.* And as for the Roman Lucius and his legions, they appear to be just so much dramaturgic machinery. But we had better beware. There is *Othello* to warn us that something seemingly insignificant, far in the dramatic background, may be poetically all-important.

Moreover, in addition to a Roman invasion of Britain, the play is full of references to Italy and Rome. As they occur in the text, scattered casually along, they excite little attention. But assembled, they assume another color and unmistakable meaning:

> What false Italian,

cries Pisanio, reading the letter from his master that accuses his mistress,

As poisonous-tongu'd as handed, hath prevail'd
On thy too ready hearing?

> My husband's hand!

exclaims Imogen, when she first sees the same letter,

> That drug-damn'd Italy hath out-craftied him,

and a moment later,

> Some jay of Italy,
> Whose mother was her painting, hath betray'd him!

When Posthumus, coming to his senses near the end, tears off his clothes, his cry is,

> I'll disrobe me
> Of these Italian weeds,

and when Iachimo—"Italian fiend" as Posthumus calls him—looking back on his villainy, confesses and repents, he declares,

> mine Italian brain
> 'Gan in your duller Britain operate
> Most vilely.

These examples give the temper of practically every reference to Italy in the play, on the part at least of any character whom we respect either at the moment or throughout. They are all violently condemnatory; they all have a social-moral bearing; and they all sound more Elizabethan than early British.

But curiously—until we see the reason—the references to Rome have a different tone that discriminates them sharply from those to Italy.* These are all military-political and carry us back to the Roman Empire and the age of Augustus. Yet in spite of Caesar and the historical date, in spite of the legendary British court and of the wager, with its touch of the age of chivalry, the play impresses us as neither Augustan, nor early British, nor medieval, but reminds us, with its account of the Queen's interest in drugs and refined forms of poisoning and its picture of the cosmopolitan gathering in Philario's house in Rome, of the period of the Borgias. Its atmosphere, save for certain scenes, is that of the less delectable aspects of the Italian Renaissance and so of Shakespeare's own time in so far as it was infected by the same virus.

And this links with something else. Adding a detail not mentioned so far as I remember in his source, Shakespeare points out that, since the com-

---

* I note one seeming exception: Imogen's "some Roman courtesan," where we might have expected "some Italian courtesan." But here the reference is merely geographical, as it were.

moners were all in service elsewhere, it became necessary for the empire to recruit its "gentry" for the business of subduing the recalcitrant Britons, who had refused to pay the tribute exacted by Julius Caesar. There would be nothing especially remarkable about that, did not the poet proceed a second time, and then a third, to stress the fact that Britain is to be conquered by Italian gentlemen in combination with certain Gallic forces. Why this triple underlining of the seemingly inconsequential fact that the invasion is to be by *gentlemen?*

It will be conjectured whither all this is leading. Almost from the outset, and increasingly, Shakespeare was plainly impressed by the evil influence on England of the ideas, manners, and morals of the darker side of the Italian Renaissance, both as imported directly from Italy and indirectly from France.

To begin with, there is the Machiavellian politics of the History Plays. This at first was hardly more than the stage tradition of the Machiavel. But, as early as *King John*, it was far more than that, a clear definition of the concept of Commodity, of power politics as we call it, exemplified in detail in that assembly of vile politicians which the History Plays so largely are. Though they were not all directly Italian-taught, these Commodity-servers are all directly, or by implication, indictments of Machiavellian politics.

But the fashions, manners, and morals of Italy are condemned quite as relentlessly as its politics in a long line of young gentlemen—some Italian, some Italian-bred, others only "Italianated"—who parade through Shakespeare's plays, especially his Comedies. The Italian setting of so many of these is comment on the vogue of things Italian among the Elizabethan gentlemen who frequented the theaters, most of whom had traveled and many of whom had been educated in Italy.

There are a few Birons, Benedicks, and Romeos, to be sure, to save the lot from utter damnation, but a general sense of the Italian young gentleman and his kin and copiers in other countries is conveyed by such men as Proteus and Tybalt, Don John and Don Armado, Sir Andrew and Sir Thurio, Bertram and Parolles, Claudio (in *Much Ado*) and Gratiano, Borachio and Roderigo, yes, even Bassanio and Mercutio when their false halos are dissipated, not to mention a majority of the various and nameless, 1st, 2d, and 3d Lords, Gentlemen, and Suitors with whom the plays abound. And time or place need not prevent us from adding figures like Osric and Pandarus, or Rosencrantz and Guildenstern, to the list. "Born originals, how comes it that we all die copies?"

There is simply no escaping the implications of these characters as a group. Interested in everything human, the poet draws most of them with a gaiety and good humor befitting comedy, but underneath his tolerance for the individual—to use that word of those who do not deserve it—can be felt his unmerciful scorn for the type, for its follies and fashions and shams that either flatten out into nonentity or grow into knavery and crime. Most of these gentlemen tend to pass either off and out as social butterflies with Osric, or down and out as cowards and villains with Parolles. "Time's flies!" If there is anything in our reading of *The Two Gentlemen of Verona*, Shakespeare saw through the dash and brilliance, the wit and fine manners of these minute-jacks earlier than has been generally admitted.

Now Iachimo is one of the most illuminating embodiments of the Italian gentleman in this sense in all Shakespeare, the type at something near its best by his own standard, something near its worst by a higher one—until his repentance at the end. It is a notable compliment to both Iachimo's intelligence and his histrionic ability that Shakespeare intrusts to him what is possibly the most difficult scene to carry off successfully on the stage, so far as the acting is concerned, of any he had confronted an actor with since Richard III wooed Anne: the one in which Iachimo assails Imogen's virtue, and, having failed, restores himself to her good grace by a lightning-like shift of tactics. Unless consummately done, that scene seems absurdly improbable and breaks the play once for all at that point. But the fault is not in the psychology. The instantaneousness with which Iachimo perceives Imogen's impregnability and the combined audacity and insight with which he nevertheless proceeds are both characteristic. The effect, too, that this Sleeping Beauty's beauty has on him in the bedchamber scene, and his description of her, are not so much Shakespeare's poetry getting out of bounds, as has often been held, as ground and preparation for a belief that Iachimo's repentance at the end is sincere.

III

If this play has often been underpraised, its heroine has not. Not a few have found her the loveliest of Shakespeare's women. "The gift of the gods" her husband calls her, and she shares with Desdemona the distinction of having the word "divine" attached to her name. Gervinus declared that "Imogen is, next to Hamlet, the most fully drawn character in Shakespeare's plays," an arresting statement whether we agree with it or not. Simplicity is the most complex thing in the world, and many rereadings of the role are necessary in order to appreciate the subtlety with which Imogen is characterized. Like Hamlet, she is an epitome, uniting in herself the virtues of at least three of Shakespeare's feminine types: the naïve girl (in boy's costume part of the time), the queenly woman, and the tragic

victim. It is as if the poet had consciously set out to endow his heroine with
the finest traits of a dozen of her predecessors:

> from every one
> The best she hath, and she, of all compounded,
> Outsells them all.

It seems at first grossly inappropriate to have put into the mouth of Cloten
essentially what Paulina says of Hermione* and Ferdinand of Miranda.†
But, as with Iago and Desdemona, Shakespeare may have meant it as the
highest conceivable tribute to Imogen's beauty that even Cloten, for one
moment of his life, is sensible to it. It is one of the most hopeful notes in
Shakespeare that, however transiently, men like Iago, Edmund, Iachimo,
and Cloten find that they cannot leave the compelling power of purity out
of account. Not only this play, then, but the heroine of it, as Cloten's flash
of insight suggests, is recapitulatory; and if the result is to make Imogen at
moments a little more ideal, a little less real, than some of her predecessors, that too is in keeping with the design.

IV

To Posthumus himself, who, like Othello, was torn from his wife almost
before he knew he had one, we grant at the outset all the virtue implied in
one "poor but worthy" who is preferred by such a paragon of women to a
royal alliance and a throne. At first sight Posthumus appears a bit the victim of the plot, but Shakespeare, turning a difficulty as usual into a triumph,
keeps his hero credible by making him two men in one: the British Posthumus, who loves and has been chosen by Imogen, and the Italian Posthumus, who falls under the corrupt influence of the South. They are as
antipodal as the two Hamlets. Indeed, we are reminded of the nunnery
scene of the earlier play in the soliloquy in which the Italian Posthumus,
convinced of the faithlessness of his wife, vomits forth his opinion of the
other sex. A more terrific indictment of woman was never uttered. But
what a careless reader misses is the fact that, since its provocation and subject is the immaculate and faithful Imogen, it is a *negative* in which all the
lights and shadows are reversed as compared with nature and so, instead of
an onslaught on woman, to the same degree an unintended tribute to her.

---

* *The Winter's Tale*, V, i, 13:
> "If, one by one, you wedded all the world,
> Or, from the all that are, took something good
> To make a perfect woman, she you kill'd
> Would be unparallel'd."

† *The Tempest*, III, i, 46:
> "O you,
> So perfect and so peerless, are created
> Of every creature's best!"

What Posthumus is actually describing is the unconscious content of his own mind. The subject is Man, not Woman, Man on the "Italian" model. Posthumus makes noble amends in the companion soliloquy that opens the fifth act, when, come to his senses, he discards his "Italian weeds" forever.

V

But now, if Posthumus loves Imogen yet lets his faith in her be undermined by a villain, and if that villain attempts in vain to seduce her, there is a third suitor of far more eminent position than either of these, a queen's son, who, before Imogen's secret marriage to Posthumus, had been pursuing her under the instigation of his mother, and who continues his siege after the banishment of the husband virtually annuls the alliance in the eyes of the court. Yes, if a gentleman from abroad sought to corrupt Imogen, so did a royal representative of the court at home. There is a British as well as an Italian villain in the piece: Cloten.

Cloten. What a masterpiece! He deserves more critical attention than he has received as the final distillation of something Shakespeare had been at work on all his life. If Iachimo is his summing up of all that is ungentle in the continental gentleman, so is Cloten of all that is ignoble in the English nobility. Cloten is a sort of demonstration in advance of *The Tempest* of what happens when we try to civilize Caliban too rapidly. His virtues disappear and his vices are raised to the *n*th power. Imogen has his measure. In one of her milder moods she addresses him:

> Profane fellow!
> Wert thou the son of Jupiter and no more
> But what thou art besides, thou wert too base
> To be his groom. Thou wert dignified enough,
> Even to the point of envy, if 'twere made
> Comparative for your virtues, to be styl'd
> The under-hangman of his kingdom, and hated
> For being preferr'd so well.

> The south-fog rot him!

retorts Cloten, meaning Posthumus, and the accent is exactly that of Caliban cursing Prospero:

> All the infections that the sun sucks up
> From bogs, fens, flats, on Prosper fall, and make him
> By inch-meal a disease!

Though criticism has scarcely done justice to Cloten, some good phrases and epithets have been struck off—such as "that conceited booby lord" (Hazlitt) or "the Queen's rickety, spluttering, blustering lump of flesh"

(Hudson). Shakespeare himself gets the effect with less effort. Cloten is trying to bribe his way into Imogen's presence with gold:

LADY: Who's there that knocks?
CLO.:   A gentleman.
LADY: No more?
CLO.: Yes, and a gentlewoman's son.
LADY: (*Aside*)   That's more
         Than some, whose tailors are as dear as yours,
         Can justly boast of.

And the same note is struck at his death, when, disguised, he meets Guiderius, and, mistaking that young prince for an outlaw, accosts him with a "yield thee, thief."

GUI.: To who? To thee? What art thou? Have not I
         An arm as big as thine? a heart as big?
         Thy words, I grant, are bigger, for I wear not
         My dagger in my mouth. Say what thou art,
         Why I should yield to thee.
CLO.:   Thou villain base,
         Know'st me not by my clothes?
GUI.:   No, nor thy tailor, rascal,
         Who is thy grandfather. He made those clothes,
         Which, as it seems, make thee.

Bernard Shaw has in one of his plays an Englishman of high estate whom he describes as an imperfectly reformed burglar disguised by his tailor. He might have stolen the idea from *Cymbeline*. But doubtless there were models nearer at hand.

If Shakespeare intended Imogen as an epitome of all that is right with woman, he certainly made Cloten an epitome of all that is wrong with man, particularly when he is a member of a privileged class. Great satirists and misanthropes have disputed whether man is more the brute, the fool, or the knave. Shakespeare makes Cloten the three in one.

         That such a crafty devil as is his mother
         Should yield the world this ass!

says the same Lord who called Imogen "divine." Even the courtiers, who are used to this sort of thing in milder form, cannot stomach this creature compared with whom Rosencrantz and Guildenstern are original, Osric unself-conscious, and Parolles brave. And it is Shakespeare's unkindest cut that he is a queen's son, who, if the plot to marry him to Imogen had gone through, might have come to the crown.

The single scene in which Cloten does not appear as boor and butt is the one where Cymbeline receives the emissaries of Augustus and the question is a diplomatic one. "We will nothing pay," Cloten says in the matter of the Roman tribute, "for wearing our own noses"—rather than Roman ones presumably. "If Caesar can hide the sun from us with a blanket, or put the moon in his pocket, we will pay him tribute for light; else, sir, no more tribute, pray you now." These thrusts seem quite too good for such a nincompoop. The poet appears to be incapable of resisting the temptation to get in a dig at any of the Caesars. He will elevate even a Cloten at their expense.

But Imogen should be allowed the last word about this gentleman who aspired to her hand:

> . . . that harsh, noble, simple nothing, Cloten,
> That Cloten, whose love-suit hath been to me
> As fearful as a siege.

One can hear the withering Cordelian scorn of that "noble" and that "nothing." Yet one item in this siege that had been so fearful to her was nothing less than the playing by the musicians of

> Hark, hark! the lark at heaven's gate sings.

What did Shakespeare mean by connecting Cloten even indirectly with that incomparable lyric? Is it a last touch of irony? Or of mercy? Perhaps if this man had not had a crafty devil for a mother, some seed of celestial melody might have germinated even in him. After reading *Coriolanus* it is easy to fill in the unwritten story of The Education of Cloten.

Nor does Cloten stand alone. He is merely the dark consummate flower of a nobility and court society that is rotten to the core. The Queen is villainous, the King pusillanimous, the British lords cowardly and panicky in battle.

> To-day how many would have given their honours
> To have sav'd their carcases! took heel to do 't,
> And yet died too!

cries Posthumus, and when he meets a British lord who, far from the battle line, is going still farther, he accosts him derisively:

> Still going? This is a lord!

VI

But Shakespeare was no Jacobin. Trust him not to leave things so one-sided as they would be if this were his last word in the matter. The plan of the play is triangular, and over against the miasma of Italian gentility and the cruder corruption of the British court he has put the mountain atmosphere of Wales and that incomparable trio, Belarius-Guiderius-Arviragus, the old man and the two kidnapped princes.

These scenes are among the loveliest in Shakespeare. They are done with a gusto that shows how deeply the poet's heart was in them. We feel ourselves bounding up the rocks, leaping the brooks, drinking in the bracing air. And the two princes *who do not know they are princes* are as indigenous to their habitat as deer or antelopes (and yet subtly alien to it too): the bold, dashing, athletic Guiderius (Polydore), and the not less courageous but more imaginative and lovely Arviragus (Cadwal), as alike and yet as different and nicely discriminated as were Goneril and Regan at the opposite pole.

We may read these scenes of course for their own sakes as a delightful idyl. (The Arden editor remarks that they have "no very vital relation to the rest of the play.") But to do so is to lose much. A part may be a perfect whole in itself but that does not prevent it from being a perfect part of a whole also. These scenes have both these perfections.

To begin with, especially with Italy and the British court for contrast, they are a revealing study in the effects on a child's life of the three factors, heredity, environment, and education. Here is noble blood under conditions best suited to elicit hardihood, thrift, simplicity, and courage. And the results, we feel, would have been less happy if the blood had not been so good or the conditions had been less *natural*. But there is a third factor. Belarius—foster-father to the children and the wisest and kindliest kidnapper on record—is beautifully unaware of the fact that his memories of a more civilized life, strained through a philosophic temperament, afford just the influence and restraint that the boys need if they are to get all that is good from nature without being merely swallowed up by her bigness and wildness. He saves them from becoming young barbarians. Nor should their nurse-mother, Euriphile, dead but not forgotten, be left out. *Good blood, unconscious of its goodness, close to nature, watched over and loved by civilized experience and wisdom:* it is just the combination essential to the best results, and the fact that Shakespeare repeats it, with only minor variations, in the cases of Perdita and Miranda shows that it is not just the chance of the plot but something approaching a considered prescription for the education of youth and the production of the noblest type of man and woman. The mountains of Wales in this play are all that Italy and the British court are not.

And now into this rocky retreat comes the older sister of these princes disguised as a boy. If Imogen has shone like a star in the darkness of the British court and has appeared there a Sleeping Beauty even to the base

Iachimo, what will she be in the heart of nature? Belarius' attempts to describe her when he first glimpses her in the cave come nearest to being adequate: "a fairy," "an angel," "an earthly paragon," "divineness no elder than a boy." Though we hear of Desdemona's house affairs, Imogen is perhaps the only character in Shakespeare who successfully reconciles the functions of angel and cook—so of heaven and of earth is she at the same time. Her supposed death and the dirge her brothers sing above her add a sad beauty to this mountain idyl.

And then it is interrupted in the most incongruous manner.

Cloten, clad in the garments of Posthumus he has gotten from Pisanio, has come to the region seeking revenge, swearing to violate Imogen for her insults to him and her rejection of him. He meets Guiderius, whom, as we have seen, he takes for a mountain robber. Enraged that the youth does not quail at the mere realization of his royal presence, he starts to beat him, but, instead, is beheaded by Guiderius. And now at the end of the dirge for the dead Fidele—Imogen under her mountain name—Belarius brings in the bloody and headless corpse of Cloten and places it beside the sleeping Imogen. The others go out. Imogen, awakening from her Juliet-like slumber and recognizing the garments of Posthumus, imagines it is the body of her slain husband by which she reposes, and, after an outburst of emotion, falls in an unconscious embrace on Cloten's bloody corpse.

VII

It is the most incredible scene in Shakespeare! Or at least the reader who pronounces it such will be understood. The living purity of womanhood, the dead and bloody trunk of sensuality and brutality, brought into this disgusting physical proximity through a mistake in identity. It strikes one as one of the most inexcusable of theatrical tricks. The horrors of *Titus Andronicus*, if they are Shakespeare's, may be forgiven on the score of the author's youth. Titania embracing Bottom—"methought I was enamoured of an ass"—which somehow seems like a far-off prophecy of this scene, is both humorous and wise. But this desecrating juxtaposition of Beauty and the Beast seems to have not a shred or shadow of excuse. The gouging-out of Gloucester's eyes may be more cruel, but it is less nauseating.

The memory of that scene from *King Lear*, however, may well set us thinking. What if here, as there, the most revolting moment in the play should be the clue? What if, in relation to the whole, this scene should have its justification and significance? There is every precedent in Shakespeare for expecting it.

The ideal purity of womanhood embracing—because it is clad in the garments of the loved one—the brutal villainy of a false nobility that sought to enforce it: here is a situation that may mean more than meets the eye at first glance. (And in exploring it for over- and underintentions—in order to minimize the mere history—let us substitute England and English for Britain and British.)

Iachimo plainly stands for Italy and her malign influence, Cloten for corrupt English nobility, and Belarius-Guiderius-Arviragus for the ancient English tradition handed on, uncontaminated, to England's youngest and most genuinely noble blood. Iachimo seeks to seduce Imogen, and Cloten tries to violate her. But in vain, for Guiderius meets Cloten and beheads him, and Posthumus disarms Iachimo in a duel but spares him. Does not the parabolic quality of all this fairly shout aloud and demand that we think of Imogen as the True England wedded secretly to the poor but genuinely gentle Posthumus Leonatus, English Manhood and Valor? Posthumus himself calls Imogen almost exactly that: "Britain, . . . even thy mistress." And though the recovery of her brothers deprives her of a worldly kingdom, she remains spiritual queen.

The moment we take the leading characters of the play in this way, numberless details rush forth to fit into what we can scarcely help calling the allegorical design. The King and Queen are plainly *The Power of the English Throne* wedded to *Corruption*, who is slowly poisoning it. Their "son"—not the King's son at all—is *Degenerate Royalty* or *False Nobility* who, though he hasn't a drop of princely blood in his veins, hopes with the help of *Corruption* to attain the throne. But *True England* prefers its *True Manhood* of low estate to its *False Nobility*—and secretly weds it. That *Manhood* is banished and is temporarily deluded by an "*Italian Fiend*," who boasts in a cosmopolitan gathering in *Rome* that he can seduce *England*. The villain, first repulsed, then too ingenuously forgiven, succeeds, by theft and lies, in ruining the faith of *English Manhood* in *England*. In a frenzy of disillusionment *He* plots *Her* death, but is saved from the ultimate crime—somewhat as Lear is by Kent—by a *Faithful Servant*. *England*, meanwhile, attacked from within as well as from without, flees from the *Court* disguised as a youth, finds in the *Mountains* her true kin, her lovers and defenders, who, a *Genuine Nobility*, save her from violation by *False Nobility*. Awakening from a stupor induced by a drug (that came from *Corruption*), for a moment she embraces by mistake the dead and headless *False Nobility* that would have outraged her—because of the stolen clothes in which the corpse is clad. (How different that scene becomes when taken in this way!)

And then the Roman invasion and the battle:

Imperialism recruiting *Gentility*—an unholy alliance found throughout history because *Gentility* can hold its privileges at home only by fomenting quarrels and conquests abroad—invades England and puts to rout the English forces until *Old English Experience and Wisdom* hand in hand with her genuinely *Noble Youth* ("an old man and two boys") and joined by *English Manhood* who has put off his Italian guise and assumed that of an *English Peasant* ("a fourth man in a silly habit") make a Thermopylean stand in a narrow lane. These four, threatening to fight their own countrymen if they do not return to the combat, turn the tide of battle, and administer to the forces of *Imperialism* an overwhelming defeat—so miraculous a one, indeed, that the victors believe that "the heavens fought" on their side and that their four saviors, or three of them at least, were angels.

The particular figurative designations suggested for the various characters need not be rigorously insisted on. There can be considerable latitude there. But can anyone believe that characters and story could fit together in this fashion by chance? If anyone can, it must be because of a dogmatic conviction that Shakespeare's genius was alien to allegory.

But to believe that the myriad-minded Shakespeare should have tried dramatic allegory—even assuming that he had not flirted with it in certain of his earlier Comedies—is surely doing him far less disrespect than to hold that he fell to composing in his last days such improbable and really inconsequential stuff as *Cymbeline* is if taken merely as a story. Furthermore, there is *The Tempest*, in which scarcely anyone denies the presence of some allegory. Granted that allegory, because of its element of conscious contrivance, is on a level below the greatest poetry: still, a form used by Spenser, Bunyan, and Keats is not to be despised. Nobody thinks of claiming that *Cymbeline* is another *King Lear*.

Moreover, some such interpretation as the one suggested seems not only to harmonize with the text and evidence of the play itself but to confirm what Shakespeare has been saying almost from the beginning about "gentlemen," the inner and outer life, court and country, and most of all about imperialism in such plays as *Henry V* and *Antony and Cleopatra*.

But if this is not enough, there is something still more convincing.

VIII

There is a Roman soothsayer in *Cymbeline* who has a dream:

> Last night the very gods show'd me a vision—
> I fast and pray'd for their intelligence—thus:
> I saw Jove's bird, the Roman eagle, wing'd
> From the spongy south to this part of the west,
> There vanish'd in the sunbeams; which portends—
> Unless my sins abuse my divination—
> Success to the Roman host.

"Unless my sins abuse my divination": why did Shakespeare slip that in? Because the event, which was a British victory, shows that his sins did abuse his divination. At the end, the Soothsayer tries to save face by a second, *ex post facto*, interpretation of the dream that only makes matters worse:

> The vision
> Which I made known to Lucius, ere the stroke
> Of this yet scarce-cold battle, at this instant
> Is full accomplish'd; for the Roman eagle,
> From south to west on wing soaring aloft,
> Lessen'd herself, and in the beams o' the sun
> So vanish'd; which foreshow'd our princely eagle,
> The imperial Caesar, should again unite
> His favour with the radiant Cymbeline,
> Which shines here in the west.

This quite confirms the suspicion that the Soothsayer was a diplomatist and not a diviner, a gross licker of the royal boots. (Caesar would not have relished being only an eagle while Cymbeline was the sun!) And yet the dream itself was from the gods. Can *we* divine its meaning?

Politically the sun is a symbol of kingship or imperial power, but psychologically and poetically it means God, the source of life, love, light. When then the Roman eagle *vanishes*—a word the Soothsayer omits or perverts in his interpretations—in sunbeams, it means power being sublimated into imagination. And that is exactly the event in the play. The villain is not taken out to be tortured, as his poetical father Iago was, but is pardoned by the man he had injured.

> Kneel not to me,

says Posthumus,

> The power that I have on you is to spare you;
> The malice towards you to forgive you. Live,
> And deal with others better.

There is power vanishing in love, indeed. And Posthumus' mercy begets the same kindliness in the King:

> Nobly doom'd!
> We'll learn our freeness of a son-in-law;
> Pardon's the word to all.

There is a general reconciliation, the older generation, as in *King Lear*, kneeling to the younger. And that reconciliation is not only personal but political. Cymbeline, out from under the spell of his wicked queen, instead of exacting tribute from the defeated Romans, agrees to give freely what he had refused to have exacted of him under compulsion. It is one of Shakespeare's last words on that spirit of magnanimity in which he held that victory should be taken. Here again the Roman eagle of Imperialism *vanishes* in the sun of pardon and harmony:

CYM.:   Laud we the gods;
    And let our crooked smokes climb to their nostrils
    From our bless'd altars. Publish we this peace
    To all our subjects. Set we forward. Let
    A Roman and a British ensign wave
    Friendly together. So through Lud's town march;
    And in the temple of great Jupiter
    Our peace we'll ratify; seal it with feasts.
    Set on there! Never was a war did cease,
    Ere bloody hands were wash'd, with such a peace.

Another significant last word.

IX

If *Antony and Cleopatra* was actual, this is symbolic history. And how incomplete the former is without the latter. "The time of universal peace is near," boasted Octavius, and then Shakespeare shows him sending his imperial legions against Britain. This is a Little England play if there ever was one. But in the suggestion of a British and a Roman ensign waving together is a hint of a reconciliation and synthesis between the liberty that can be found only in the little country and the unity of the whole world, which is the redeeming ideal behind an Imperialism that, practically, always makes the mistake of letting the sunshine vanish in the eagle instead of the eagle in the sunshine.

But this play is as much a moral as a political allegory. The warning it affords England of the dangers lurking in the decadent agents of the Renaissance (what a prophecy it is of the worst features of the Jacobean drama!) goes far, as does its stress on the virtues of simplicity, to place Shakespeare, in his latest phase, with Milton and the Puritans. He was little enough of a puritan in the popular derogatory sense of the term. I detect not one trace of false asceticism in his nature. But when Posthumus, still supposing he has been the cause of Imogen's death, discards his Italian garments and assumes those of a British peasant, allegory or no allegory, we catch intimations not only of the Puritans, but of Rousseau, Wordsworth, and even Tolstoy. It is like a poetical Reformation denouncing a poetical Renaissance that has proved traitor to the very beauty she thought she worshiped. We have been too blind to this side of Shakespeare. The last lines of Posthumus' speech, on the edge of battle, ring out as one of the supreme spiritual utterances of

England's supreme poet, and, by that fact, of England. And as it happens there is proof that they embody that poet's own sentiments as much as they do those of the man in whose mouth he places them. Posthumus is addressing the gods:

> Imogen is your own; do your best wills,
> And make me blest to obey! I am brought hither
> Among the Italian gentry, and to fight
> Against my lady's kingdom. 'Tis enough
> That, Britain, I have kill'd thy mistress; peace!
> I'll give no wound to thee. Therefore, good heavens,
> Hear patiently my purpose: I'll disrobe me
> Of these Italian weeds and suit myself
> As does a Briton peasant; so I'll fight
> Against the part I come with; so I'll die
> For thee, O Imogen, even for whom my life
> Is every breath a death; and thus, unknown,
> Pitied nor hated, to the face of peril
> Myself I'll dedicate. Let me make men know
> More valour in me than my habits show.
> Gods, put the strength o' the Leonati in me!
> To shame the guise o' the world, I will begin
> The fashion: less without and more within.

While the whole passage has the accent, its last two lines have also almost the identical language of that unique and supreme sonnet, the 146th, which comes as close as anything Shakespeare ever wrote to being a personal religious creed. What that sonnet, like the passage from *Cymbeline*, says of sin, of the transitoriness of life, of the falsity and futility of outward show, of the all-importance of the soul and its power to conquer death, could have been underwritten by any of the great Puritans or Quakers of the next generation:

> Poor soul, the centre of my sinful earth,
> [Cow'd by] these rebel powers that thee array,
> Why dost thou pine within and suffer dearth,
> Painting thy outward walls so costly gay?
> Why so large cost, having so short a lease,
> Dost thou upon thy fading mansion spend?
> Shall worms, inheritors of this excess,
> Eat up thy charge? Is this thy body's end?
> Then, soul, live thou upon thy servant's loss,
> And let that pine to aggravate thy store;
> Buy terms divine in selling hours of dross;
> Within be fed, without be rich no more:

So shalt thou feed on Death, that feeds on men,
And Death once dead, there's no more dying then.

X

Through the symbolic connection between England and Imogen that it sets up, *Cymbeline* suggests that those two age-old combats between lust and purity, and between empire and liberty, are at bottom the same. The latter struggle will go on, Shakespeare seems to say, until those opposites, envy and privilege, on which it depends, recognize with shame their identity under their apparent difference and repent like Iachimo:

> Knighthoods and honours, borne
> As I wear mine, are titles but of scorn.

Those who rest in them "scarce are men," while those who do not are "gods."

> England! awake! awake! awake!
>   Jerusalem thy Sister calls!
> Why wilt thou sleep the sleep of death
>   And close her from thy ancient walls? ...
>
> Bring me my Bow of burning gold:
>   Bring me my Arrows of desire:
> Bring me my Spear: O clouds unfold!
>   Bring me my Chariot of fire.
>
> I will not cease from Mental Fight,
>   Nor shall my Sword sleep in my hand
> Till we have built Jerusalem
>   In England's green & pleasant Land.

If I am not mistaken, these incomparable stanzas from two of William Blake's poems say in a very different way the same thing as *Cymbeline*, and *Cymbeline* says the same thing as they. It sometimes seems as if their author were a reincarnation not only of Milton, as he himself believed, but of the visionary Shakespeare. There are many Shakespeares. The visionary Shakespeare, like Blake, is an eagle that vanishes in sunshine.

Chapter XXXV

The Winter's Tale

I

Like *Much Ado about Nothing*, *What You Will*, and *As You Like It*, the title *The Winter's Tale* might seem to be the author's hint to us to take his play as pure entertainment, like a story told to a group around the fire of a winter's night.

> A sad tale's best for winter. I have one
> Of sprites and goblins,

says the boy Mamillius. "Come on," says his mother, taking him up,

> and do your best
> To fright me with your sprites; you're powerful at it.

> There was a man . . .

Mamillius begins,

> Dwelt by a churchyard. I will tell it softly;
> Yond crickets shall not hear it.

But the tale is never told, for just then the boy's father enters and turns from narrative into drama his boy's tale of sprites and goblins, the first chapter of which he has himself already enacted. He, too, is "powerful at it," and does his best to fright Hermione. Leontes and his son are alike in the capacity to summon out of nothing things that both are and are not there. All of which goes to show that the title is linked with the theme and characters as well as with the plot.

There are several other allusions to the title in the text. "This news which is called true," says a Second Gentleman, referring to the recovery of Perdita, "is so like an old tale, that the verity of it is in strong suspicion." "Like an old tale still," says a Third Gentleman a little later.

> That she is living,

cries Paulina of Hermione at the end,

> Were it but told you, should be hooted at
> Like an old tale.

The reiteration has its purpose. We are more inclined to accept an impossible story if the teller frankly confesses his awareness of the strain to which he is subjecting our credulity.

The Winter's Tale, unless we take it as such a story, does indeed subject us to this strain if for no other reason than that it is such a heterogeneous mixture, a stranger one than even *A Midsummer-Night's Dream*. It is a fairy tale—it is fact. It is romantic—it is realistic. It is tragic—it is comic. It is Christian—it is pagan. It is harsh and crabbed—it is simple and idyllic. It is this—it is that. It is a welter of anachronisms. Its geography is in spots fantastic. It has not only gods, but a bear, a storm, and a yacht, from the machine. And as for its construction, if it had been expressly written to defy the classic unities, it could hardly have violated them more flagrantly. It plays the old witch with time and space and compactness of action, sprawling from Sicilia to Bohemia-with-a-seacoast, leaping over sixteen years in the middle, and (apparently at least) so dividing the interest that many have called it two plays tied by the slenderest of threads rather than one. Yet, as is usual with Shakespeare, these diversities serve a purpose, and the play has more seriousness, unity, and singleness of effect than is immediately apparent. For like a complex musical composition that strikes us at first as full of discords but that we eventually come to like, *The Winter's Tale* has the gift on more intimate acquaintance of insinuating its way into the affections and understandings of many who were originally unsympathetic or even repelled by its heterogeneities. Autolycus expresses it perfectly:

> And when I wander here and there,
> I then do most go right.

It might be Shakespeare's "apology" buried just where one might expect Shakespeare to bury it, in a song.

II

The suddenness with which Leontes becomes suspicious of his innocent wife, Hermione, inevitably invites both comparison and contrast with Othello. Othello, a man just married, succumbs to suspicion only under the manipulations of a fiendishly skilful villain who builds up what looks like a convincing case against the Moor's wife. Leontes, happily married so far as everything appears, with one child already and expecting another, is his own Iago and becomes instantaneously the victim of an insane jealousy for no other reason than the trifle that his friend from boyhood, Polixenes, who has refused to prolong his visit at Leontes' request, agrees to stay at the solicitation of Leontes' wife. Within a matter of minutes, we might almost say of seconds, he is so beside himself that he is actually questioning the paternity of his own boy and his mind has become a chaos of incoherence and sensuality. Unmotivated, his reaction has been pronounced by critic after critic, and so it is, if by motive we mean a definite rational incitement to action. But there are irrational as well as rational incitements to action, and what we have here is a sudden inundation of the conscious by the unconscious, of which the agreement of Polixenes to prolong his visit is the occasion rather than the cause.

> I am a feather for each wind that blows,

Leontes confesses of himself later when he changes his mind and decides to have the child to whom Hermione has given premature birth exposed rather than burned—a line that sums up his emotional instability as well as anything in the play.

A reading of *Much Ado about Nothing* with full attention to the meaning of the word "nothing" both in the title and in the text is the best possible introduction to the first act of *The Winter's Tale*.

> Is whispering nothing?
> Is leaning cheek to cheek?

asks Leontes, attempting to convince Camillo of the guilt of his wife and his friend, and after listing all the physical and psychological intimacies between the two which his "weak-hing'd fancy" (Paulina's phrase) has conjured up out of nothing, he concludes,

> Is this nothing?
> Why, then the world and all that's in 't is nothing;
> The covering sky is nothing; Bohemia nothing;
> My wife is nothing; nor nothing have these nothings,
> If this be nothing.

Leontes is exactly right, but not in the sense he intends, for it is precisely out of the vast realm of Nothing—of pure possibility—that he has summoned these nothings.

> Affection! thy intention stabs the centre,

he cries, pushing absurdity quite beyond bounds in seeming to question his son's paternity,

> Thou dost make possible things not so held,
> Communicat'st with dreams;—how can this be?—
> With what's unreal thou co-active art,
> And fellow'st nothing.

He could not have diagnosed his own case more correctly: emotion, he declares, brings within the realm of possibility things nonexistent. But, continuing, he hopelessly confuses cause and effect:

> Then 'tis very credent
> Thou mayst co-join with something; and thou dost,
> And that beyond commission, and I find it,
> And that to the infection of my brains
> And hardening of my brows.

Since emotion can give reality to "nothing," he argues, it is very credible that that "nothing" should join on to "something" in the external world (that the idea of a faithless Hermione should fit Hermione herself). And that thought, he confesses, infects his brain. But the truth of course is the other way around: it is the infection of the brain that has fitted the fantasy to the present instance.

> Your actions are my dreams,

he says later to Hermione, little dreaming how consummately he has condensed the truth and psychology of his own affliction into five words. Fully as almost everyone else sees through him, it is Leontes himself who without knowing it is the best expositor of his own nature and weakness. But Camillo's diagnosis is worthy of notice too—and Paulina's.

> . . . you may as well
> Forbid the sea for to obey the moon,

says the former, informing Polixenes that Leontes has appointed him to murder him.

> As or by oath remove or counsel shake
> The fabric of his folly, whose foundation
> Is pil'd upon his faith, and will continue
> The standing of his body.

Camillo perceives that Leontes is possessed and moved by forces transcending consciousness too tremendous to be amenable to reason, and he wisely brushes aside Polixenes' request to know how the man's mad conduct is to be explained in favor of instant escape from impending death. Leontes' jealousy of Polixenes is like Shylock's hatred of Antonio (and Shakespeare uses the same two metaphors of wind and waves to convey it). In that case nothing personal, but centuries of mistreatment of the Jews, was the "motive." In this case nothing personal, but the whole history and inheritance of human jealousy, is the cause. What we are dealing with here is nature in the raw, with the fantasy-making of the unconscious mind and the emotional fury it engenders. Leontes' mind is like a fiery furnace at such a temperature that everything introduced into it—combustible or not—becomes fuel. That he threatens in turn to have his wife, the child, and Paulina *burned* is significant repetition and detail that indicate the volcanic depth from which his passion comes. And, appropriately, it is coincidence, not reason—the coincidence of the judgment of Apollo and his son's death—that convinces him of his mistake.

> I have too much believ'd mine own suspicion.

One line and he emerges from his obsession as suddenly as he had succumbed to it. The man is a victim of fantasy, the vehicle of a sort of inverted and infernal, as his wife is of a celestial, faith.

Indeed *The Winter's Tale* might have been written to expound the difference between fantasy and imagination, between infatuation and faith. Leontes, in the first half of the play, shows what happens when one reverts to the instinctive fears that send a small child or a primitive man into a panic,

> Fancies too weak for boys, too green and idle
> For girls of nine,

as Paulina (confirming Camillo) well describes them. Hermione, on the contrary, shows what happens not just when one uses his reason (though she does that of course) but also when one surrenders to those finer and loftier instincts that are as much a part of our inheritance as are our lower and grosser ones, however much rarer they are and less potent they appear. If Leontes is a feather to be blown about by every gust, Hermione is a sail to take advantage of even the most adverse wind, without which the rudder of reason would be of no avail. Nothing can undermine her combined modesty and pride, blur her insight and sympathy, or shake her trust that truth will triumph in the end. And except for her husband the faith of others in her is almost equal to her faith in herself. She seems to lift others above their natural level. Unlike the obsequious and fawning courtiers to be found in some of Shakespeare's other plays, these people stand up for the truth and their Queen in the very face of the King. And even when he subjects her to the degradation of insults and the ignominy of an open trial she preserves the serene dignity and repose which, without being cold, insensibly prepare us for her role as statue in the fifth act.

The murderous division that comes between Polixenes and Leontes is the more tragic because the two had grown up together:

> Two lads that thought there was no more behind
> But such a day to-morrow as to-day,
> And to be boy eternal . . .
> We were as twinn'd lambs that did frisk i' the sun,
> And bleat the one at the other. What we chang'd
> Was innocence for innocence.

This world of innocence, of frisking lambs, of boys eternal, when all days are alike because all days are perfect, seems gone forever. But no, Shakespeare brings it back, if with a few differences and if not for these two, in the fourth act of his play, one of the longest he ever wrote, expressly contrived, one would think, for the sharpest contrast with the three that preceded it. If they were earth, this is heaven, or, more precisely, if they were earth with a few touches of heaven, this is heaven with a few touches of earth: flowers, lambs, songs and ballads, dances, masquerades, shepherds and shepherds' daughters, princes and princesses, lovable pickpockets, simplicity and happiness under a dozen aspects even including a delectable brand of imbecility. Quite too lovely to be true, or at least to last. What wonder that this is held to be two plays rather than one! How shall this Bohemia ever be reconciled with that Sicilia? It is fortunate that Shakespeare has a fifth act in which to suggest how that miracle may take place. Thesis. Antithesis. Synthesis. If this turns out to be the scheme of the play, it cannot justly be charged with lack of unity. A man asleep often bears little resemblance to the same man awake. Yet they are somehow one.

III

For sheer joy in life and breath at the present moment, the fourth act of *The Winter's Tale* is one of Shakespeare's pinnacles. Perdita alone would be enough to make it so. But there is Autolycus too, who is as far beyond good and evil in his roguery as she is in her innocence—a childlike not a childish innocence, be it noted. And thrown in for full measure is Florizel, most faithful and poetically articulate of princely lovers (we would like to think that Shakespeare stole phrases for him from the memories of his own love-making), ready to sacrifice his royal prospects for a shepherd's daughter. And then there are those two minor masterpieces, the old shepherd and his clownish son. All in all it is a very superfluity of comic and romantic riches.

Perdita (whose name in view of what she is could be taken to imply that she is the Paradise Lost of human nature) has beauty both of countenance and of character, and that beauty is infectious in the sense that it seems to endow all who come near her, if it does not strike them dumb, with the power to say something beautiful about it. An anthology of such utterances from the play would exceed in loveliness even the one she herself makes of the flowers. Camillo wants to gaze at her forever. Florizel wants her to continue doing without end whatever she happens to be doing at the moment. When the King praises her dancing, her shepherd-father says she does anything as well. And even after Florizel's father has revealed his identity and turned on the young couple all the fury at his command, he cannot even castigate her without complimenting her in the same breath. "Fresh piece of excellent witchcraft," he calls her, ". . . enchantment," and threatens to have her beauty scratched with briars. Camillo accepts correction from her on the question of the effect of adversity on love and confesses she has attained wisdom without schooling:

> I cannot say 'tis pity
> She lacks instructions, for she seems a mistress
> To most that teach.

The gentleman who announces her arrival in Sicilia speaks of her as

> the most peerless piece of earth, I think,
> That e'er the sun shone bright on. . . . This is a creature,
> Would she begin a sect, might quench the zeal
> Of all professors else,

and her own father, before he recognizes his daughter, calls her "goddess." If she were not Florizel's, he would beg her for himself.

The best thing we can say about Perdita is that she lives up to all this adulation and seems no whit hurt by it. She unites the simplicity of a shepherd's daughter with the poise and grace of a princess. Her blood can make her blush or speak boldly as fits the occasion. When the enraged King threatens her with death if she ever embraces his son again, though she dismisses her dream instantly and announces that she will go back to milking her ewes, she is not at all put out by the King's tirade:

> I was not much afeard; for once or twice
> I was about to speak, and tell him plainly
> The self-same sun that shines upon his court
> Hides not his visage from our cottage, but
> Looks on alike.

This is the Shakespearean equivalent of Melville's great theological justification of spiritual democracy—"His omnipresence, our divine equality!"— and is enough in itself, in the light of what Perdita is, to wipe out for good and all a multitude of the silly things that have been said and written about the poet's "snobbery." And Florizel is as true a son of Shakespeare as Perdita is daughter. Nothing is altered between us, he assures her when the blow falls. "What I was, I am." It might be Shakespeare's own vow in the 123d sonnet, "No, Time, thou shalt not boast that I do change," or his dictum in the 116th:

> Love is not love
> Which alters when it alteration finds,

though it is the father here, not the loved one, who has brought the alteration. Let the succession go, Florizel boldly protests, "I am heir to my affection." "Be advis'd," cautions Camillo. "I am, and by my fancy," Florizel retorts:

> If my reason
> Will thereto be obedient, I have reason;
> If not, my senses, better pleas'd with madness,
> Do bid it welcome.

Fancy here of course means love. It is one of the plainest of a number of passages in the later Shakespeare showing that as against his earlier ideal of a balance between instinct and reason ("blood and judgment") he had come to believe that reason should be obedient to the imagination—or to imaginative love, as some may prefer to call it here. The person on this occasion whose reason is subdued to madness in another sense than Florizel's is the infuriated father whose sudden outburst seems to be put in as a counterpart of the royal explosion of Leontes in the first act. The Jealous Husband, the Patriarchal Father: there seems little to choose between these ancestral types in the matter of emotional unbalance. Polixenes has more excuse on the grounds of dynastic custom, but less excuse in the fact that his loss of temper is deliberately planned and timed.

In view of Perdita's simplicity it is interesting that she has what is perhaps the most complicated role in Shakespeare in the matter of disguise. But this is in keeping with the fact that true simplicity is the most complex thing in the world. The disguise the poet uses in Perdita's case is not disguise for its own sake or for purely theatrical purposes, as in the early Comedies, but disguise fairly overflowing with symbolic significances. Perdita is by blood a princess, King Leontes' daughter. Exposed as a babe, she is found and brought up by a shepherd as his own child. On the occasion of the sheep-shearing this princess who supposes herself a shepherd's daughter impersonates the goddess Flora, pausing incidentally at her "father's" request, while still in her costume as goddess, to act as combined hostess and servant to the guests at the sheep-shearing, a part the shepherd's wife had often played when she was living. Here is a mixture indeed of high and low, of human and divine. To complete the picture, this princess-shepherdess-housekeeper-goddess is wooed by a king's son disguised as a country swain (with a remote suggestion that he is also Apollo) who is so serious in his intentions that, as we have seen, he is willing to surrender his hope of the throne rather than give up the girl he loves. And to keep the comedy abreast of the romance, the rogue Autolycus is transmuted into a gentleman by exchange of clothing with the prince. It is all good fairy-tale stuff and admirable "theater." But it is also a summation of much that Shakespeare has been saying most of his life on the interrelations of what we now call democracy and aristocracy, of humanity and divinity.

Through much of this idyllic festivity that representative of reality, the Father, is present in disguise, ready at the proper moment to break the iridescent bubble with one breath of paternal authority. While still in the role of casual visitor at the feast, Polixenes can admire and compliment his son's sweetheart as enthusiastically as anyone:

> This is the prettiest low-born lass that ever
> Ran on the green-sward,

and even instinctively detect her secret:

> Nothing she does or seems
> But smacks of something greater than herself,
> Too noble for this place.

Quite as unconsciously she rebukes his recognition of artificial distinctions with regard to human nature by boldly asserting her preference for natural flowers as against those artificially crossed. The lines in which he answers her are among the most famous on art in Shakespeare:

> Yet nature is made better by no mean
> But nature makes that mean; so, over that art
> Which you say adds to nature, is an art
> That nature makes. You see, sweet maid, we marry
> A gentler scion to the wildest stock,
> And make conceive a bark of baser kind
> By bud of nobler race. This is an art
> Which does mend nature, change it rather, but
> The art itself is nature.

This reads like an explicit blessing on a union between this king's son and this shepherd's daughter—a gentle scion married to wild stock—but Polixenes is not acute enough to get the application of his words to the present situation. His general doctrine of the relation of art and nature is true or false according as we choose to use the word "nature" in an all-inclusive or in a restricted sense, to contrast art with nature or subsume it under it. If I say, "It is the nature of art to add to nature," the opposite meanings of "nature" are evident. Usage generally, and etymology specifically, seem to be against Polixenes. Shakespeare waits for the fifth act to make his comment. Meanwhile, Perdita, with a bewitching mixture of feminine docility and stubbornness, assents to this stranger's idea in the abstract but refuses to have anything to do with it in the concrete:

POL.: The art itself is nature.
PER.:   So it is.
POL.: Then make your garden rich in gilly-flowers
         And do not call them bastards.
PER.:   I'll not put
         The dibble in earth to set one slip of them,

any more, she adds, than I would paint my own cheek to lure a lover. And then follow her memorable words about the flowers Proserpina let fall from Dis's wagon,

                    daffodils,
         That come before the swallow dares, and take
         The winds of March with beauty . . .

and so on, words lovely in their own right, lovelier still in their mythological echoes, but loveliest of all in their elusive allusiveness to Perdita herself, who in more senses than one is a spring flower who dared come ahead of time.

                    Sure this robe of mine
         Does change my disposition.

We are ready to take her at her word and to believe that a touch of the goddess Flora has entered into her from her costume, for clothes can be creative when treated as poetic symbols just as they can be degrading when taken as mere insignia of social rank.*

IV

As a reward for his extraordinarily successful fourth act, Shakespeare finds himself, when the fifth act opens, with two heroines on his hands. He has fascinated us more or less equally with mother and daughter, and

* This theme is elaborated in the parts of Autolycus, the Old Shepherd, and Clown. The Shepherd's son mistakes Autolycus for a great courtier merely because he is dressed in Florizel's clothes, but the Old Shepherd detects the fact that the garments

so has prepared for several highly dramatic recognition scenes: one between the father and his lost daughter, another between the husband and his "dead" wife, a third between the mother and her lost daughter, and a fourth between the other King and his prospective daughter-in-law, not to mention the reunion between the two Kings themselves which involves another type of recognition. This was too much of a good thing even for Shakespeare, who had recently tried something of the kind in the last act of *Cymbeline* and apparently was not in a mood for the same sort of congestion again in a fifth act. So, though it must have hurt him to do it, he sacrifices the daughter to the mother dramatically by narrating instead of presenting the reunion of daughter and father (and incidentally the meeting of the two Kings). The spectator or reader feels a bit deprived, and at the same time a bit impatient while others are being enlightened about what he already knows, but the poet was undoubtedly right in deciding that the highlight of his act should be the scene in which Hermione, posing as her own statue, returns to life and is reunited with her husband and her daughter.

It is a scene which if taken prosaically is open to a flood of objections, but if taken poetically is near perfection. It is effective on several levels. Theatrically it is a masterpiece of suspense. Dramatically it rounds out every character who participates in it. Symbolically it ties together all the play has said or suggested concerning the relation of art and nature, and so, by implication, of the worlds of reality and romance, of Sicilia and Bohemia. And last of all it is a veritable whispering gallery of literary and mythological echoes. In a way it is the story of Pygmalion and Galatea over again; in another it is a reincarnation of the great scene that concludes the *Alcestis* of Euripides in which his dead wife is restored to Admetus. How much or how little Shakespeare may have known of this scene there is no way of telling. But however that may be, here is a remarkable example of the unity of all imaginative literature wherever or whenever written. A work of art is a world unto itself, but all works of art belong to one world. We are considering Shakespeare's *The Winter's Tale;* yet only those who are acquainted with another work of another poet written two thousand years earlier are in a position to catch all the overtones and undertones of this one. Leontes, as truly as Admetus, had let his wife sacrifice her life to his selfishness. Hermione, as truly as Alcestis, had accepted her fate with unselfishness, nobility, and calm. Paulina, as truly as Heracles,

do not fit the man. Later, when both father and son are themselves clad as gentlemen, the Old Shepherd feels that his gentleman's clothing carries with it an obligation to be gentle, while his son thinks it merely grants him license to swear and lie.

had snatched away death's prey before it was too late. Paulina, who is an example of good impulsiveness as Leontes is of bad, has been praised at length by many commentators for her honesty, her outspokenness, and her bravery, and has time and again been justly likened to Kent in *King Lear*. But perhaps the highest tribute that can be paid to her heroism is merely to point out that she is the counterpart in Shakespeare's play of Heracles in Euripides'.

The defeat of death is the main problem of humanity. That defeat may be effected either by the direct imitation of divinity by man (the way of religion) or by the indirect imitation of it through the creation of divine works (the way of art), though practically it must be by a combination of the two, for it is only the religion that speaks artistically that is articulate and only the art that is pervaded by a religious spirit that is redeeming. As Perdita impersonated the goddess Flora, so Hermione imitates an artistic incarnation of herself as a work of sculpture. Sixteen years in which to rehearse the effect of adversity on love have made her a living proof of her daughter's words in her own moment of adversity:

> I think affliction may subdue the cheek,
> But not take in the mind.

From *Hamlet* on, Shakespeare had been saying, sometimes in poetic and sometimes in religious language, that life must unite with spirit, reason must become the servant of imagination, nature must imitate art.

> Alla bell' arte che, se dal ciel seco
> Ciascun la porta, vince la natura,

as Michelangelo puts it, for it is nature that must be subsumed under art, not, as Polixenes contended, the other way around, though of course if we want to call that art a higher kind of nature there is nothing to prevent our doing so.

Perdita achieved that subsumption unconsciously by making every moment perfect:

> What you do
> Still betters what is done. When you speak, sweet,
> I'd have you do it ever; when you sing,
> I'd have you buy and sell so, so give alms,
> Pray so; and for the ord'ring your affairs,
> To sing them too. When you do dance, I wish you
> A wave o' the sea, that you might ever do
> Nothing but that; move still, still so,
> And own no other function. Each your doing,

> So singular in each particular,
> Crowns what you are doing in the present deeds,
> That all your acts are queens.

These words of Florizel's might be dismissed as the illusion of a young lover—but for two things. In the first place, everyone else, though all cannot express it as well, seems to feel about Perdita in this respect much as Florizel does, and secondly, there is everything to indicate that Shakespeare considered such "illusions" the highest kind of reality, or at least the promise of it. It is not a question of youth or age, but of awakened or un-awakened imagination, imagination being the illusion nothing can shatter. As Florizel feels intuitively about Perdita, so Leontes, after long suffering, comes to feel about the lifelike statue of his wife—that he would like to keep it, to look on her just as she is, forever. And so would Perdita.

> PAUL.: He'll think anon it lives.
> LEON.: ... *Make me to think so twenty years together!* ...
> PAUL.: ... Shall I draw the curtain?
> LEON.: *No, not these twenty years.*
> PERD.:   *So long could I*
>   *Stand by, a looker on.*

This thirst for the continuance of life just as it is at the significant instant is the very heart of art. It is also the natural attitude of childhood. Thus art is an attempt to recover childhood in a form that will not be transient.

> Two lads that thought there was no more behind
> But such a day to-morrow as to-day,
> And to be boy eternal.

So early did Shakespeare introduce into his play the theme of the *puer aeternus*, or what is the same thing, of the eternal moment. There, at the beginning, how casually he slips it in, a few notes played by the flute or a single violin. But we forget it at our peril—the peril of not getting the connection when the full orchestra takes it up, modulated from the key of childhood to the key of art, in the last scene of the last act. Back there, it had to do with art in its embryonic form of play, where it is still indistinguishable from life. Here it has to do with play in its mature form of art, an art again in this case indistinguishable from life—the statue that is a woman—the goal alike of both art and life. Like so many of the characters in this play, what a long detour humanity has to make to arrive as it were at the spot from which it set out—or, more strictly, *above* the spot from which it set out, for the movement from childhood to art is not a circle but a spiral, a passage from a first innocence, through adversity, to the second innocence of universal forgiveness.

With the first three acts and the fifth act put in this light, how perfectly the fourth act, with its humor and romance, fits between them, a sort of *scherzo*. Autolycus especially! No longer does he appear as just a picaresque figure introduced for the entertainment of the groundlings, but as an embodiment on his own level of the main idea. He is knavery sublimated into play, "crime" de-moralized for purely comic consumption. He passes from one "perfect crime" to another with casual ease. He is like the childlike and elfin half of Falstaff come back to a world freed of all ethical complications—and excess fat. Who would not rather have his pocket picked than not by such a fascinating rascal? When this snapper-up of unconsidered trifles gets to heaven, be certain he will be found picking the pockets of the angels, cheating them with his ribbons, and inducing them to discard their hymns and try out his latest ballad on their golden harps. And they will be the first to forgive him and take his tricks as just celestial fun.

In all these variations on this theme of the eternal moment—comic, tragic, romantic, religious—Shakespeare clasps hands across the centuries with Goethe: "Verweile doch! du bist so schön!" Tarry! thou art so fair! The Faustian test is the only valid test of happiness. The moment is the model of eternity, and only by a prolongation of the perfect moment, or, better, by an integration of many perfect moments, can Eternity be attained.

This concentration on the present is the art of something better than forgiving, namely, forgetting. The reconciliations with which the last act is filled are illustrations of this art. It is appropriate that a play whose crisis involves Apollo and the Delphic Oracle should have its climactic scene take place in a chapel and sound a religious note.

Over and over in the concluding lines of his play Shakespeare strikes off, mostly through Paulina, brief aphoristic imperatives that reiterate its leading idea in mingled religious and artistic language:

> It is requir'd
> You do awake your faith.
>
> Music, awake her.
>
> Be stone no more.
>
> Fill your grave up.*
>
> Bequeath to death your numbness.

"And Death once dead, there's no more dying then," as the poet himself says.

* This is not an imperative in the text ("I'll fill your grave up"), but the sense justifies its being included as one.

Euripides permits no word to the revived Alcestis. Shakespeare grants the restored Hermione one speech.

> You gods, look down,

she says,

> And from your sacred vials pour your graces
> Upon my daughter's head!

A natural prayer—answered in advance—yet it sums up in another tongue just what the poet himself has expressed through the "statue." That which is art from the point of view of humanity is, from the point of view of heaven, grace. But all this need not be dwelt on further here, for Shakespeare himself dwells on it at length in *The Tempest*.

Chapter XXXVI

The Tempest

God knows there are desert islands enough to go round—the difficulty is to sail *away* from them—but dream islands . . . they are rare, rare.—KATHERINE MANSFIELD on *The Tempest*.

I

It is customary to set *The Tempest* beside *A Midsummer-Night's Dream* as Shakespeare's mature compared with his more youthful treatment of fairyland. Its connection with *Macbeth*, if less obvious, is profounder, the earlier play revealing the relation to human life of the darker part of the spiritual world as the later one does the brighter. But a still more interesting, if more unusual, way of taking *The Tempest* is as a sequel to *King Lear*:

> We two alone will sing like birds i' the cage.

The Enchanted Isle is like a bird cage only in a certain sense and Prospero and Miranda bear no personal resemblance to Lear and Cordelia. But there they are—they two alone—father and daughter, transmigrated and altered as they might be in a dream. For what other name than Wonderful could fit Cordelia after the miracle of her "death" and what compensation better suit the angry and irrational old King than power to command the winds of which he formerly had been the victim? Yet even this little runs the risk of making too particular an analogy that should be left vague. Enough if we feel that the storm that rocked *King Lear* all but to the end is not unrelated to the tempest that is just about to blow itself out as this play begins. In *Othello* and *King Lear* we thought we caught glimpses into a region on the Other Side of the Storm. Nearly all of this play takes place there. In that sense—but in that sense only—*The Tempest* is *King Lear in Heaven*.

II

The opening scene of *The Tempest*—the shipwreck—is like an overture throughout which we catch echoes, like distant thunder, of the themes that dominated the historical and tragic music dramas of Shakespeare's earlier periods. It is an extraordinary epitome. "What cares these roarers for the name of king?" Into that question—or exclamation, if you will—the disdainful Boatswain condenses not only *King Lear* but all that Shakespeare ever said on the subject of worldly place and power. Here are a group of "great ones"—from king down—up against it. "The king and prince at prayers!" The mingled surprise, humor, and consternation in those words of old Gonzalo says it all. When kings and princes are reduced to prayer, then indeed is the day of doom near. The roaring Boatswain—a kind of emancipated and active twin of Barnardine in *Measure for Measure*—is the one man who shines in this crisis, his combined cheerfulness, energy, resourcefulness, and contempt being just the brew needed in the situation. Even the master of the boat relies on him to carry ship, mariners, passengers, and master himself through on his lone shoulders. Emergencies crown their own kings. As the Bastard needed no title in *King John*, so this man can stand on his own feet. Nature hands him the command and everybody of any account concurs. "Keep your cabins; you do assist the storm," he orders his royal passengers. There is a symbolic diagnosis of war in eight words, with a prescription for peace thrown in. Let "great ones" go below and leave the decks to the boatswains and their mariners. It is still sound advice. Even the good Gonzalo, with his philosophy, strikes us as a bit superfluous at the moment. "You are a counsellor," says the Boatswain; "if you can command these elements to silence, and work the peace of the present, we will not hand a rope more; use your authority . . . Cheerly, good hearts! Out of our way, I say." Again Shakespeare amends Plato: not when philosophers are kings, but when boatswains are. William James declared that the best thing education can impart is the power to know a good man when you see him. In that case these scions of royalty are not educated, for all they can call this genius of the storm is bawling, blasphemous, incharitable dog, whoreson, insolent noisemaker, and cur. What fools! What a man! What a scene!

Commentators have long been tempted to identify Prospero with Shakespeare and to find in his farewell to his art, with the breaking of his wand and the drowning of his book, the poet's farewell to the stage. The magician's summary of his deeds—the graves he has opened, the wars of the elements he has fomented, the oaks he has rifted with lightning-bolts, on to the heavenly music he is even now "requiring," which might so easily be

The Tempest itself—fits the masterpieces of the poet so exactly that the inference seems all but inescapable. (And then there are Miranda and Judith Shakespeare.) But a parallelism, however close at one or two points, is a different matter from a full identification, and we can easily believe that Shakespeare had his own retirement from the theater in mind when he wrote this particular speech, without committing ourselves to the idea that Prospero is the author throughout. Indeed it is hard to see how anyone who has attended to the whole of Prospero's role could entertain such a notion for a moment.

For there are two Prosperos in this play, the man and the magician, Prospero the father of Miranda, and Prospero the master of Caliban and Ariel, fomenter of tempests. Miranda's father is an antitype of Hamlet's father (as ghost) in his treatment of his child, beginning, in this respect at least, where King Lear left off. From this angle *The Tempest* might be entitled *The Education of Miranda* and be put over against *The Education of Coriolanus*. But there should be no hasty inference that children should be brought up by their fathers rather than their mothers, for though Prospero calls himself Miranda's schoolmaster, I imagine that, like Cadwal and Polydore, she was brought up mainly by a woman, Nature. Prospero, like Belarius, probably merely added a touch of wisdom here or exerted the restraining hand of experience there, so little, under healthy conditions, does civilization need to interfere with the natural impulses of a gifted child. And he was rewarded. Miranda plainly taught him more than he did her, and laid in him that basis of love and wonder which made possible the miraculous change that comes over him in the end. His discarding of his magic mantle in her presence in the first scene of the play is clearly a preparation for his final discarding of it in the last scene. (There is a reason for Shakespeare's careful attention to stage directions in *The Tempest*.)

But Prospero the magician is a being of a different order from Miranda's father. He can be traced to the former Duke of Milan, the recluse so absorbed in his books that he was unconscious of the conspiracy of the brother who deposed him. Now in exile, this master of strange lore can emerge from solitude to issue stern commands and rebukes. Those who nonchalantly equate him with Shakespeare have not only his treatment of his abhorred fetcher of fuel to come to terms with, but the more difficult fact of his sharp words to Ariel. "Dull thing"—of all things to this spirit of fire and air!—"Thou liest, malignant thing!" His threat to imprison his winged servant if he murmurs is enough in itself to put any identification with the author out of court.

How shall we reconcile these opposites—the loving father and the harsh taskmaster?

III

The Tempest has an unrivaled power to inspire in almost all sensitive readers a belief that it contains a secret meaning. Even those who make no attempt to search it out retain the feeling that it is there and that if it could only be found it would lead close not merely to the heart of Shakespeare's convictions about life but close to the heart of life itself. Naturally I have no reference here to the many minute and elaborate allegorical interpretations of the play that have been offered, which, even if they were convincing within their own limits, could have only a historical, biographical, or other subpoetical interest. What I have in mind rather are more modest attempts to connect and elucidate the main themes and symbols around which the poem is obviously built and which seem to have in peculiar degree the power, in Keats's words, to "tease us out of thought as doth eternity." To set out to interpret *The Tempest* (which I do not intend to do) is one thing; to point out certain aspects of its symbolism and thematic structure with which any satisfactory interpretation must come to terms as a sort of minimum requirement is another and much less ambitious undertaking.

To begin with, this play is centrally concerned with the three things that Shakespeare had perhaps come to value most highly in life: liberty, love, and wonder—the identical trinity, by the way, that Hafiz, long before Shakespeare, had also chosen. Concerned with realities rather than with names, the poet not only gives examples of these things but, to make clear what they are in their purity, shows us what they are in their perversions: license is set over against liberty; lust against love; banality, but more particularly "wonders," against wonder.

And the play has also what might be called a biological theme. As has often been pointed out, the characters are arranged in a sort of evolutionary hierarchy from Caliban, who is a kind of demi-creature of water and earth, up through human strata of various stages of development to Ariel, who is all fire and air—though it is made clear that where human nature becomes degenerate it seems to sink to a level lower than that of Caliban.

Closely allied to this, yet distinct from it, is a psychological interest. The play is fairly saturated with references to sleep and waking—and to various states of consciousness and unconsciousness between the two, drowsiness, daydreaming, dreaming, trance, hallucination, and other hypnagogic conditions. Likewise *The Tempest* is filled from end to end with noises and music—from the thunder and roaring of the storm itself, the howling of beasts, through the sounds and sweet airs of the Enchanted Isle that could charm even Caliban, through every variety of human utterance from the cries and coarse ballads of drunkards to the voices of lovers, up finally to the songs of Ariel. And Shakespeare seems interested not only in these two things, sleep and music, but even more in the relation between them—in the relation, to put it more pedantically, between music and the unconscious mind. The voices of the isle could induce such sleep in Caliban that when he waked he cried to dream again. Miranda falls asleep on the entrance of Ariel and awakens on his exit. The same is true in some degree of the other good characters, but not of the baser ones, who become victims on at least one occasion of an evil form of waking hallucination. All these reactions turn on the receptivity of the unconscious mind.

These various themes and symbols are inextricably interwoven, and, seen from a slightly different angle, give us Shakespeare's final word on a subject that had engaged his attention from the beginning: the different kinds of power that men possess and are possessed by. Here the political and religious aspects of the story merge as we are carried all the way from the demonic tyranny of the witch Sycorax to the reign of pure goodness in old Gonzalo's ideal commonwealth. More specifically, we have within the main action of the play: the political and military power of Alonso and Antonio, the magical power of Prospero, the alcoholic power of Stephano, the unveiling power of love in Ferdinand and Miranda, and the musical power of Ariel. (Nor am I omitting, though I may seem to be, the religious power of forgiveness.)

The play culminates in three emancipations—of Caliban from the enthralment of the drunken Stephano, of Prospero from his magic, and of Ariel from the service of Prospero in the cause of that magic (not to mention the emancipation from moral bondage of Alonso and his companions). What might be called, grotesquely, the biography of Ariel gives at least an intimation of what these interrelated emancipations mean, though we must beware here not to fetter the play within any rigid allegory. For twelve years—"years" doubtless comparable to the "days" of creation in Genesis—Ariel was imprisoned in a cloven pine by the witch Sycorax because he was

> a spirit too delicate
> To act her earthy and abhorr'd commands.

This imprisonment, once imposed, Sycorax is powerless to undo and Prospero with his art must come to the rescue. What does this signify? Might it not mean that when imagination is enslaved by the senses superstition usurps its function—and the senses become powerless to release it? It must be set free by knowledge and reason. But that is not the end of the story.

Out from under the domination of the senses, imagination now becomes the slave of the very intellect that rescued it. Prospero is now master and the delicate spirit he has set free from Sycorax is impressed into the service of his magic—even at one point at the threat of a second imprisonment, in a cloven oak, of like duration as the first, if he complains. Here, again, is a Prospero remote enough from anything we associate with Shakespeare.

What is the character of Prospero's magic? If it is not black art, it certainly is not "white" in the sense of being dedicated unreservedly to noble ends. Prospero was indeed the victim of injustice. But his main miracle, the raising of the tempest, appears to have been undertaken primarily to get his enemies within his power for purposes of revenge. Moreover, his magic banquets and charmed swords have an element of mere display about them that is reminiscent of the "wonders" of the common conjurer. The higher the nature of the miracle sought, the more Prospero seems to intrust its execution to Ariel's improvisation, as in the saving of Gonzalo and most of all the falling in love of Ferdinand and Miranda. Prospero willed this love affair, but the bringing of it into being was plainly Ariel's work, and his success so delights Prospero that he promises his servant his freedom as a reward:

> PROS.:   It goes on, I see,
> As my soul prompts it.

(Not, notice, "as I ordered" but "as my soul prompts"!)

>   Spirit, fine spirit! I'll free thee
> Within two days for this!

And as if he would not have us miss the point, the poet repeats it a moment later:

>   At the first sight
> They have chang'd eyes. Delicate Ariel,
> I'll set thee free for this!

He sees that this is Ariel's accomplishment—nothing of his own magic at all. (From Prospero's command to his servant to summon his "rabble" of spirits and "incite them to quick motion" we seem entitled to think that even the wedding masque is mainly the latter's doing.) As in the case of Lear and his Fool, the servant has become the master of the master, a fact that comes out emphatically when Prospero has his enemies at his mercy. He is then in the same position as was the banished Coriolanus, except that the force at his command is knowledge and magic rather than the sword.

> Now does my project gather to a head,

he cries triumphantly in the first line of the last act. His foes, along with some innocent ones entangled with them, are powerless to budge, and we feel that he is now about to get even for the injustices they formerly inflicted on him. And then, like Virgilia with her kiss, Ariel speaks:

ARIEL: Him that you term'd, sir, "the good old lord, Gonzalo,"
His tears run down his beard like winter's drops
From eaves of reeds. Your charm so strongly works them
That if you now beheld them, your affections
Would become tender.
PROS.:   Dost thou think so, spirit?
ARIEL: Mine would, sir, were I human.
PROS.:   And mine shall.
Hast thou, which art but air, a touch, a feeling
Of their afflictions, and shall not myself,
One of their kind, that relish all as sharply
Passion as they, be kindlier mov'd than thou art?
Though with their high wrongs I am struck to the quick,
Yet with my nobler reason 'gainst my fury
Do I take part. The rarer action is
In virtue than in vengeance. They being penitent,
The sole drift of my purpose doth extend
Not a frown further. Go release them, Ariel.
My charms I'll break, their senses I'll restore,
And they shall be themselves.

Prospero thinks it is his reason that overcomes his fury. But what has just happened contradicts him. It was his angel that whispered the suggestion in his ear. And a man's angel or genius is not to be confused with the man himself.* Indeed this very one of Prospero's is a spirit whose independence he is about to declare. Crying, "My charms I'll break," he invokes the elves and demi-puppets—"weak masters" who have helped him to do only such trifles as to bedim the sun and call forth winds—and bids farewell forever to them and magic. Ariel, his strong master, enters on the instant, with music, to displace them. And forthwith follows a wonder that genuinely deserves the name—the forgiveness and reconciliation that Prospero has just resolved on. Here is a divine right of kings to which even the strictest equalitarian could not object—the intervention of one of those angels in whom Richard II, because he was unworthy, trusted in vain. Here is the counterpart and antithesis of Macbeth's surrender to the Witches. As they tempted him to crime and death, so Ariel tempts Prospero to forgiveness and life.

* "Thy demon—that's thy spirit which keeps thee" (*Antony and Cleopatra*, II, iii, 19).

How all this illuminates what has gone before! The stages in Ariel's estate now stand out unmistakable. While he was subjected to Sycorax, he was imprisoned and powerless. While he obeys Prospero, he performs material wonders—though even then, if the initiative is left to him, he goes beyond them. Finally, when it is he who whispers the hint in Prospero's ear and Prospero obeys *him*, the wonder of a spiritual miracle occurs. Music replaces magic; Ariel's songs achieve what is beyond the scope of Prospero's wand.

Those who, once powerful, suffer defeat, are restored to power, and then might take revenge but do not—they hold the keys of peace. That is what the end of *The Tempest* seems to say, as Shakespeare himself said it in the 94th sonnet:

> They that have power to hurt and will do none . . .
> They rightly do inherit heaven's graces.

It is an old truth—no discovery of Shakespeare's. But crowning as it does the last act of what was probably the last full play he ever wrote, backed up by hundreds, we might almost say thousands, of minute particulars from his previous works, and embodied in his own practice of understanding rather than judging all humanity from saint to sinner, it acquires the character of a revelation.

> Be cheerful
> And think of each thing well.

By itself, that could sound commonplace or even banal. But against the inferno of the Tragedies, it is no silly philosophy of smiling evil out of existence.

IV

> Where the bee sucks, there suck I,

sings Ariel when Prospero tells him the moment of his release is near,

> Where the bee sucks, there suck I.
> In a cowslip's bell I lie;
> There I couch when owls do cry.
> On the bat's back I do fly
> After summer merrily.
> Merrily, merrily shall I live now
> Under the blossom that hangs on the bough.

This angel will not use his freedom to fly away to some distant heaven: he will hide under the nearest flower. The world of spirit, in other words, is not Another World after all. It is this world rightly seen and heard. From end to end *The Tempest* reiterates this. To innocent senses the isle itself is pure loveliness; to corrupted ones it is no better than a swamp:

ADRIAN: The air breathes upon us here most sweetly.
SEBASTIAN: As if it had lungs, and rotten ones.
ANTONIO: Or as 'twere perfumed by a fen.
GONZALO: Here is everything advantageous to life.
ANTONIO: True; save means to live.

Even in Caliban an Ariel slumbers. He loves the voices of the isle, and his moral awakening at the end—

> What a thrice-double ass
> Was I, to take this drunkard for a god
> And worship this dull fool!

—though passed over swiftly is as hopeful a note as is struck in the entire play. Prospero was wrong in thinking that Caliban was impervious to education.

But it is Miranda of course, of the human inhabitants of the isle, who gives supreme expression to the way the world looks to uncontaminated senses and imagination:

> O, wonder!
> How many goodly creatures are there here!
> How beauteous mankind is! O brave new world,
> That has such people in 't!

Imagination, as dreams show, is something that awakens in most of us only when the senses are put to sleep. It is only when *they* awaken refreshed at sunrise that we occasionally see the world for a moment as God intended us to. But really, Shakespeare is telling us in *The Tempest*, sense and spirit are as much made for each other as lovers are. It is appetite and intellect that have put an abyss between them. That is what Prospero the Magician learned from Ariel and his own child. Miranda did not need to read *King Lear*. But unless we have a child or angel to teach us, we do. We must go to Shakespeare and the other poets—for poetry, as Shelley said, "lifts the veil from the hidden beauty of the world and makes familiar things as if they were not familiar."

But whatever may be true of the rest of us, why does a poet need poetry? It is easy to see why a young poet does. But why should an old one?

We have noted how Shakespeare's need for drama in the narrower sense yielded to his need for poetry. Was his need for poetry now yielding to his need for life? It was the moment after Prospero listened to his spirit that he decided to break his staff and drown his book. Perhaps Shakespeare at last perceived that dramatic compositions, even poetic ones, are only airy charms. Perhaps he said to himself,

> ... this rough magic
> I here abjure:

I will return from the necromancy of art to the wonder of life itself. Whatever he said or didn't say, he must have come to realize what creative minds in the end are almost bound to see: that the arts are to men only what toys are to children, a means for the rehearsal of life. And so, paradoxically, the object of art is to get rid of the arts. When they mature, the art of life will be substituted for them—as children outgrow their toys.

> Merrily, merrily shall I live now
> Under the blossom that hangs on the bough.

Perhaps Shakespeare had himself in mind when he wrote those lines of Ariel's. I picture him retired to Stratford lying under a plum tree in May doing "nothing." "Had I a little son," said Charles Lamb, "I would christen him Nothing-to-Do; he should do nothing." Shakespeare would have understood. "Nothing brings me all things."

V

Shakespeare could have bidden farewell to the theater in no better way than through Ariel, for no figure he ever created more utterly transcends the stage. How shall Ariel be acted? The most graceful girl to be found for the part, the most charming boy, will instantly blur or erase the Shakespearean conception. Which, indeed, should play the role, if it is to be played, boy or girl? And what pronoun should be resorted to in referring to this spirit of music and the dance? The paucity of language compels us, as in the case of the angels, to use either the masculine or the feminine. But neither will do. Ariel is above sex. In that respect this ultimate creation of the poet's genius seems like the culmination of something he had been seeking all his life. From Adonis and the Young Man of the Sonnets, through Rosalind and Hamlet, Desdemona and Cordelia, on to Imogen, Florizel and Cadwal, Ferdinand and Miranda (remember her willingness to carry logs!), Shakespeare is bent on finding men and women who, without losing the virtues and integrity of their own sex, have also the virtues of the other. If Shakespeare had no admiration for the womanly woman in the sense of the clinging vine, neither had he any for the manly man as embodied in what our generation refers to as the "he-man" or the "red-blooded man." He scorned the gentleman, but all his best men are gentle men. Whatever else he may be, Ariel is a symbol of this union of the masculine and feminine elements of the soul.

But what makes Ariel even more akin, if possible, to the spirit of his maker is the capacity to assume any form or shape, to perform any function, to be at home in any element. By universal consent this is close to Shakespeare's supreme gift. And there is no better example of it than his creation (along with Caliban) of this very Ariel—a creature so unique that he seems to have sprung full-blown from the head of his maker. But even Ariel has been prepared for. From Puck with his flower juice squeezed in lovers' eyes, to the Fool with his wise folly whispered in Lear's ear, Ariel has seldom been far away in Shakespeare wherever spiritual force from without comes to the rescue of weak or foolish or proud humanity. Who shall say that Ariel was not there when the God Hercules left Antony and music was heard in the air, or when Cleopatra herself turned to fire and air?

VI

Of the many universal symbols on which *The Tempest* is erected that of the island is fundamental. An island is a bit of a higher element rising out of a lower—like a fragment of consciousness thrusting up out of the ocean of unconsciousness. Like a clearing in the wilderness or a walled city, like a temple or a monastery, it is a piece of cosmos set over against chaos and ready to defend itself if chaos, as it will be bound to do, tries to bring it back under its old domination. It is a magic circle, a small area of perfection shutting out all the rest of infinite space. What wonder that an island has come to be a symbol of birth and of rebirth, or that from the fabled Atlantis and that earthly island, the Garden of Eden, to the latest Utopia, an island, literal or metaphorical, is more often than any other the spot the human imagination chooses for a fresh experiment in life!*

Like Ariel himself, this island play, *The Tempest*, is so *sui generis* that we do not easily see how naturally it emerges from the rest of Shakespeare. In its emphasis on parent and child and the theme of reconciliation, its kinship with the others in the group of plays that begins with *Pericles*, it is true, is a commonplace. But its roots go deeper than that.

Prospero, Duke of Milan, deprived of his dukedom and exiled on an island, is restored at the end to his former place, a man so altered by his experience that henceforth, he declares, every third thought shall be his grave. Obviously, this is the pattern of *As You Like It* with the Forest of Arden in place of the Enchanted Isle and with the difference that the Senior Duke is in no need of regeneration. But, less obviously, this theme of the King, Prince, Duke, or other person of high estate losing his place or inheritance only to recover it or its spiritual equivalent, after exile or suffering, in a sense in which he never possessed it before, is repeated by Shakespeare over and over. All stemming in a way from that early and under-

* A rarely beautiful and subtle example is Green Island in Sarah Orne Jewett's *The Country of the Pointed Firs*.

valued study of King Henry VI, *Measure for Measure, King Lear, Timon of Athens, Coriolanus, Antony and Cleopatra*, and parts of *Pericles, Cymbeline* and *The Winter's Tale* are built on this situation. They all, in one way or another, contrast with and supplement *Hamlet*, whose hero propounds the same problem, wavers on the edge of a fresh solution, only to offer in the end the old erroneous answer. They all, in various keys, reiterate the theme of Timon: "Nothing brings me all things."

But it is not just those who have lost worldly kingdoms in a literal sense who come to realize this truth. Shakespeare uses the same idea metaphorically. Over and over in his plays when the object valued or the person loved is taken away, an imaginative object or person, more than compensating for the loss, appears in its place.

Friar Francis in *Much Ado about Nothing* formulates the psychology of it. Hero, accused at the marriage altar by Claudio of unfaithfulness, falls unconscious—dead, it is thought at first. Give it out that she is dead, advises Friar Francis later, and you will perceive a miracle: the real Hero will be reborn in Claudio's soul.

> So will it fare with Claudio.
> When he shall hear she died upon his words,
> The idea of her life shall sweetly creep
> Into his study of imagination,
> And every lovely organ of her life
> Shall come apparell'd in more precious habit,
> More moving-delicate and full of life,
> Into the eye and prospect of his soul,
> Than when she liv'd indeed.

And so it proves, when the supposedly dead Hero, posing as her own cousin, is produced, and Claudio, seeing now with his imagination, superimposes his purified memory on the new bride and cries, "Another Hero!" Another Hero indeed, and yet the same. Beatrice and Benedick, too, are toppled out of their pride and disdain by a variation of the same psychology. Listening to "lies" about each other and themselves that are nearer the truth than the counterfeit personalities their wit has created, and shaken into sincerity by Claudio's mistreatment of Hero, they bid farewell to contempt and confess their love. And as if fascinated by the situation, Shakespeare relies on it yet again in *All's Well That Ends Well*, when Bertram resees the "dead" Helena at the end. In the light comedy of these over-theatrical plays, however, Claudio and Bertram have acted so outrageously that their conversions are to many modern readers or spectators unconvincing. Some will suspect the poet himself of skepticism or irony in these happy endings.

But the moment we pass to tragedy we accept this psychology without question. Romeo falls in love with Juliet at first sight but he loves her utterly only when she lies "dead" at his feet. Hamlet* realizes what Ophelia is to him only when he has driven her to madness and death and is literally with her in her grave. Othello recognizes the divinity of Desdemona only after he has killed her. Lear "sees" Cordelia fully only when she is dead in his arms. Antony bcomes conqueror of himself only when he believes that Cleopatra has committed suicide, and Cleopatra is translated into fire and air only when her Emperor has proved his faith by taking his own life. The number of repetitions of this theme or situation in the Tragedies is startling and it is continued in modified form in the last group of plays. Posthumus discards his Italian weeds and his shame only when he believes he has murdered Imogen. Leontes falls truly in love with the "dead" wife he has wronged only when she is transformed into a statue. Symbolically this last instance might stand for all. The "illusion" of loss permits the senses to see life as if it were a work of art. In how many cases imagination is the child of death: in tragedy generally of death itself, in comedy often of a false report of death—death being the supreme "nothing" that brings "all things." In the dramatic romances especially Shakespeare seems to be asking whether some great shock short of death cannot awaken the imagination as death itself does in the Tragedies. In banishment, exile, or separation Shakespeare finds such shocks, but even these understudies of death, as they might be called, are rather the necessary condition than the cause of the awakening. Prospero on his island is not enough. There must be a Miranda too. And in all the plays where this theme of exile is conspicuous, of which The Tempest is the typical and terminal one, we never fail to find childhood or a childlike innocence preserved into maturity as seed for the soil that has been plowed by adversity. It is not chance that in these last plays there are so many children, unspotted maidens (and young men) together with older women and old men who have attained the wisdom of a renewed childhood: young Mamillius, Cadwal and Polydore, Perdita and Florizel, Marina, Imogen, Ferdinand and Miranda, Hermione, Paulina, Belarius, the Old Shepherd, and Prospero himself. (The innocent Desdemona is in a sense the tragic mother of them all.) One of the certainties about the later Shakespeare is his conviction of the reciprocal necessity of childhood to age and of age to childhood. Confirming King Lear, these plays assert that where the older generation has sinned it must seek pardon of the younger generation:

ALONSO: But O! how oddly will it sound that I
Must ask my child forgiveness!

* This case, it is admitted, is debatable.

but where it has kept virtuous, as Belarius did, its function is to help keep the younger generation uncontaminated by the world—uncontaminated by it, be it noted, not unacquainted with it. For Shakespeare is the last one to advocate the closing of eyes to fact. Only he keeps faith in the power of imagination to subdue fact to its own shape. *The Tempest* seems like the summation and consummation of what he has been saying on that subject all his life. Prospero, when expelled from his dukedom, is a narrow and partial man. Thanks to his child, the island, and Ariel, he gives promise of coming back to it something like a whole one. But an integrated man is only another name for an imaginative man. And so the marriage of Ferdinand and Miranda is not the only union this play celebrates, nor is the island the only symbol of wholeness. On this isle we have all found ourselves, Gonzalo proclaims in the end, "when no man was his own." In this location of spiritual treasure within the self ("The Kingdom of Heaven is within you") as well as in its emphasis on childhood and forgiveness, together with the note of humility and the appeal for mercy on which its epilogue ends, *The Tempest* is a profoundly Christian play.

VII

When we consider out of what this poem is woven, is it any wonder it produces the effect it does? Its action takes place on an enchanted island. Its main human character is a magician. Its most celestial figure is the very spirit of metamorphosis. Its most earthy one undergoes a seemingly impossible transformation—an extreme example of the moral regeneration that comes to a number of others in the play. Its atmosphere throughout is as insubstantial as a rainbow. (Iris herself actually appears at one point.) The best-remembered sentence from its best-remembered speech is

> We are such stuff
> As dreams are made on.

Shakespeare must have known what would happen within the minds of readers and auditors to such a diaphanous and ethereal thing. Life, as he had long since discovered, reveals as much of herself to any man as he brings to her—and no two bring the same. Bright or dark, the world seems contrived to confirm whatever idea of it we conceive it under. A poem, in proportion as it is like life, like that world, will do the same. What else than this is the ultimate meaning of the Shakespearean firmament at which we have been gazing—this human universe we have been passing in review —wherein hundreds of stars, though they inhabit the same sky, differ in glory each from each? A single universal symbol invites projection as surely as a mirror does reflection. *The Tempest* is crowded with such symbols from end to end. How inevitable that it should tempt the sensitive reader, as the stories of Belarius did Cadwal, to "strike life" into it and "show much more his own conceiving"! So long as we reverence and do not neglect its text, what *The Tempest* means, then, is what it means to you or to me. And it will never mean when we are in one mood precisely what it does when we are in another, or mean tomorrow precisely what it does today. And so, as in the case of *Hamlet*, and in due degree of the other plays, each age will find its own interpretation of *The Tempest*, and, miraculously, it will seem to have been written for each age. A main thing it says to our age ought to be plain. Its great opposed symbols are the tempest of Prospero, which Ariel made as Prospero's slave, and Ariel's music, which Ariel made of his own free will. The former is the result of necromantic science or theurgy. The latter is a spontaneous overflow of joy in life. The one creates an opportunity for revenge. The other resolves the situation thus created. What that says to a generation that has used its own science to make an atomic bomb is as illuminating as a flash of lightning by night.

VIII

If lovers of Shakespeare were asked to select a single passage from his works best representative of both his poetry and his philosophy of life, there would probably be nearly unanimous agreement in choosing Prospero's lines beginning,

> Our revels now are ended. . . .

through

> We are such stuff
> As dreams are made on, and our little life
> Is rounded with a sleep.

In their context, as Prospero utters them, they are susceptible of a profoundly sad, not to say pessimistic, interpretation. But as Shakespeare's words the world has on the whole refused to take them so, finding in them rather a supreme expression of the mystery and wonder of life. "Rounded with a sleep" can mean several other things than ended with a sleep, and when did a dream ever exist without a dreamer?

There is one little word here, of only two letters, that makes all the difference. Most commentators explain that "We are such stuff as dreams are made on" means according to Elizabethan usage, as indeed it may, "We are such stuff as dreams are made of." But it may also mean just what it says to the unlearned modern mind. Whether we are such stuff as dreams are made of is at best a matter of opinion or conviction, even though Shakespeare's authority is supposed to support the assertion. But that we are such stuff as dreams are made on is a matter of fact. It is indeed the one datum of consciousness—more nearly ultimate even than Descartes's *Cogito, ergo sum.* The science of our age seeks to explain the constitution of matter. But perhaps the final secret and definition of matter will turn out to be not some mathematical formula but simply this: Matter is that stuff on which dreams can be imprinted, that substance, in other words, on which creative energy can be projected. How else could things as frail as dreams have survived the tempest and chaos of material evolution?

> How with this rage shall beauty hold a plea,
> Whose action is no stronger than a flower?

A question that contains its own answer.

Harold C. Goddard died without naming his book, and the title was given by the publisher.

Acknowledgments

Acknowledgment of permission to reprint passages from copyrighted material is made to the following persons and organizations:

George H. Doran Company for permission to quote from *Anton Tchekhov; Literary and Theatrical Reminiscences*, translated and edited by S. S. Koteliansky, 1927.

E. P. Dutton and Company for permission to quote from *Life and Habit* by Samuel Butler and *The Note-Books of Samuel Butler*; and from *William Shakespeare, a Commentary*, by M. R. Ridley, copyright 1936 by E. P. Dutton and Company.

Ginn and Company for permission to quote from *Julius Caesar*, edited by George Lyman Kittredge, copyright 1939 by George Lyman Kittredge; and from *The Hudson Shakespeare*, with Introduction and Notes by Henry Norman Hudson, copyright 1909 by Ginn and Company.

Harcourt, Brace and Company for permission to quote from *The Art and Life of William Shakespeare* by Hazelton Spencer, copyright 1940 by Harcourt, Brace and Company.

Harper and Brothers for permission to quote from *Bolts of Melody: New Poems of Emily Dickinson*, edited by Mabel Loomis Todd and Millicent Todd Bingham, copyright 1945 by Millicent Todd Bingham.

Henry Holt and Company for permission to quote from the *Complete Poems of Robert Frost*, copyright 1930, 1949 by Henry Holt and Company.

Houghton Mifflin Company for permission to quote from *The Life and Letters of Emily Dickinson* by Martha Dickinson Bianchi, copyright 1924 by Martha Dickinson Bianchi; from Joseph Quincy Adams' "Commentary" to his edition of *Hamlet*, published in 1929 and copyright 1929 by Joseph Quincy Adams; and from *John Jay Chapman and His Letters* by M. A. DeWolfe Howe, copyright 1937 by M. A. DeWolfe Howe.

Alfred A. Knopf, Inc., for permission to quote from *The Letters of Katherine Mansfield*, copyright 1932 by Alfred A. Knopf, Inc.

Little, Brown and Company for permission to quote from *The Complete Poems of Emily Dickinson*, edited by Martha Dickinson Bianchi, copyright 1890 by Roberts Brothers.

Longmans, Green and Company for permission to quote from the works of William James. Permission granted by Paul R. Reynolds & Son, 599 Fifth Avenue, New York 17, New York.

The Macmillan Company for permission to quote from *Shakespearean Tragedy* by A. C. Bradley, copyright 1904 by The Macmillan Company; from *William*

Shakespeare by George Brandes, published in 1920; from *Shakespeare Studies* by Elmer Edgar Stoll, published by G. E. Stechert and Company, 1942, copyright 1927 by The Macmillan Company; from *What Happens in Hamlet* by John Dover Wilson, copyright 1935 by The Macmillan Company; from *The Fortunes of Falstaff* by John Dover Wilson, copyright 1944 by The Macmillan Company; from the Constance Garnett translations of the stories of Anton Chekhov, *The Duel and Other Stories*, 1920, and *The Lady with the Dog*, 1917; from the Constance Garnett translations of the novels of Fyodor Dostoevsky, *The Brothers Karamazov*, 1929; *The Possessed*, 1931; *A Raw Youth*, 1923; *Crime and Punishment*, 1929; and from the Constance Garnett translation of *War and Peace* by Leo Tolstoy.

The Massachusetts Historical Society for permission to quote from *The Education of Henry Adams, an Autobiography*, copyright 1918 by the Massachusetts Historical Society.

Methuen and Company for permission to quote from *The Sacred Wood* by T. S. Eliot.

W. W. Norton and Company for permission to quote from *Hamlet and Oedipus* by Dr. Ernest Jones, copyright 1949 by Dr. Ernest Jones.

Oxford University Press for permission to quote from the Gilbert Murray translation of Euripides' *The Trojan Women*, copyright 1915 by Oxford University Press.

Routledge and Kegan Paul Ltd. for permission to quote from *Dostoevsky Portrayed by His Wife: The Diary and Reminiscences of Mme. Dostoevsky*, translated and edited by S. S. Koteliansky.

Charles Scribner's Sons for permission to quote from *The Poetical Works of George Meredith*, copyright 1912 by Charles Scribner's Sons.

Simon and Schuster, Inc., for permission to quote from *In Defence of Sensuality* by John Cowper Powys, copyright 1930 by John Cowper Powys.

Index

INDEX